DESIGNING PHARMACEUTICAL INNOVATION AROUND PATIENT ACCESS AND RESPONSIBILITY

Why Early Decisions Determine Who Gets Treated

TONY TOKS AKIWUMI MBA, PGDIP, FCMI

Book cover design by Tony Toks Akiwumi

Book formatting by HMDPublishing.com

ALDER & STONE
GROUP

DEDICATION

For those who make innovation human and insist that it reaches the people it was meant for.

EPIGRAPH

"The true measure of innovation is not what we invent, but who it reaches."

- Anonymous health economist, Geneva roundtable, 2024

OTHER BOOKS BY TONY TOKS AKIWUMI

Non-fiction (strategy, leadership, innovation)

The Same Molecule: Two Different Fates

How Mindset, Strategy, and Culture Decide the Destiny of a Drug

How to Lead When You're Not the Boss

A guide to building credibility, trust, and impact through insight and collaboration rather than position

Satirical works

Egbert Floppercough and The Chronicles of Pharma

A witty and revealing journey through the strange realities of innovation, ambition, and absurdity in the pharmaceutical world

CONTENTS

PART IV - LEADERSHIP AND SYSTEM CHANGE

PART V - THE PRACTITIONER'S TOOLKIT

LIST OF FIGURES

LIST OF TABLES

HOW TO USE THE TOOLS

This book includes a set of tools designed to support access-related decision making in real organisational settings. They are not templates to be completed or checklists to be followed mechanically. They are prompts to think more clearly about how access is designed, negotiated, and sustained.

Each tool addresses a different moment in the access lifecycle. Some are diagnostic, helping teams understand where they are today. Others are exploratory, designed to surface assumptions, trade-offs, and blind spots. None of them produce a single right answer. Their value lies in the quality of the conversation they enable.

The tools can be used in three main ways.

First, as individual reflection aids. Many of the tools work well when used by a single person preparing for a decision, review, or discussion. They help clarify what matters, where uncertainty lies, and which questions remain unanswered.

Second, as team discussion frameworks. Several tools are designed to be used in cross-functional meetings, portfolio reviews, or planning sessions. Used this way, they help align perspectives across clinical, economic, access, and leadership roles and make trade-offs explicit.

Third, as learning and governance supports. Some tools are most useful when revisited over time, particularly those linked to maturity, metrics, and learning loops. They support consistency and institutional memory rather than one-off decisions.

The tools are introduced in the chapters where their underlying logic is explained. They are listed together in the front matter for easy reference. You do not need to read the book in sequence to use them, but understanding the surrounding chapters will help you apply them more effectively.

If a tool feels uncomfortable or exposes disagreement, it is probably doing its job.

FOREWORD

Few questions in the development and delivery of medicines are more important than whether patients will have access. Have we met our main objective if patients cannot access the treatment? Every therapy that is underutilized - whether due to lack of clinical impact or access – is a tragic failure. Resources are wasted, but perhaps most importantly, time is lost.

For years, the pharmaceutical world has mistaken discovery for progress. The more novel the molecule, the more ambitious the science, the louder the celebration. However, strong science without medical value is not a solution, and medical value without patient access is equally useless.

In Designing Innovation Around Access, Patients and Responsibility: Why Early Decisions Decide Who Gets Treated, Tony Toks Akiwumi asks a critical question: what happens when we build science that the system cannot absorb? Drawing on decades of experience at the junction of research, policy, and practicality, he shows that success in healthcare can't stop at regulatory approval. Every therapy that arrives to market but remains out of reach to patients, whether due to affordability or other barriers to access, is a moral failure dressed up as progress.

What makes this book stand out is its intelligence and honesty. Tony unpacks, in an easy-to-understand manner, the machinery of access: the economics, the evidence, and the culture that decides who will benefit. Yet he never loses sight of the human cost hidden in the spreadsheets.

This book is relevant to a broad constituency; truly, anyone who has attempted to move an idea through a complicated system will find his logic illuminating. Whether you are a scientist, clinician, payer, or work in the policy space, you will find the concepts in this book clear, quietly provocative, and actionable.

Tony's dryly humorous voice has that rare mix of warmth and precision: sharp enough to cut through jargon, grounded enough to make you nod in recognition. He doesn't posture as a rebel; he writes as a reformer. His argument is both simple and uncomfortable in equal measure and should be pinned to the corkboard above every desk in pharma and healthcare delivery: access isn't a communications problem, it's a design problem.

As medicine races into an era of AI, biomarkers, and digital diagnostics, the question of access will only become more complicated. Regulators and payers are evolving toward dynamic evidence, and patients rightly expect a seat at the table. In that shifting ground, Designing Innovation Around Access, Patients and Responsibility: Why Early Decisions Determine Who Gets Treated, is both compass and conscience.

To be sure, this is not a manifesto or a corporate handbook. It's a reality check, written by someone who has been inside the process long enough to see both its brilliance and its blind spots. It reminds us that the next frontier in medicine won't be biological; it will be structural.

As we progress, technology will drive discovery, but humanity will decide its impact. That's why I strongly recommend this book be read by anyone involved in developing the next solution and by those tasked with deciding access and availability to those in need. You will benefit, as will our patients.

Anthony J. Yanni, MD, MBA,
Founder and Chief Executive Officer of Lucid Health Solutions
Author of A Bandana and a Bluebird:
The Path to a Patient-Centric Healthcare System

PREFACE

A Note from a Recovering Optimist

When I joined the pharmaceutical industry, I believed that good science would naturally find its way to patients. If a molecule worked, I assumed regulators would value the evidence, payers would recognise the benefit, clinicians would prescribe it, and somewhere a patient would experience the result. Innovation, I thought, carried its own momentum.

For a while, that belief felt justified. I sat in meetings celebrating breakthrough therapies where the data looked strong, the dossiers were polished, and the headlines seemed almost written in advance. We congratulated one another and spoke about impact as if it were inevitable, confident that the hard work had already been done.

Then the celebrations ended.

Reimbursement stalled, health systems hesitated, and clinicians stayed with familiar options. Within a year, forecasts were revised downward and the excitement quietly evaporated. The therapy had not failed in the laboratory, but it had failed in life.

That experience was not unusual. It revealed something deeper about how our industry still operates. For all its sophistication, it often follows a twentieth century script in which approval is treated as success and access is treated as someone else's problem. Patients, however, do not live on development timelines. They live in real systems that are political, constrained, and full of competing priorities, and those systems do not bend to optimism.

Hope matters in this industry. You cannot spend a decade pursuing a molecule without believing it might change lives, but there is a fine line between optimism and complacency, and we cross it more often than we like to admit. We tell ourselves comforting stories that innovation will speak for itself, that value will be obvious, and that alignment will follow. Too often, it does not.

The problem is not talent or intent, it's design. Our processes were built to achieve regulatory efficiency, not real-world adoption, and we still treat discovery, approval, and access as sequential steps when in practice they are interdependent parts of the same system. Access is an upstream responsibility.

That became clear to me during a European payer meeting. Our clinical data were rigorous and our models elegant, at least on paper. After reviewing the slides, a payer smiled and said, "You have shown that it works. Now show that we can afford it." We could not. Our endpoints made sense to regulators but not to health systems, and our economics collapsed once local realities were applied. The therapy reached patients two years later than expected, two years filled by competitors and by waiting for people who did not have two years to spare.

From that moment, I stopped seeing access as a department and started seeing it as a condition for innovation.

Over time, access came to feel less like a function and more like a way of thinking. It begins with different questions about who will use a therapy, what they will value, who will pay for it, and who might be excluded. An access mindset means designing trials, evidence, and pricing as one coherent story, and it means involving regulators, payers, and patients before protocols are fixed rather than after decisions harden.

This way of working often feels uncomfortable. It demands humility, transparency, and shared ownership, and it requires different success measures from those the industry has traditionally celebrated. Approvals are easy to mark because they come with dates and certificates. What matters more is quieter and harder to track, including how many patients were treated, how many were excluded, and how many clinicians changed practice. These numbers rarely headline a slide deck, yet they define real impact.

This book exists because too many people work in the gaps between functions. Research, health economics, medical affairs, policy, and access teams each see part of the picture, but few are encouraged to see the whole. Access-First Innovation connects those pieces. It is written for people who are tired of launch surprises, confused forecasts, and confidence that dissolves on contact with reality. It is deliberately practical, occasionally blunt, and sometimes humorous, because the work is serious enough already.

Despite everything, I remain an optimist. This industry still does something remarkable by turning data into life, and that deserves belief. But belief must mature into responsibility. We cannot keep applauding breakthroughs that never reach the bedside, and we need success measures that reflect how well discovery turns into delivery rather than how quickly approval is achieved.

I believe in Access-First Innovation which is about that conversion. It argues that empathy and evidence are not opposites but partners, and it makes space for irony because anyone who has survived a launch readiness meeting where fifteen teams argue about whose slides are correct will understand why humour can be a professional survival skill. Irony is not cynicism. It creates room for change.

Science is accelerating. New technologies and therapies are transforming what is possible, yet dazzling science still needs a path into practice. Without access, it remains trapped in journals and headlines, impressive but inert.

Our challenge now is not discovery. It is delivery.

This book is my contribution to that challenge. If it sparks uncomfortable conversations in leadership rooms, good. If it brings access thinking into decisions earlier, even better. And if it helps one therapy reach one more patient who might otherwise have waited, that is enough.

I am still an optimist. I simply no longer confuse hope with design. Here is to science that works in the real-world, to medicines that are not only approved but used, and to treating approval as the beginning rather than the end.

A NOTE ON EGBERT FLOPPERCOUGH

From time to time, brief observations attributed to Egbert Floppercough appear throughout this book.

Egbert is not a character in the conventional sense. He is a device for capturing familiar organisational moments that are often recognised but rarely named. His remarks reflect recurring patterns rather than the behaviour of any individual or institution.

These short reflections are not instructions or conclusions. They are intended to create pause. They sit alongside the main argument as quiet observations about what happens when good intentions meet organisational reality.

Readers may recognise some of these moments. That recognition is the point.

HOW TO USE THIS BOOK

This book is not a manifesto; it is a working document. It's meant to be used, argued with, scribbled on, and quietly referenced when someone in a meeting says, "We'll think about access later."

It's a field guide for people who want to get medicines to patients faster, more fairly, and more intelligently. Whether you are a head of market access, a clinical development leader, a policymaker, or a commercial lead wondering why your latest launch did not quite land, this book gives you both the language and the logic to fix it.

The pharmaceutical world is full of bright people solving the wrong problem in the right way. *Designing Innovation Around Patient Access and Responsibility* aims to reverse that. It helps you see the entire system, from discovery through patient access, and act on it in a coordinated way.

How the Book Is Organised

The book has five parts, each tackling a different side of the access challenge. You can read it from start to finish or go straight to the part that keeps you awake at night.

Part I – The Access Imperative

This section dismantles the old success myth that regulatory approval equals victory. It explains why so many "successful" launches fail in practice and how the world's definition of value has changed. It might make you a little uncomfortable. That means it is working.

Part II – Building the Access-First Blueprint

Here, the tone moves from critique to construction. It shows how to design access into the molecule from the start through smarter trials, early economic modelling, meaningful endpoints, and genuine co-creation. This is the practical engine room of the book. If you work in clinical development, HEOR, medical affairs, or market access, this may become your new favourite manual and your best reason to rewrite a few SOPs.

Part III – Execution and Acceleration

This part turns ideas into delivery. It explores how to convert approval into adoption, manage reimbursement efficiently, generate real-world evidence, and measure what truly matters. You will find frameworks to track performance and examples of what effective, coordinated execution looks like. If your organisation often says, "We are launch ready," start here.

Part IV – Leadership, Culture, and the Future

The fourth part looks beyond process to mindset. It is about leadership that values impact over ceremony, systems over silos, and humility over hierarchy. It ends with a challenge: to define success by lives reached, not labels achieved.

Part V – Tools, Scenarios, and Practical Applications

The final part moves from theory to hands-on application. It gathers the frameworks, case studies, exercises, and templates that turn the book's ideas into day-to-day practice. You will find diagnostic checklists, access dashboards, and scenario-based learning guides that help teams embed access thinking in real time. If you want to translate insight into action, start here, or return here often.

Features to Look Out For

Each chapter ends with an Executive Checklist, a concise list of actions you can start next Monday morning.

You will also find Access in Practice boxes with short, real-world cases that show theory meeting reality, sometimes elegantly, sometimes awkwardly.

Diagrams such as the Access Equation, Value–Affordability Matrix, and Precision Access Pipeline are there for you to copy, adapt, or wave in meetings when logic needs a visual ally.

The appendices and Access-First Toolkit at the back include templates, dashboards, and checklists you can actually use. They turn philosophy into process.

How to Read It

Read actively. Question what applies to your context and what does not. Mark the pages that irritate you; they often point to an inconvenient truth. Discuss the ideas with your teams, especially the ones you rarely meet until Phase III.

You do not have to agree with every argument, but you do need to stay open to thinking differently by the end.

This is not a book about compliance or slogans. It is about alignment: of science, value, and humanity. It is for people who want to build the next generation of pharmaceutical organisations that are evidence-led, patient-centred, and system-savvy.

One Final Note

You will notice the language is plain and the humour deliberate. That is intentional. There are already enough documents in this industry written in corporate Esperanto. This one speaks human.

So, keep a pencil handy. Challenge the frameworks. Annotate the margins. Quote the lines that make you laugh. Most importantly, use what you learn to change something in your team, your company, or your health system.

Because if one idea from these pages helps one therapy reach one more patient faster and fairer, the book will have done its job.

Now turn the page to Chapter 1 and the question that still defines our industry: Why do we still think approval is the finish line?

PART I

THE ACCESS IMPERATIVE

CHAPTER 1

APPROVAL ISN'T THE FINISH LINE

"Approval creates permission, not impact. Impact begins when someone receives the medicine."
– Egbert Floppercough

This chapter reframes approval as a regulatory milestone rather than a measure of success. It argues that impact emerges only when therapies are adopted within real health systems. Access is not a downstream administrative function. It is a system outcome shaped by decisions made long before submission.

The Launch That Wasn't

The atrium was filled with applause. A large screen displayed one word in bold letters: APPROVED. Speeches followed, photographs were taken, and congratulatory messages circulated across the organisation. Years of development had culminated in regulatory clearance. By every traditional measure, the programme was a success.

Six months later, uptake was negligible.

Reimbursement had stalled in key markets. Health technology assessment bodies had raised comparative and cost-effectiveness concerns that had not been expected. Clinicians hesitated, uncertain how the therapy fitted into existing treatment pathways. Forecasts were revised quietly downward.

Nothing had failed in the laboratory. The failure occurred at the interface between evidence and economics.

In a subsequent payer meeting, the disconnect became explicit. Data showed efficacy under trial conditions, but committee members asked a direct question: how does this therapy improve outcomes relative to current practice, and at what cost to the system? Submission materials addressed the first part only partially and the second inadequately, revealing that the evidence had been designed for regulatory scrutiny rather than system adoption. Market conditions were not the problem; the development strategy was incomplete.

The Structural Misalignment

For decades, regulatory approval functioned as a proxy for value. If a therapy met standards of safety, quality, and efficacy, it entered the market. That model assumed expanding health budgets, limited therapeutic competition, and relatively permissive pricing environments. Those conditions no longer hold.

Today, approval marks the beginning of a second evaluation phase rather than the end of development. Regulators determine whether a therapy can be marketed. Payers, clinicians, and health systems determine whether it will be used. Their criteria differ materially. Safety and efficacy are necessary conditions. They are not sufficient ones.

Most development processes remain optimised for the first decision and under-prepared for the second. Evidence is generated to satisfy regulatory endpoints, often without parallel consideration of comparative effectiveness, affordability, infrastructure requirements, or real-world integration. When those questions arise post-approval, organisations attempt to retrofit answers onto data that were never designed to address them.

This sequence produces delays, renegotiations, and erosion of first-mover advantage. More importantly, it postpones patient access.

Impact as a System Outcome

Impact cannot be inferred from approval status. It depends on adoption within the constraints of real systems.

A therapy may show strong clinical performance yet fail to secure reimbursement in a budget-constrained environment. It may receive positive health technology assessment but encounter operational barriers such as diagnostic capacity, prescribing restrictions, or pathway inertia. It may achieve reimbursement but remain under-used because the evidence did not resonate with practising clinicians.

In each case, the scientific achievement remains intact. The system integration fails.

The relationship can be expressed simply: impact is the product of innovation and adoption. If adoption approaches zero, impact collapses regardless of scientific merit. Innovation generates potential. Adoption converts it into a measurable benefit.

This is not a communication problem. It is a design problem.

The Missing Middle

Between regulatory approval and patient treatment lies a decision space often treated as secondary. This "missing middle" includes health technology assessment, pricing negotiations, budget impact modelling, clinical guideline integration, and operational readiness. Each stage imposes criteria distinct from regulatory review.

When development teams operate sequentially, handing assets from R&D to access functions late in the lifecycle, misalignment is predictable. Clinical endpoints may lack comparative relevance. Economic models may rely on assumptions unsupported by trial design. Pricing strategies may ignore fiscal realities in specific jurisdictions.

These are not unforeseeable obstacles. They are foreseeable consequences of fragmented planning.

The challenge, therefore, is not to work harder after approval but to work differently before it. Trial design, comparator selection, endpoint choice, economic modelling, and stakeholder engagement must evolve in parallel rather than in sequence. Access must be treated as a condition of innovation rather than a negotiation that follows it.

The Stakes

Delays between approval and reimbursement now extend from weeks to years across comparable health systems. The variation is not primarily scientific. It reflects differences in evidence alignment, economic modelling, and system negotiation.

The consequences are measurable. Launch underperformance can eliminate projected returns on multibillion-dollar investments. More critically, delayed access translates into deferred or foregone patient benefit. The gap between approval and use is where trust either strengthens or erodes.

When approved therapies remain inaccessible, the public does not observe procedural complexity. It observes inequity.

Approval, therefore, should be understood not as the point at which impact is achieved, but as the point at which responsibility intensifies. From that moment onward, the central question shifts from whether a therapy works to whether it will reach those who need it.

The rest of this chapter examines how that responsibility can be operationalised, and how organisations can redesign development to close the gap between innovation and adoption.

Approval, Adoption, and the Missing Middle

Most failures between approval and adoption follow a familiar pattern. Evidence packages built entirely for regulators prove inadequate for health technology assessment agencies. Clinical endpoints that meet statistical significance fail to resonate with payers or clinicians. Pricing models that look solid in Excel collapse under the weight of real-world budgets. The real challenge lies in what I call the missing middle, the space between approval and access where scientific logic must meet system reality. Regulators evaluate risks and benefits. Payers evaluate value and affordability. Patients evaluate relevance and fairness. Bridging those perspectives requires more than data; it requires design.

The traditional linear approach, where functions work in isolation and hand off to one another, cannot keep pace with the complexity of modern healthcare. Clinical Development, Health Economics and Outcomes Research, Medical Affairs, and Market Access: If these functions still operate as a relay team, access failure is guaranteed.

In the chapters ahead, you will see that integration in practice: trial designs built for real-world endpoints, early evidence strategies that pre-empt payer questions, and access plans that treat affordability as a design feature rather than an afterthought.

The Stakes of Getting It Wrong

Every delay in access has measurable consequences. The clinical cost is hard to quantify, but the economic cost of a failed launch can exceed two billion dollars in lost investment and opportunity.

In oncology, reimbursement delays shorten survival at a population level, not metaphorically but measurably. Studies of access to new cancer medicines across Europe show this clearly. In countries with slower reimbursement systems, patients lose years of cumulative survival compared to those in faster markets such as Germany.

In rare diseases, delay can mean the difference between a child walking or never walking. Beyond economics and outcomes lies a deeper cost: trust. When approved therapies sit unused while patients wait, public confidence in the entire system erodes. People see injustice, not complexity. Advocacy groups lose faith, while policymakers question motives. The public narrative hardens against the industry. That is why access is not simply a market access problem; it is a moral one.

The Access Equation in Practice

Translating the Access Equation into practical strategy means confronting the uncomfortable truth that most barriers to access are predictable. They are not acts of fate or quirks of the market. They are design choices. Once that is accepted, the path to improvement becomes clearer. The solution is not to work harder after approval but to work differently before it.

In practice, this requires a shift in both process and mindset. Teams must move from sequential handovers to parallel collaboration, where clinical, economic, and practical evidence evolve together. Market Access and HEOR should no longer be downstream functions waiting for data but co-architects shaping the evidence package from the earliest phases. Medical Affairs must act as the bridge between science and society, bringing real-world relevance into development rather than translating it afterward. And leadership must treat access not as an outcome but as a core design principle.

To help teams make this shift, I use a simple visual: The Access Equation becomes not a slogan but an operating system. Its two components, innovation and adoption, represent the dual engines of impact. The greater the synchronisation between them, the greater the lift.

This shift is not theoretical. It has already been demonstrated in multiple case studies where foresight and alignment turned potential failures into successful access stories.

Case Studies in Access-First Thinking

Case Study 1: The Oncology Mirage

Question: Why is regulatory approval often a trap, not a triumph?

A cancer therapy won rapid European approval based on promising progression-free survival data from a small Phase III trial. The company celebrated what looked like a textbook success: speed, scientific credibility, and first-to-market advantage.

Yet, when the health technology assessment reviews began, the picture changed completely. Payers in France, Italy, and the Netherlands all asked the same questions: Where was the comparative evidence against the local standard of care? Where was the mature survival data? Neither existed. The dossier was strong for regulatory purposes but weak for reimbursement.

The company spent the next eighteen months gathering real-world data to answer those questions. By the time reimbursement was secured, two competitors had also launched. The therapy that was once first became third and largely forgotten.

Lesson: Regulatory success does not equal market readiness. The evidence that satisfies regulators rarely satisfies payers.

Case Study 2: The Orphan Drug That Planned Ahead

Question: How can uncertainty in early development be managed to earn trust and faster access?

A small biotech developing a therapy for a rare blood disorder faced a classic problem: a tiny patient population, surrogate endpoints, and considerable uncertainty.

Instead of following the usual approach (complete trials, submit, then negotiate), they invited representatives from health technology agencies to review their evidence framework early. Together, they agreed on a post-launch data collection plan and a shared understanding of how to handle uncertainty. Patient groups were involved to help define outcomes that mattered in daily life, such as transfusion independence, not just laboratory markers.

When the dossier reached review, it did not hide uncertainty. It showed a credible plan to reduce it over time. The result was conditional reimbursement within months of approval. The therapy reached patients faster, and the evidence base continued to evolve.

Lesson: Transparency earns more trust than perfection. A well-planned evidence roadmap signals credibility in ways flawless but incomplete datasets never can.

Case Study 3: Two Gene Therapies, Two Fates

Question: Can pricing and payment models be treated as innovation, not just commerce?

This case failed because... Company A treated access as a commercial hurdle.

Two companies launched gene therapies for similar rare diseases within a year of each other. Both offered transformational efficacy. Yet their fates diverged. Company A priced its therapy aggressively, confident that its curative claim would compel payers to pay. Company B took a different route.

During development, Company B began discussions with payers about affordability and sustainability. Together, they explored new payment models, including annuity-style payments linked to long-term outcomes.

When approval arrived, Company A celebrated but could not secure reimbursement in most markets. Company B moved smoothly through negotiations and achieved reimbursement in multiple countries within twelve months. Its therapy was adopted widely and became a reference point for future gene therapy discussions. The difference was not science but strategy.

Lesson: Treating access as part of innovation, exploring flexible payment models and long-term value, accelerates adoption and market entry.

Case Study 4: The Value of Humour in Hard Truths

Question: What is the simplest way to introduce humility into the launch process?

At a leadership offsite, one team suggested creating a laminated card for every new launch listing the reasons it might fail. "You mean a post-mortem in advance?" someone asked. Everyone laughed, but they also recognised the point.

Most access failures are predictable and therefore preventable. The exercise of articulating potential failure points *before* launch forces teams to confront realistic access hurdles (e.g., "The local guidelines will reject our surrogate endpoint," or "Our price point assumes global volume we won't achieve"). By making the fear explicit and slightly absurd, they made the discussion safer. They shifted from avoiding potential failure to actively mitigating it.

Lesson: A little humility early can save a great deal of regret later. Making potential failure points explicit is the first step toward preventing them.

From Insight to Action

Turning these lessons into everyday practice requires structure. It is easy to talk about designing for access; the challenge lies in operationalising it. To make the idea tangible, I encourage teams to use three tools: the Access-First Checklist, the Access Maturity Matrix, and the Evidence Planning Map. These are simple frameworks, not bureaucratic templates, designed to help organisations think in systems rather than silos.

The Access-First Checklist acts as a quick diagnostic for any development programme. It includes six straightforward questions. Do our trial endpoints align with what payers and clinicians consider meaningful? Is the comparator used in trials the same as that used in real-world practice? Have we tested our proposed price range against realistic health-economic models? Do we understand the operational requirements for uptake, such as diagnostics or infrastructure? Have we engaged with health technology assessors, payers, and patients early enough to shape their expectations? And finally, how will we measure adoption once the product is available? If any of these answers are uncertain, the programme is at risk.

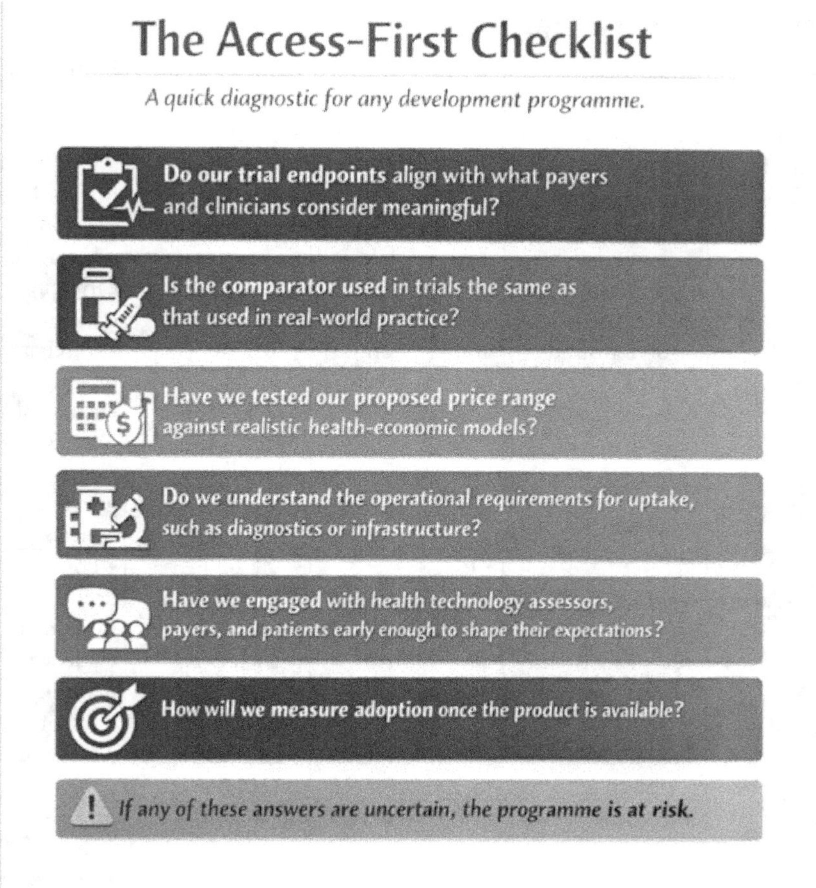

Figure 1.1 The Access-First Checklist

The Access Maturity Matrix helps leaders assess where their organisation stands. In the approval-first stage, teams focus almost exclusively on regulatory milestones. Market Access enters late, and evidence gaps appear after submission. At the access-aware stage, early dialogue occurs, but integration remains inconsistent. The organisation begins to recognise the issue but has not yet institutionalised change. The access-first stage represents full alignment, where cross-functional planning, payer input, and adaptive evidence planning are standard practice. Moving from stage one to stage three is not a question of more process but of earlier curiosity.

Access Maturity Matrix

Stage	Description	Typical Behaviours	Risks and Limitations	Path to Next Stage
Stage 1: Approval-First	Access is treated as a post-launch activity focused on reimbursement paperwork. The organisation's success metrics revolve around regulatory milestones and time to approval.	• Market Access teams join late in development. • Trial endpoints designed solely for regulators. • Limited understanding of payer needs or health system constraints.	• Delays between approval and reimbursement. • Data gaps discovered post-launch. • Reactive pricing strategy and strained payer relationships.	• Bring Access and HEOR into early asset planning. • Introduce early payer dialogue and scenario testing. • Establish joint R&D–Access governance reviews.
Stage 2: Access-Aware	Access considerations are recognised but inconsistently applied. Teams discuss access during Phase II or III, often without integration into evidence planning.	• Payer engagement begins mid-development. • Basic health-economic models built late. • Access teams still viewed as support functions.	• Misaligned data packages. • Moderate launch delays and patchy adoption. • Occasional success dependent on individual champions.	• Formalise cross-functional evidence planning. • Integrate payer and patient insights into trial design. • Make time-to-access a standard KPI.
Stage 3: Access-Integrated	Access thinking shapes scientific, clinical, and commercial decisions from the start. Payer and patient perspectives are built into trial endpoints, comparators, and post-launch evidence plans.	• Unified access roadmap across functions. • Early health-technology assessment (HTA) simulation. • Scenario testing for price, value, and equity.	• Potential internal friction as priorities shift. • Increased workload for evidence generation.	• Build real-world data capabilities. • Expand multi-stakeholder co-creation frameworks. • Establish outcome-based performance incentives.

Stage	Description	Typical Behaviours	Risks and Limitations	Path to Next Stage
Stage 4: Access-First Organisation	Access defines the organisation's culture, metrics, and leadership model. Success is measured by speed, equity, and sustainability of adoption. Innovation and access are inseparable.	• Access and R&D functions fully integrated. • Real-world evidence and policy engagement run continuously. • Leadership rewards linked to patient reach and access metrics.	• Requires sustained investment and external trust. • Complex governance models to manage multi-country equity.	• Maintain adaptive learning loops through continuous evidence generation. • Share best practices externally to shape industry standards.

Table 1.1: The Access Maturity Matrix

The Evidence Planning Map expands on this thinking. It helps teams design, align, and communicate evidence generation across multiple decision-makers; regulators, HTA bodies, payers, clinicians, and patients, from the earliest stages of development.

Evidence that convinces one audience rarely satisfies another. Regulators need proof of safety and efficacy. Payers need comparative and economic value. Clinicians want relevance and usability. Patients care about quality of life, dignity, and access.

The Evidence Planning Map creates a shared visual language across these audiences, ensuring that data generated once can work many times.

Evidence Planning Map

Audience	What They Need to Know	Preferred Evidence Types	When to Engage	Success Indicator
Regulators	Is the therapy safe, effective, and of consistent quality?	Randomised controlled trials (RCTs), pharmacovigilance plans, chemistry–manufacturing–controls (CMC) data.	Preclinical through Phase III; continuous during lifecycle.	Approval granted with minimal queries or conditional obligations.
HTA Bodies	Is the therapy better or more efficient than current standards of care?	Comparative effectiveness studies, cost–utility analyses, and budget impact models.	Early dialogue during Phase II; pre-submission alignment.	Positive or conditional HTA recommendation within 6–12 months of approval.
Payers	Can the system afford it, and what is the value for money?	Economic models, real-world data, scenario-tested pricing analyses, managed-entry agreements.	From Phase II onwards; pricing rehearsals pre-launch.	Reimbursement granted promptly with acceptable terms.
Clinicians	Does it work for my patients in real-world settings?	Pragmatic trials, practice-relevant endpoints, patient-reported outcomes, and usability data.	Throughout trials and post-launch evidence generation.	Prescriber confidence, guideline inclusion, sustained uptake.
Patients and Advocacy Groups	Will it improve my life, and can I access it fairly?	Quality-of-life measures, long-term follow-up, equitable access data, and patient experience research.	From design stage to lifecycle management; continuous feedback loops.	Improved adherence, satisfaction, and engagement in research design.

Table 1.2 The Evidence Planning Map

How to Build an Evidence Plan Using the Map

Step 1: Define the Core Claim of Value

What is the single most important statement you want every stakeholder to believe about your therapy?

For example: *This treatment reduces hospital stays by 30 percent compared with current care.*

Write this clearly. Every evidence activity must support it.

Step 2: Identify Audience Priorities

For each stakeholder group, list their decision criteria. Regulators look for risk control, payers for economic impact, clinicians for practical benefit, and patients for lived outcomes.

Step 3: Map Evidence to the Development Timeline

Overlay your evidence plans onto the drug development timeline. Ensure that the right data types are collected early enough to answer payer and HTA questions, not after approval.

Step 4: Plan for Real-World Continuity

Every evidence plan should include post-launch follow-up: registries, real-world studies, patient-reported outcomes, and system-level performance metrics.

Step 5: Align Internally

Create a single evidence narrative that integrates regulatory, clinical, economic, and patient perspectives. Consistency is credibility.

The Evidence Planning Map – Template Example

Development Phase	Objective	Evidence Activities	Primary Audience	Secondary Use	Planned Outputs
Preclinical	Define mechanism and safety profile.	Proof-of-concept studies; basic economic scoping.	Regulators	Payers, HTA	Early narrative of innovation potential.
Phase I	Establish safety and dosing.	Safety endpoints; exploratory biomarkers.	Regulators	Clinicians	Dose rationale and early differentiation story.
Phase II	Demonstrate preliminary efficacy and relevance.	Comparative trials; exploratory PROs; pilot cost analysis.	Regulators, HTA	Payers	Phase IIb dataset linked to payer modelling inputs.
Phase III	Confirm efficacy and generate regulatory submission data.	Global pivotal RCTs; quality-of-life studies; early HEOR integration.	Regulators, HTA	Clinicians	Integrated Clinical and Economic Dossier (ICED).
Pre-Launch	Align pricing, access, and adoption plans.	Health-economic models; payer rehearsals; managed entry scenarios.	Payers	Regulators, HTA	Pricing justification narrative and reimbursement toolkit.
Post-Launch	Sustain adoption and monitor outcomes.	Real-world studies; long-term registry data; patient satisfaction surveys.	Payers, Clinicians, Patients	Regulators	Evidence refresh for lifecycle extension and HTA reassessment.

Table 1.3 The Evidence Planning Map - Template Example

How to Use This Map in Practice

1. *Make it visual.*
   Print or project the map in your evidence planning meetings. Plot each data type and timeline together to spot gaps early.
2. *Run evidence rehearsals.*
   Before Phase III completion, simulate HTA and payer questions. See whether your current data would survive scrutiny.
3. *Integrate it into governance.*
   Make the Evidence Planning Map part of your portfolio review pack. Each asset should show how its data supports adoption, not just approval.
4. *Update continuously.*
   Evidence planning isn't a one-off event. Review and adjust your plan every six months based on new real-world data or regulatory feedback.

Common Pitfalls and How to Avoid Them

Pitfall	**Consequence**	**Prevention Strategy**
Collecting data that regulators value but payers ignore.	Delayed reimbursement and low adoption.	Map every evidence activity to at least one payer or HTA question.
Treating real-world evidence as a post-launch afterthought.	Lost momentum and missed learning cycles.	Plan registries and follow-up studies during Phase II or III.
Keeping economic modellers separate from clinical teams.	Fragmented story and inconsistent assumptions.	Create integrated evidence sprints involving both groups.
Neglecting patient input.	Unrealistic endpoints or weak adherence evidence.	Involve patient representatives in trial and PRO design.

Finally, here is a set of five **Leadership Reflex Questions** that can be used in governance meetings to embed access thinking in decision making. Who will decide whether this therapy is used? What evidence will they trust most? What uncertainty will they fear most? How can we reduce that uncertainty before launch? And how quickly can we move from approval to the first patient treated? When leaders ask these questions regularly, they prevent 80 percent of the most common access failures.

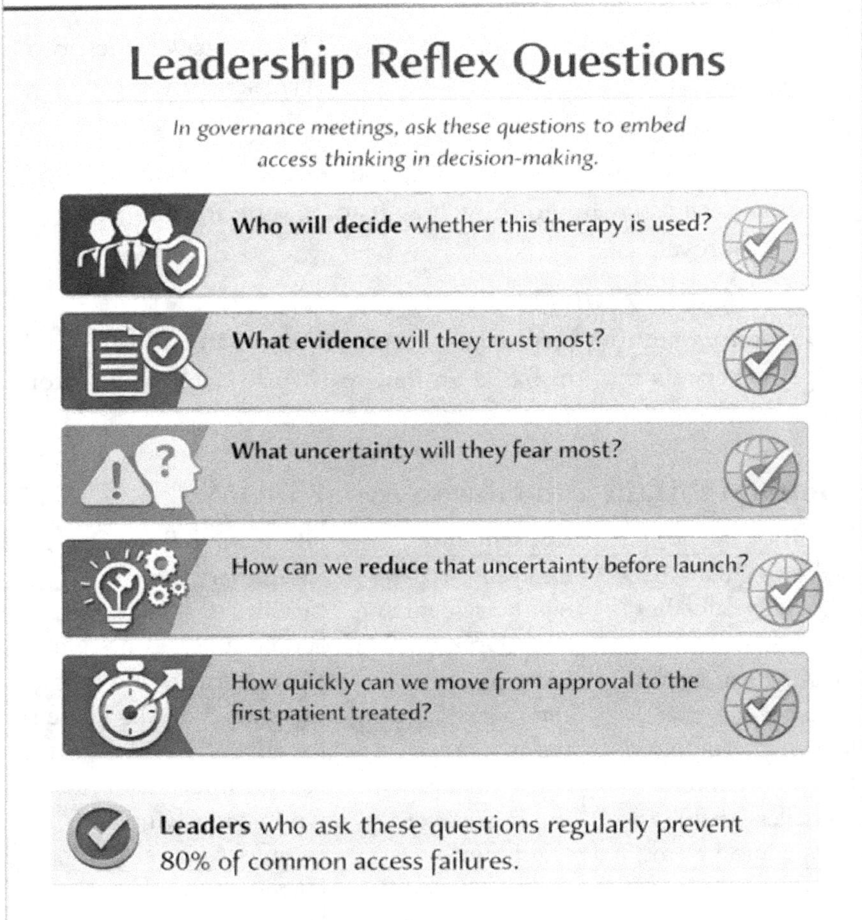

Figure 1.2 Leadership Reflex Questions

Why Frameworks Matter

These frameworks may seem simple, but they work because they replace assumption with clarity. They force teams to articulate what value means from the perspective of the people who decide on access. They also promote humility, a quality not always abundant in scientific cultures. When a cross-functional team can look at an evidence plan and say, "We have strong data for regulators but weak relevance for payers," it marks a maturity that separates high-performing organisations from the rest.

Embedding access in this way changes behaviour. Conversations in programme review meetings begin to sound different. Instead of "When will we submit to the regulator?" people start asking "When will patients start treatment?" The difference seems small but is transformative. It signals that success is being measured not by certificates on walls but by use in real life.

Evidence from Across the Industry

Data from recent access studies reinforce why these frameworks are necessary. Analysis of oncology medicines approved in Europe between 2016 and 2021 found a median reimbursement delay of more than four hundred days across seven high-income countries. Germany achieved reimbursement in three days, while Belgium took more than seven hundred. Only Germany met the European Union's 180-day target. These figures underline the fragmentation and complexity of access in supposedly similar systems. The causes were rarely scientific. They were procedural, economic, or evidence related.

Another case, involving lenalidomide for a rare myelodysplastic syndrome with a specific chromosomal deletion, illustrates how well-planned real-world evidence can make the difference between rejection and approval. The manufacturer complemented limited trial data with survival and treatment duration data from real practice. This persuaded NICE to recommend the therapy despite residual uncertainties. It was a success built on preparation rather than persuasion.

A broader study of cancer medicines in Central and Eastern Europe revealed long delays between approval and access even for drugs with substantial clinical benefit. Some waited up to three years for reimbursement. The analysis confirmed that high clinical value alone does not guarantee fast access. Systems with constrained budgets delay decisions regardless of evidence. This reinforces the need to design affordability into the strategy rather than treat it as a post-approval negotiation.

Even outside oncology, the principle holds. The global rollout of COVID-19 vaccines demonstrated that approval and supply are not enough to guarantee access. Studies by University College London and The University of Manchester highlighted stark inequalities in geographical reach and uptake among ethnic groups, even within the same country. These findings show that access depends on infrastructure, trust, and public engagement as much as regulatory clearance.

Each of these examples supports the same conclusion: the bridge between innovation and adoption must be built deliberately and early.

The Strategic and Ethical Dimension

Access is not only a question of commercial performance. It is the bridge between scientific promise and social legitimacy. Every company claims to be patient centred, but that claim is tested not at the moment of approval but at the moment of access. If a therapy exists but patients cannot reach it, society does not see innovation; it sees inequity. The gap between approval and use is where public trust either grows or erodes.

Health systems today operate under extraordinary pressure. Ageing populations, rising expectations, and budgetary constraint have created an environment where every new therapy must prove not only that it works but that it is worth it. Governments and payers now share the role once held solely by regulators. They are no longer passive recipients of data but active participants in defining value. For companies, that means the scientific argument is no longer enough. It must be supported by an economic, operational, and moral one.

The moral argument is simple. Innovation that does not reach people fails its purpose. When reimbursement delays stretch into years, patients lose hope and clinicians lose faith. A study published by ISPOR estimated that delayed reimbursement for two breast cancer medicines in Spain translated into thousands of years of survival lost across the population. Behind those statistics are lives that could have been extended or improved. Numbers matter because they make the invisible visible. They quantify the cost of inertia.

The economic argument is equally compelling. The average cost of developing a new medicine is estimated to exceed two billion dollars. When that investment does not translate into patient use, value evaporates. The sunk cost remains, but the return never arrives. Investors become cautious. Portfolio decisions become defensive. Innovation slows. The system that was built to encourage progress ends up punishing it.

Trust as the New Currency

The industry's reputation has long fluctuated between admiration for scientific achievement and suspicion of commercial intent. In recent years, that balance has shifted decisively towards scepticism. High prices, delayed access, and inconsistent equity have all contributed to a perception that innovation serves profit before people. The only way to reverse that perception is through transparency and accountability.

Access-First strategies naturally foster trust because they align company goals with public outcomes. When developers engage payers early, share data openly, and adapt pricing models to real-world constraints, they signal respect for the system and for the people it serves. When they insist on secrecy and rigidity, they invite confrontation. The former approach builds credibility, but the latter burns it.

Transparency does not mean surrendering commercial advantage. It means sharing uncertainty honestly. Most payers and policymakers accept that not all evidence can be perfect at launch. What they cannot accept is being misled. A company that admits what it does not yet know and presents a clear plan to resolve it is far more likely to earn cooperation. In contrast, one that pretends every question has been answered will face scrutiny and delay.

Patient Perspectives

The most powerful insights into access rarely come from boardrooms. They come from the people waiting for treatment. A patient advocate once told me, "It's strange. We celebrate new medicines on the news, but most of us never see them." That single sentence captures the essence of the access problem better than any slide deck could. For patients, the difference between discovery and delivery is not an abstract process. It is the difference between hope realised and hope deferred.

In many health systems, patients have become the most effective catalysts for access reform. Advocacy groups are increasingly sophisticated in their understanding of reimbursement processes and evidence requirements. They are no longer passive recipients of information but active shapers of it. When companies involve them early, both sides benefit. The evidence becomes more relevant, the communication more credible, and the outcome more sustainable.

Policy and System Alignment

Governments and payers are already developing policies to reward access-first thinking. Performance-based agreements, value-based pricing, and outcome-linked reimbursement schemes are now part of the mainstream in many regions. These mechanisms recognise that value is not static but dynamic. They encourage collaboration rather than confrontation.

For companies, this evolution presents both a challenge and an opportunity. It demands flexibility, new data capabilities, and a willingness to share risk. But it also rewards those who can show real-world impact. The companies that learn to navigate this environment effectively will not only achieve faster access but will also secure stronger, longer-term relationships with health systems.

This is where the practical meets the ethical. The shift from volume to value aligns commercial sustainability with social responsibility. A company that designs for access is not only doing the right thing morally; it is also doing the smart thing strategically.

Equity and Global Responsibility

Access inequity remains one of the most persistent problems in global health. Wealthy and less wealthy nations show differences in time to reimbursement that measure in years. The pandemic exposed how fragile access really is when supply chains, budgets, and trust are strained simultaneously. While no single company can fix these systemic issues alone, each can choose to contribute to the solution.

Building equity into access planning means thinking beyond regulatory markets. It means considering affordability tiers, differentiated pricing, and partnerships with public agencies to extend reach. It also means investing in infrastructure, diagnostics, and health literacy in the regions where the burden of disease is highest. Access is not only about price; it is about preparedness.

The Organisational Shift

Internally, an access-first culture requires a change in incentives and mindset. Organisations tend to celebrate visible milestones such as regulatory submissions and approvals. Access milestones are often quieter, less glamorous, and harder to measure. Yet they define real impact. Senior leaders must make it clear that the true measure of success is not the number of labels achieved but the number of patients reached.

To embed this, companies can adapt their performance metrics. Time to reimbursement, time to first patient treated, and equity of uptake should sit alongside traditional measures such as time to approval and revenue. When teams know that access outcomes affect their recognition and reward, their priorities shift. They view access not as someone else's problem but as their own.

From Reflection to Action

The shift from approval-first to access-first sounds conceptually simple, yet it challenges habits that have been built over decades. The traditional model was designed for a world in which regulators were the primary audience and data moved slowly. It prioritised control and predictability over speed and collaboration. That model protected patients from harm, but it also built walls that now impede progress. To move forward, the industry must dismantle some of those walls.

Cross-functional collaboration must become the default, not the exception. Payer engagement should begin during the design of pivotal trials, not at the point of submission. Real-world evidence generation must be planned from the outset, not treated as a rescue operation after rejection. And communication with patients, policymakers, and clinicians must be ongoing, not transactional.

The change is cultural as much as procedural. It requires humility, curiosity, and empathy. The best innovators in the coming decade will not be those who produce the most data but those who understand what data others need.

A Quick Reality Check

Whenever I review a portfolio plan, I use a simple test. Imagine standing in front of a group of patients still waiting for a product and explaining that your company considers its launch a success. Would they agree? If the answer feels uncomfortable, you are probably closer to the truth than you think. That discomfort is not a weakness. It is a sign of awareness.

Key insight

Approval is not the point at which impact is achieved. It is the point at which responsibility begins. Innovation only becomes meaningful when it is adopted within real health systems and reaches patients in practice. When organisations optimise for approval alone, they create the illusion of success while leaving access to chance.

Reflection

Think about the last approval your organisation celebrated. What assumptions were made at that moment, about access, reimbursement, and uptake?

Consider whether those assumptions were tested explicitly or simply inherited from previous launches. Notice how the definition of success shaped what happened next.

Try this

- Identify one recently approved or late-stage asset and map the path from approval to the first patient treated.
- List the assumptions made about reimbursement, affordability, and adoption.
- Ask which of those assumptions were evidence-based and which were hopeful.
- Review when Market Access and HEOR were first involved in shaping the programme.
- Decide what would need to change to design for access earlier next time.

Summary

- Approval grants permission, not impact.
- Impact depends on adoption, not celebration.
- Access failures are usually predictable and preventable.
- Designing only for regulators strands innovation downstream.
- Early integration reduces delays and rework.
- Success should be measured by patients reached, not milestones achieved.
- Champagne is optional. Access is not.

If approval is no longer the accurate measure of success, the obvious question is why the industry continues to behave as if it were. The next chapter examines how success has been defined in modern pharma, and how those definitions quietly reinforce approval-first behaviour.

CHAPTER 2

THE ACCESS IMPERATIVE: REDEFINING SUCCESS IN MODERN PHARMA

"Access rarely fails loudly. It simply never arrives, having been excluded quietly by earlier decisions."
– Egbert Floppercough

This chapter examines how traditional success metrics continue to privilege regulatory milestones over patient reach, and how those definitions quietly shape behaviour. It establishes access as an operational aim rather than a moral aspiration.

The Conversation in Geneva

At a global health policy forum in Geneva, a senior civil servant said something most executives prefer not to hear. "The problem isn't that you're not innovative," he said. "It's that you keep innovating in ways the system can't pay for." The executives around him smiled politely but said nothing. There was nothing to argue. He was right.

Back in their offices, those same executives were preparing to launch dozens of new therapies. Most were scientifically impressive but commercially uncertain. The press releases would speak of breakthrough designations and record approvals. Yet between those headlines and the hospital wards, many of those therapies would stall. They would become trapped in reimbursement reviews, delayed in price negotiations, or suspended in endless cycles of further clarification. Those launches did not stall because the science was weak, but because affordability was never designed.

That quiet remark over coffee captured the access problem in one sentence. The industry is living through its most productive scientific era and its most constrained economic one. We have learned to create miracles but not to sustain them. We can design therapies that transform biology but struggle to design systems that can afford them. The result is a widening gap between what science can achieve and what health systems can deliver.

Redefining Success

The Access Imperative begins with a necessary question. What does success mean in today's pharmaceutical world? For much of the twentieth century, success was defined narrowly by discovery and approval. The most admired companies were those that produced the most new medicines, secured the most approvals, and generated the most revenue. The model rewarded volume and speed. It worked in an era when regulators were the primary arbiters of value, health budgets were growing, and pricing power was largely unquestioned. That era has ended.

In its place is a new reality where innovation must compete not only for regulatory approval but also for fiscal viability, social legitimacy, and ethical accountability. Health systems no longer reward novelty. They penalise irrelevance. Regulators may approve a therapy because it meets standards of safety and efficacy, but payers ask whether it improves outcomes in ways that justify cost and displace existing practice. Patients ask whether it changes lives, not just test results. Policymakers ask whether it is sustainable.

This shift demands a redefinition of success. The companies that thrive will not be those that produce the most molecules, but those that ensure those molecules are actually used. They will measure progress not in labels achieved but in lives reached.

Traditional assumption		Access-first reframing
Approval defines success	→	**Patient use** defines success
Access follows approval	→	**Access** is designed upstream
Market access is a function	→	Access is a system outcome
Evidence is generated once	→	**Evidence** evolves over time
Pricing is a commercial decision	→	**Pricing** is a system design choice
Equity is a policy issue	→	**Equity** is a design constraint

Leaders who ask these questions regularly prevent **80%** of common access failures.

Figure 2.1 Access Reframing

The Productivity Paradox

By almost any scientific measure, the pharmaceutical industry has never been more productive. Advances in genomics, artificial intelligence, and precision medicine have created an unprecedented pipeline of potential cures. The number of novel drug approvals has increased steadily across major markets. Clinical development tools are faster, data are richer, and translational science has blurred the line between discovery and application.

Yet the paradox is that access to these innovations has become slower, not faster. A recent European review of oncology therapies found that while the number of new approvals continues to rise, the median time from regulatory approval to reimbursement has grown longer. Some countries deliver access within weeks. Others take years. The bottleneck is rarely scientific. It is organisational.

This paradox reveals an uncomfortable truth. Innovation alone no longer guarantees success. Without affordability, integration, and adoption, scientific progress becomes stranded potential. The system cannot absorb infinite innovation without reforming the way value is defined, measured, and rewarded.

The Core Challenge

The core problem is simple: development is optimised for approval, not adoption. Pharmaceutical development remains largely optimised for regulatory approval. Evidence is generated to prove that a product is safe and effective under controlled conditions. That evidence satisfies regulators but often fails to satisfy payers, who need proof that the therapy delivers value in real-world practice relative to alternatives and within finite budgets.

This misalignment is not just procedural; it is cultural. Many organisations still treat Market Access as the department responsible for fixing whatever evidence gaps remain once development is complete. Access is the outcome of every decision made from the earliest stages of research onwards. Trial design, endpoint selection, comparator choice, pricing assumptions, and even corporate narratives all shape whether a therapy will eventually be adopted. Treating access as an afterthought guarantees delay.

The New Value Triangle

To realign innovation with adoption, companies must expand their definition of value. The New Value Triangle defines how modern pharmaceutical value is created, demonstrated, and sustained. Traditional value models focused almost entirely on clinical efficacy - the ability of a therapy to work under ideal conditions.

Today, value must be proven across three equally weighted dimensions: Clinical, Economic, and Societal. Together, these form the New Value Triangle - a model that integrates patient benefit, system efficiency, and societal legitimacy into one coherent measure of impact.

Most organisations believe they address all three. Very few do.

1. Clinical Value – The Foundation of Trust

Key Question:

Does the therapy meaningfully improve patient outcomes compared with current standards of care?

Definition:

Clinical value represents the therapeutic benefit established through robust evidence: safety, efficacy, durability, and quality of life. It remains the foundation on which all other forms of value are built, but it is no longer enough on its own.

Evidence Sources:

- Randomised controlled trials (RCTs)
- Real-world effectiveness studies
- Patient-reported outcomes (PROs)
- Comparative data against local standards of care

Indicators of Excellence:

- Clinically significant endpoints validated by independent experts
- Clear linkage between trial outcomes and patient-relevant benefits
- Transparent reporting of uncertainty and follow-up plans

Strategic Message:

Strong science earns approval. Credible translation earns adoption.

2. Economic Value – The Engine of Sustainability

Key Question:

Can the health system afford it, and does it deliver measurable efficiency or savings over time?

Definition:

Economic value connects clinical outcomes to resource impact, the balance between cost, affordability, and benefit. It captures not just price, but productivity, system savings, and opportunity cost.

Evidence Sources:

- Cost–effectiveness models (e.g. QALY or cost per responder)
- Budget impact analyses
- Health resource utilisation studies
- Productivity and workforce participation metrics

If these data appear after Phase III, access failure is already locked in.

Indicators of Excellence:

- Early integration of health-economic modelling (by Phase II)
- Transparent scenario testing with payers
- Local adaptation of models to reflect national budgets
- Real-world validation of predicted cost savings

Strategic Message:

Value that can't be financed is value that can't be delivered.

3. Societal Value – The Measure of Legitimacy

Key Question:

Does the therapy contribute to a fairer, stronger, and more resilient health system?

Definition:

Societal value determines whether innovation earns legitimacy or resistance. It captures the broader benefits - equity, trust, access, and contribution to long-term health resilience.

Evidence Sources:

- Equity impact assessments
- Access and inclusion metrics across demographics
- Public trust and transparency indicators
- Evidence of local capacity-building or system investment

Indicators of Excellence:

- Reduced disparities in access or outcomes across populations
- Inclusion of underserved or minority groups in research and adoption
- Partnerships that strengthen diagnostic or delivery infrastructure
- Measurable social return on investment (SROI)

Strategic Message:

Innovation earns legitimacy when it improves fairness as well as function.

The Integrated View – Balancing the Triangle

In the old model, clinical data drove everything, while economic and societal factors were treated as afterthoughts. In the New Value Triangle, **balance** is the defining feature. True access-first innovation exists only when all three dimensions are in alignment.

Dimension	Core Question	Success Indicator	Strategic Focus
Clinical	Does it work and for whom?	Evidence of meaningful, reproducible outcomes.	Patient benefit.
Economic	Can it be sustained within budgets?	Positive cost–effectiveness and affordability models.	Efficiency.
Societal	Does it strengthen trust and fairness?	Demonstrated inclusion, transparency, and equity impact.	Legitimacy.

Table 2.1 The New Value Triangle Framework

When one corner dominates, imbalance follows:

- A **clinically strong** therapy that is **economically weak** becomes unaffordable.
- An **economically sound** therapy that is **clinically marginal** loses credibility.
- A **scientifically brilliant** therapy that is **socially inequitable** loses trust.

  Balance isn't compromise, it's coherence.

The New Value Triangle Leadership Behaviours in Practice

1. *Assess Early*
   Map your programme across all three dimensions during Phase II. Ask: which corners of the triangle are strongest and weakest?
2. *Align Evidence Generation*
   Use the Evidence Planning Map to ensure that every study or data source contributes to at least two dimensions.
3. *Frame Communication*
   Structure your value narrative around the three pillars. For example: *Clinically superior, economically viable, socially equitable.*
4. *Monitor Continuously*
   Post-launch, track real-world metrics that reflect all three corners: outcomes, affordability, and reach.

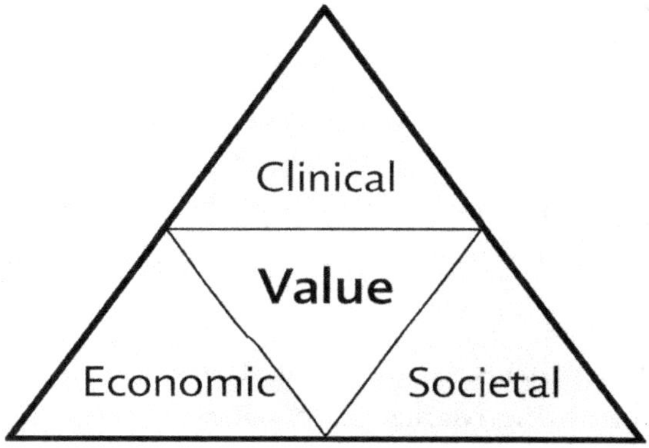

Value is a balance of clinical, economic, and societal impact.

Source: Author framework.

Figure 2.2 New Value Triangle Communication

Example Application: The Case of Two Cell Therapies. Both companies believed they had solved access. Only one had.

Therapy	Clinical Value	Economic Value	Societal Value	Outcome
Company A	High efficacy in early trials	High upfront cost, weak long-term data	Limited global access strategy	Delayed reimbursement, narrow adoption
Company B	Moderate efficacy, strong durability	Outcomes-based pricing model	Investment in diagnostic access in lower-income markets	Broad reimbursement, sustained adoption

Table 2.2 The New Value Triangle Framework Application

Lesson:

Company B won not by outspending, but by aligning all three dimensions of the triangle.

The Cultural Shift

Embracing the Access Imperative requires more than new frameworks; it requires a change in mindset. If your organisation values certainty over relevance, access will remain elusive. Access-first culture values curiosity, transparency, and adaptability. The first rewards internal validation; the second rewards external relevance. The difference is subtle but profound.

Organisations that succeed in this transition tend to share three traits. First, they bring Market Access and HEOR into development governance early, not as advisors but as co-decision makers. Second, they integrate Medical Affairs as a listening function, gathering insights from clinicians and patients to shape design. Third, they hold leaders accountable for access outcomes, not just approvals.

The result is a different kind of conversation at the leadership table. Instead of asking, "Are we on track for submission?" people ask, "Are we on track for reimbursement and adoption?" Instead of celebrating the number of trials completed, teams measure how many patients have been reached.

From Mindset to Method

To make this mindset operational, companies need a disciplined approach that connects intent with execution. The Access Equation introduced in the previous chapter provides the conceptual foundation. The New Value Triangle adds the framework for defining what matters. Together they create the rationale for rethinking processes, incentives, and governance.

In the sections that follow, we will examine how these principles translate into practical tools for aligning innovation with access. We will look at real cases where companies redesigned their development strategies, evidence plans, and partnerships to deliver both value and viability. We will also explore what happens when they fail to do so.

The Access Imperative is not a slogan. It is a strategic necessity. It recognises that innovation has little meaning if it cannot be used.

Putting the New Value Triangle into Practice

The New Value Triangle provides a structure for evaluating success that goes beyond traditional measures of efficacy and cost. It recognises that access is achieved not through isolated excellence but through balance. A therapy that delivers strong clinical outcomes but destabilises a health system financially will struggle to gain traction. Likewise, a product that fits a budget but fails to address unmet need will not endure. True success sits at the intersection of these three dimensions.

Operationalising this balance requires practical tools. The first is an explicit recognition that value is dynamic, not static. Clinical data evolve, budgets fluctuate, and societal expectations shift. Companies that build flexibility into their value frameworks can adapt more easily to changing evidence and policy environments. Those that do not are forced into reactive adjustments that delay access and damage credibility.

The second is alignment. Each internal function must understand how its decisions affect all three dimensions of value. Research and Development define clinical potential. Health Economics and Outcomes Research quantify affordability. Market Access and Policy teams interpret social and system impact. Medical Affairs translates across these domains. When these functions operate in isolation, the result is duplication and drift. When they align early, they create coherence and speed.

Framework: The Value Integration Map

A useful tool for embedding the New Value Triangle into everyday operations is the Value Integration Map. It helps teams visualise how evidence, engagement, and decision making interact across the three dimensions of value.

Clinical Dimension – Focused on efficacy, safety, and patient outcomes. Key activities include robust trial design, selection of meaningful endpoints, and inclusion of representative patient populations.

Economic Dimension – Concerned with cost-effectiveness, budget impact, and long-term sustainability. This includes early health-economic modelling, scenario analysis, and pricing simulations.

Societal Dimension – Encompasses equity, system readiness, and ethical responsibility. This means planning for infrastructure, diagnostics, health literacy, and affordability across different markets.

The map is not a checklist but a diagnostic. It allows teams to ask whether their evidence package and strategic plans support all three dimensions simultaneously. A strong clinical story unsupported by credible affordability or equity data signals imbalance. A product designed for short-term gain without long-term sustainability undermines both reputation and impact.

Case Studies: Success and Shortfall

Case 1: The High-Impact but Low-Adoption Oncology Drug

A multinational company developed a targeted therapy that showed remarkable efficacy in clinical trials. Regulators approved it rapidly under an accelerated pathway. The company's leadership anticipated rapid uptake and invested heavily in launch activities.

However, reimbursement stalled in several European markets. Payers requested comparative effectiveness data against existing standard treatments, long-term survival evidence, and real-world quality-of-life outcomes. None were available. The clinical data were strong, but the evidence package lacked economic and societal credibility.

The result was predictable. The therapy remained confined to a few academic centres while competitors with broader evidence and flexible pricing gained wider coverage. The product was scientifically successful but commercially and socially invisible.

Lesson: Excellence in science must be matched by relevance in value. If development does not anticipate payer expectations, innovation becomes stranded potential.

Case 2: The Integrated Rare Disease Programme

A smaller biotech company developing a therapy for a rare neuromuscular disorder took a different path. From the outset, the team involved patient associations, clinicians, and health economists in trial design. They worked with HTA bodies to agree on outcomes that could be measured meaningfully in small populations. They built a global patient registry before launch and committed to publishing outcomes annually.

When the therapy reached the reimbursement stage, the evidence was transparent, the uncertainty acknowledged, and the real-world data already flowing. Payers approved conditional reimbursement in multiple countries. The therapy reached patients within months of regulatory approval.

Lesson: Early integration of stakeholders across all dimensions of value builds trust and accelerates access. Planning for evidence continuity from trial to real-world use transforms uncertainty into confidence.

Case 3: Two Gene Therapies, Two Fates

Two companies launched gene therapies for similar inherited disorders within the same year. Both offered potentially curative outcomes. Both carried high price tags.

Company A treated access as a negotiation, assuming that the transformational nature of the therapy would justify its cost. Company B treated access as a design principle. It co-created payment models with payers, offering multi-year annuity contracts and outcome-based adjustments. It provided transparent assumptions about durability and committed to follow-up studies.

Eighteen months after launch, Company B's therapy was reimbursed in several markets and had reached hundreds of patients. Company A's product remained largely unused, awaiting funding decisions that never came.

Lesson: Value is not what a company declares; it is what the system accepts. Flexible pricing and shared risk demonstrate partnership and earn adoption.

Building an Organisation that Can Deliver Access

The difference between companies that achieve access and those that do not often comes down to structure and culture. An access-first organisation operates through alignment rather than hierarchy. It treats information as a shared resource rather than a territorial asset.

1. *Governance and Decision Making*
   Access-first organisations establish cross-functional governance for early development. Instead of sequential sign-offs from Research, Development, Medical, and Market Access, they use integrated evidence boards. These forums review every new asset through the lens of the New Value Triangle. They ask whether the evidence is fit not only for regulators but also for payers and patients.
2. *Incentives and Metrics*
   Traditional performance systems reward milestone achievement and cost control. Access-first systems reward outcomes such as time to reimbursement, equity of uptake, and quality of stakeholder relationships. This does not mean abandoning financial metrics; it means balancing them with measures that reflect real impact.
3. *Skills and Mindsets*
   Many teams lack the language and confidence to discuss value beyond their own domain. Clinical scientists may not feel equipped to engage with economic modelling. Market Access specialists may not understand trial design constraints. Access-first companies invest in cross-training. They develop generalists who can connect disciplines without diluting expertise.

4. *Transparency and Feedback Loops*
   An access-first culture depends on constant learning. Launch experiences must feed directly into early development planning. Post-launch evidence gaps should trigger systematic change in how future trials are designed. In many organisations, lessons remain trapped in PowerPoint decks. The best companies institutionalise feedback by design.

Practical Framework: The Access Performance Dashboard

To track progress towards access-first maturity, leadership teams can use a simple dashboard built around three categories: adoption, affordability, and alignment.

Adoption Indicators – Time from regulatory approval to reimbursement; time from reimbursement to first patient treated; uptake trajectory in the first twelve months.

Affordability Indicators – Payer satisfaction with pricing agreements; proportion of population covered; equity of access across regions.

Alignment Indicators – Early payer and HTA engagement completed; cross-functional access planning in place before Phase III; post-launch evidence commitments met on time.

Each indicator can be colour-coded to provide a visual summary of where access is progressing and where intervention is needed. Unlike traditional launch metrics, which focus on promotional activity, these indicators focus on real-world outcomes. They reflect the health of the access system, not just the success of the marketing plan.

The Leadership Imperative

Access-first innovation is not achieved by process alone. It depends on leadership behaviour. The leaders who succeed in this environment are those who combine strategic vision with empathy. They can hold scientific excellence and social responsibility in the same conversation.

Leadership in this context means asking harder questions. Instead of "What can we prove?" it becomes "What will the system believe?" Instead of "How fast can we launch?" it becomes "How fast can we reach patients?" Instead of "What price will maximise revenue?" it becomes "What model will sustain trust?"

This mindset requires courage. It sometimes means challenging internal assumptions or accepting short-term trade-offs for long-term credibility. But the reward is lasting legitimacy. Health systems remember the companies that helped them solve problems, not the ones that created them.

Case Example: Redesigning Development Culture

A European mid-sized pharma company decided to transform its entire governance model after repeated reimbursement failures. The new CEO commissioned an audit of every recent launch and found a pattern. In each case, clinical development teams had made strong scientific decisions but weak access ones. Endpoints were chosen for regulatory ease, not payer relevance. Comparator choices reflected internal convenience rather than clinical practice.

The company created a cross-functional Access Council that reviewed every pivotal study before final design. The council included representatives from Market Access, HEOR, Medical Affairs, and Regional Policy. Within three years, the average time from approval to reimbursement fell by 40 percent. Payer relationships improved, and the company's reputation for credibility increased.

Lesson: Structural change only works when accompanied by cultural humility. The Access Council did not replace expertise; it connected it.

The Broader Impact

The Access Imperative is reshaping what it means to lead in pharmaceuticals. It challenges the industry to measure success not by activity but by outcome. It also reframes competition. In the access era, the true competitors are not other companies but inefficiency, inertia, and mistrust. The organisations that can eliminate those will become the new leaders.

Strategic Implications

The Access Imperative reshapes every aspect of pharmaceutical strategy. It compels organisations to think in systems rather than sequences. Discovery, development, approval, reimbursement, and adoption are not linear stages; they are interdependent parts of one continuous process. When one part fails, the whole system suffers.

Strategically, this means three things. First, planning must become multidimensional. Teams should design products, evidence, and partnerships with the New Value Triangle in mind from the beginning. Second, accountability must be distributed. No single function owns access; every function contributes to it. Third, measurement must evolve. Success cannot be judged by regulatory milestones alone but by the speed, breadth, and equity of real-world adoption.

To support this shift, companies are beginning to adopt integrated access plans that run in parallel with clinical development plans. These documents define not only how the therapy will be tested but also how it will be understood, funded, and used. They specify the payer dialogues, evidence commitments, and system readiness requirements that will make access achievable. When done well, they serve as the connective tissue linking scientific ambition to patient impact.

Rethinking Organisational Design

Many companies still operate under a model designed for the twentieth century. It is efficient at generating regulatory submissions but ineffective at generating access. The boundaries between R&D, Medical Affairs, HEOR, and Market Access are rigid. Information flows upward but rarely sideways. Each function measures success by its own metrics, and collaboration is often reactive.

The organisations that thrive in the next decade will look different. They will be flatter, more transparent, and more externally engaged. They will measure performance not by functional success but by collective impact. They will invest in data systems that connect clinical evidence with real-world outcomes and in people who can translate between scientific, economic, and policy languages.

A company that achieves this alignment does more than accelerate access. It becomes a credible partner to health systems. It moves from defending its prices to justifying its value, from reacting to policy changes to helping shape them. It earns a seat at the table not through lobbying but through evidence and integrity.

The Leadership Philosophy of Access

True leadership in this context is about creating clarity in complexity. It is about helping teams see beyond the next milestone and understand how their work contributes to the system as a whole. Access-first leaders model humility and curiosity. They listen to what regulators, payers, clinicians, and patients actually need rather than assuming they already know. They also understand that speed is not the same as progress.

In access-first organisations, leaders ask different questions. They no longer ask, "How do we convince payers?" but "How do we work with them?" They no longer ask, "How can we maximise short-term revenue?" but "How can we create sustainable value that strengthens the system and secures long-term trust?" These are not philosophical luxuries. They are strategic necessities in a world where public scrutiny, affordability pressures, and data transparency define competitiveness.

Leadership also involves courage. It means challenging traditional habits and being willing to admit when the company is part of the problem. Many executives talk about patient centricity; fewer are willing to measure it honestly. The most effective leaders are those who make patient access the ultimate definition of performance.

Key insight

Access failure is not an exception in modern pharma. It is a systemic outcome of how success is defined and rewarded. When organisations treat access as a downstream activity rather than a design objective, delays and inequities become normalised. Redefining success is therefore not philosophical. It is operational.

Reflection

How does your organisation define success today? Which achievements are celebrated publicly, and which outcomes are quietly tolerated or explained away?

Reflect on whether access outcomes are treated as core indicators of performance or as complications to be managed after the fact.

Try this

- Review the KPIs used to assess late-stage development success.
- Identify which metrics reward speed to approval versus speed to patient use.
- Ask where access outcomes appear in leadership dashboards, if at all.
- Consider what behaviours your current success measures encourage.
- Identify one metric you would change to signal access-first thinking.

Summary

- Access delays are systemic, not accidental.
- Traditional success metrics reinforce approval-first behaviour.
- Redefining success changes upstream decisions.

- What gets measured shapes what gets prioritised.
- Access must be treated as a primary outcome, not a downstream task.
- Cultural change begins with metric change.

Changing what organisations aim for does not automatically change how they behave. The next chapter explores how organisational structures, incentives, and hand-offs create the persistent gap between innovation and access, even when intentions are good.

CHAPTER 3

THE INNOVATION–ACCESS GAP

"Organisations do not fail at access because they lack intent. They fail because their structures reward something else."
– Egbert Floppercough

Redefining success does not automatically change outcomes. This chapter explains why well-intentioned organisations still struggle to translate innovation into access. It introduces the innovation–access gap as a consequence of organisational design, incentives, and hand-offs rather than scientific failure.

A Brilliant Failure

In a glass meeting room overlooking the Thames, the development team stood before the board to present the culmination of a decade's work. Their new therapy for a rare autoimmune disease had achieved every milestone. The trial data were solid, the regulators were supportive, and the approval had arrived exactly on schedule. For a moment, there was a sense of quiet triumph.

Eighteen months later, that optimism had faded. The therapy had been approved but not adopted. Reimbursement had been secured in only a few markets. In one major country, negotiations had stalled because payers doubted whether the clinical endpoints used in the trials reflected outcomes that mattered in practice. In hospitals, the product sat unused because diagnostic pathways were incomplete and clinicians were uncertain about patient selection.

The executives in charge reviewed the disappointing uptake and called it an access problem. In truth, it was an alignment problem. The company's structure and strategy had been built for an earlier era, when approval was the finish line. The evidence generated had been perfect for regulators but irrelevant for payers. The market access plan had been designed too late to influence development decisions. The result was a scientifically excellent therapy that made little real-world difference.

Traditional assumption		Access-first reframing
Approval defines success	→	**Patient use** defines success
Access follows approval	→	**Access** is designed upstream
Market access is a function	→	**Access** is a system outcome
Evidence is generated once	→	**Evidence** evolves over time
Pricing is a commercial decision	→	**Pricing** is a system design choice
Equity is a policy issue	→	**Equity** is a design constraint

Leaders who ask these questions regularly prevent **80%** of common access failures.

Figure 3.1 Access-First Reframing

This was not an isolated case. It was a familiar pattern repeated across the industry: products that clear regulatory hurdles but stall in the real-world. The innovation–access gap is not about science failing; it is about systems failing to connect.

Understanding the Gap

The innovation–access gap is not a mystery. It is the predictable result of decisions made early and defended later. It represents the loss of impact that occurs when the scientific, economic, and operational elements of development fail to align.

This gap does not emerge from a single mistake. It is the cumulative result of dozens of small disconnections between teams, incentives, and timelines. Each decision may seem rational in isolation, but collectively they create a system that excels at innovation and struggles at adoption.

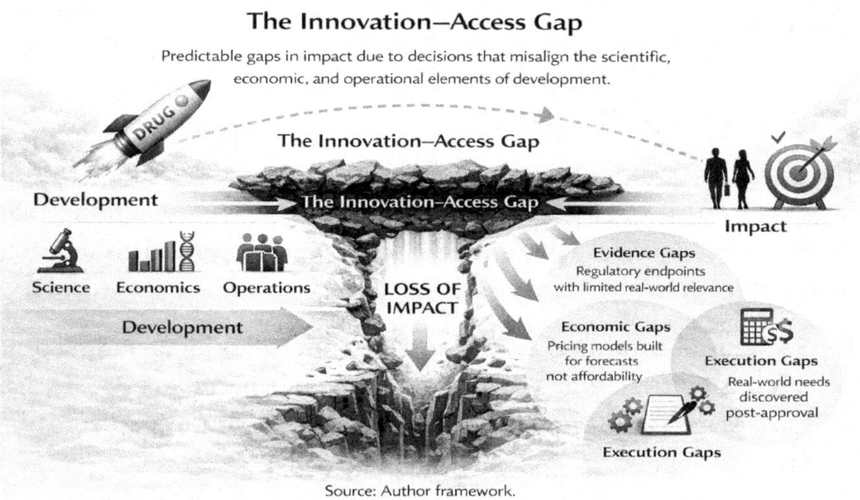

Figure 3.2 The Innovation Access Gap

To understand why the gap persists, it helps to examine its three most common forms: evidence gaps, economic gaps, and execution gaps.

Evidence gaps occur when data collected for regulatory approval do not satisfy the expectations of payers, HTA agencies, or clinicians. Regulators ask whether a therapy is safe and effective under controlled conditions. Payers ask whether it improves outcomes in real life at a cost the system can bear. When those questions diverge, time is lost rebuilding evidence that could have been designed in.

Economic gaps arise when pricing and reimbursement strategies are based on internal value assumptions rather than external market realities. Companies often price for innovation rather than affordability, overlooking the thresholds that determine actual patient access.

Execution gaps appear when infrastructure, training, and system readiness are not in place. Even reimbursed therapies can remain out of reach if clinicians are unprepared or if diagnostic services are limited.

Each of these gaps is avoidable. Yet they persist because the industry's operating model remains built around regulatory logic rather than system logic.

Why the Gap Persists

The gap persists because leadership tolerates it. Many organisations still view access as a stage rather than a philosophy. It is something that happens after development, once the science is complete. This mindset creates three systemic weaknesses:

1. **Sequential thinking.** Teams work in a linear fashion, handing over responsibilities from research to development to market access. Each stage is optimised for efficiency but disconnected from the one that follows.
2. **Fragmented governance.** Decision-making bodies are organised by function rather than by outcome. R&D, HEOR, and Market Access operate on separate timelines, each with its own success metrics.
3. **Misaligned incentives.** Individuals and departments are rewarded for achieving regulatory milestones or publication targets, not for achieving patient reach or equity of access.

These habits produce well-intentioned activity without coherent direction. They make it possible for a therapy to be technically perfect yet practically unusable.

Case Study 1: The Oncology Setback

A European oncology company achieved conditional approval for a therapy targeting a rare tumour subtype. The data were statistically strong, and the company celebrated being first to market. However, payers quickly raised questions. The pivotal trial had used a surrogate endpoint that did not clearly demonstrate overall survival benefit. The comparator chosen for the study was not the one used in local clinical practice.

Health technology assessment agencies requested additional analyses, delaying reimbursement by more than a year. During that time, two competing products entered the market with clearer value propositions and stronger comparative evidence. The therapy that had been hailed as a breakthrough became an afterthought.

The lesson was clear: accelerated approval does not guarantee accelerated access. Without early payer input and comparative data that reflect clinical reality, regulatory success can lead to commercial failure.

Case Study 2: The Rare Disease Success

A small biotechnology company working on a treatment for a rare neuromuscular disorder took a different approach. From Phase II onwards, they involved patient groups and national reimbursement bodies in the design of their evidence plan. They agreed to collect long-term outcome data through patient registries and designed their pivotal trial to include quality-of-life measures identified as meaningful by patients and clinicians.

When the therapy reached review, the submission was transparent about uncertainty but credible in its plan to address it. Conditional reimbursement followed within months of approval. The company had not eliminated uncertainty but had replaced it with trust.

The success was not due to luck but to method. By embedding access thinking early, the company avoided the usual post-launch scramble to fill evidence gaps.

The Evidence Paradox

At the heart of the innovation–access gap lies an uncomfortable paradox. Pharmaceutical development generates more data than ever before, yet decision-makers often feel less informed. The volume of evidence grows, but its relevance does not.

This occurs because evidence is still designed primarily for regulatory approval, not for health system adoption. Endpoints that satisfy regulators routinely fail payers, yet they continue to be chosen. The populations enrolled in trials may not reflect those who will use the therapy in practice. The time horizons of studies may not capture long-term value or affordability.

Bridging this gap requires a different mindset. Evidence must be seen as a shared currency rather than a departmental output. Regulators, payers, clinicians, and patients all hold legitimate perspectives on what counts as value. The task of modern development is to integrate those perspectives rather than choose between them.

Framework: The Innovation–Access Alignment Model

To address this challenge, organisations can use a structured approach that links scientific development with system adoption. The Innovation–Access Alignment Model provides a practical framework built around three stages: design alignment, evidence alignment, and delivery alignment.

Design alignment begins with defining value in system terms. It requires selecting comparators and endpoints that reflect real clinical practice and including diverse populations that represent the intended users.

Evidence alignment ensures that data generated across the lifecycle serve multiple audiences. This means planning health-economic analyses and real-world data collection from the outset rather than retrofitting them later.

Delivery alignment focuses on readiness. It anticipates the operational, educational, and logistical needs that determine whether patients can actually receive the therapy.

These three dimensions transform access from an afterthought into a discipline. Together, they reduce uncertainty, accelerate reimbursement, and build credibility with payers and policymakers.

Case Study 3: Alignment in Action

A mid-sized company developing a biologic for chronic inflammatory disease adopted this model. A cross-functional steering group, including representatives from R&D, HEOR, and Market Access, met monthly to review development through the lens of design, evidence, and delivery alignment.

They engaged non-binding feedback from HTA agencies in two European countries, who advised on endpoint selection and comparator choice. They built a patient registry before launch to capture real-world outcomes. When reimbursement submissions began, the evidence package addressed nearly all anticipated questions.

Approval to reimbursement took less than six months. Payers praised the transparency and the relevance of the evidence. Adoption was strong from the outset because clinicians and health systems had been involved early.

The approach did not slow development; it made it smarter.

The Cost of the Gap

Every delay between approval and adoption carries a cost that extends far beyond balance sheets. It is measured in lost revenue, wasted investment, and most importantly, in time lost for patients. The innovation–access gap undermines not only commercial success but also public trust in the entire healthcare ecosystem.

A recent multi-country analysis of oncology medicines approved by the European Medicines Agency between 2016 and 2021 found that the median time to reimbursement exceeded 400 days. In Belgium, the wait was more than 700 days. Germany, with its early access pricing model, reimbursed new therapies within days. The disparity showed how structural and procedural differences, not scientific ones, determine the speed of access.

For the companies behind these products, the delays eroded exclusivity periods and reduced lifetime revenue potential. For patients, they meant uncertainty and unequal access to treatments already proven effective. Every delay becomes a silent loss of health outcomes.

Economically, the gap represents inefficiency. Global R&D expenditure has doubled over the past decade, but the proportion of therapies achieving broad market access within a year of approval remains low. The mismatch between innovation output and adoption input is now one of the biggest drains on productivity in the industry.

Socially, it erodes credibility. When the public sees headlines announcing new cures while patients continue to wait, faith in both industry and institutions declines. The reputational risk is as tangible as the financial one.

Why Traditional Models Fall Short

The problem is not that pharmaceutical companies lack intelligence or resources. It is that they optimise for the wrong end point. Traditional development systems were designed for regulatory compliance, not for health system adoption. They produce evidence that is necessary but not sufficient.

The metrics of success reinforce this distortion. Teams celebrate approval dates, publication counts, and trial completion milestones, while access-related indicators such as time to reimbursement or geographic coverage are treated as secondary. The result is a culture of completion rather than connection.

This culture also discourages cross-functional collaboration. Teams focus on defending their evidence rather than integrating it. Meetings become negotiations between silos rather than conversations about shared outcomes. The irony is that every function in the company is trying to serve patients, yet their separate processes prevent them from doing so effectively.

Organisational Remedies

Closing the innovation–access gap requires structural, procedural, and cultural reform. The goal is to build systems where access thinking is embedded in every stage of decision-making.

1. *Integrated Strategy Development*
   Each new asset should begin with an access strategy that sits alongside the clinical development plan. This document defines what success will mean not just for regulators but for patients, payers, and society. It outlines key value hypotheses, payer evidence needs, pricing principles, and potential access barriers. It is a living document that evolves as data emerge.
2. *Early Evidence Planning*
   Evidence planning should occur before Phase II, when trial design and endpoints are still flexible. At this stage, HEOR and Market Access experts can identify which outcomes will matter most to HTA bodies. This allows the clinical team to incorporate meaningful endpoints and comparators early, reducing the need for additional studies later.
3. *Cross-Functional Governance*
   Governance structures should bring together R&D, Medical Affairs, HEOR, and Market Access in shared decision forums. These groups should review trial design, economic models, and stakeholder engagement strategies together rather than in sequence. The key is not to slow decisions but to make them coherent.
4. *Continuous Learning Loops*
   Launch experiences should be analysed and fed back into early development. Real-world evidence, payer feedback, and clinician insights can inform the next wave of assets. This creates a virtuous cycle where every launch improves the next.
5. *Cultural Reinforcement*
   Access-first behaviour must be rewarded. Performance reviews and incentives should include metrics such as time to reimbursement,

equity of access, and stakeholder satisfaction. Leadership must communicate that the goal is not just approval but impact.

Practical Tools

The Access Alignment Checklist

Before each development milestone, ask five questions:

1. Do our clinical endpoints align with what payers and clinicians consider meaningful?
2. Have we validated our economic models with real-world cost data?
3. Are our comparators reflective of current standards of care in target markets?
4. Have we involved HTA bodies, patients, or clinicians early enough to shape evidence expectations?
5. Are we measuring adoption readiness as rigorously as we measure trial success?

A "no" to any of these questions signals an emerging gap that should be corrected before proceeding.

The Integration Scorecard

Companies can use a simple scorecard to assess their access maturity.

Dimension	Description	Maturity Indicator
Design	Access principles are built into early development plans	Percentage of Phase II trials with payer input
Evidence	Data meet the needs of regulators, payers, and clinicians	Number of submissions accepted without major post-hoc analysis
Delivery	Systems and infrastructure ready for real-world use	Time from approval to first patient treated
Governance	Cross-functional decision-making in place	Frequency of integrated access reviews

Dimension	Description	Maturity Indicator
Culture	Access-first mindset embedded in leadership and incentives	Inclusion of access metrics in performance reviews

Table 3.1 The Integration Scorecard

Tracking these dimensions helps leadership identify where the organisation must evolve.

The Leadership Imperative

Leaders play a central role in closing the innovation–access gap. They must create alignment across functions and clarity of purpose across levels. Leadership in this context is less about authority and more about translation. It involves helping scientific teams see the policy landscape, helping commercial teams understand the science, and ensuring that every decision links back to patient access.

Effective leaders ask questions that reframe assumptions. Instead of asking, "Are we ready for submission?" they ask, "Are we ready for adoption?" Instead of focusing on how to persuade payers, they focus on how to collaborate with them. The shift may seem subtle, but it changes how teams think, plan, and measure success.

Access-first leadership also requires courage. It means acknowledging that the company's own processes may be part of the problem. It demands openness to dialogue with sceptical payers, transparency about uncertainty, and willingness to test new pricing or evidence models.

Above all, it requires humility. No company can deliver access alone. It takes partnerships across governments, regulators, health systems, and patient communities. Leadership in this context is about convening rather than controlling.

Key insight

The gap between innovation and access is created by organisational design, not by a lack of intent. Structures, incentives, and hand-offs determine whether access considerations shape decisions early or surface as problems late. Access outcomes reflect how organisations are built, not what they say they value.

Reflection

Think about how decisions move through your organisation. Where do hand-offs occur, and what information or accountability is lost at each transition?

Notice whether access-related questions are raised early, or only when problems become visible and costly.

Try this

- Map the decision pathway for a single development asset across functions.
- Identify where access perspectives enter the process and where they do not.
- Examine how incentives differ across R&D, Medical, and Access teams.
- Ask where accountability for access outcomes truly sits.
- Consider one structural change that would reduce late-stage surprises.

Summary

- The innovation–access gap is organisational, not scientific.
- Intent does not overcome misaligned structures.
- Late access involvement guarantees rework and delay.

- Incentives shape behaviour more powerfully than strategy statements.
- Integration must be designed, not requested.
- Access performance mirrors organisational architecture.

If access outcomes are shaped by organisational design, the practical question becomes where that design first exerts influence. The next chapter turns to trial design, showing how early scientific choices quietly determine downstream access possibilities.

PART II

DESIGNING FOR ACCESS

CHAPTER 4

DESIGNING TRIALS FOR ACCESS

"Most access problems are not discovered after approval. They are designed into trials long before it."
– Egbert Floppercough

If organisational design shapes access outcomes, the earliest and most influential design choices occur in clinical development. This chapter shows how trial design decisions quietly determine what evidence will later be possible. It explains why trials optimised solely for approval often constrain access long before launch.

The Trial That Missed the Point

The conference room was filled with confidence. On the screen, the Phase III results looked flawless. The trial had met every primary endpoint, achieved statistical significance, and passed all safety thresholds. The regulatory affairs lead described it as "a model of excellence". The team congratulated itself on what it believed was a perfect clinical package.

Then the payer reviews began.

The therapy was approved by regulators within months. Payers were unconvinced. The endpoints used in the pivotal trial were surrogate biomarkers, not outcomes that reflected real patient benefit. The comparator arm did not represent local standard of care. The population studied was narrower than the population that would ultimately be asked to use the therapy.

The dossier that had once seemed perfect now looked exposed. Reimbursement was delayed by eighteen months while the company gathered real-world evidence it could have planned for earlier. By the time market access was secured, two competitors had entered with stronger evidence packages.

The problem was that the trial had been designed for approval, not for adoption.

What Trial Design Really Does

Every clinical trial tells a story. It describes how a therapy works, for whom, and why it matters. But in modern healthcare, the audience for that story is no longer just regulators. It includes payers, policymakers, clinicians, and patients, each with different questions about value. If the story fails to speak their language, even strong science fails.

Designing trials for access means building that broader narrative from the start. It means anticipating the needs of those who decide not only whether a therapy can be sold, but whether it will be used.

The old logic treated clinical and economic evidence as separate worlds. Today, they are inseparable. A trial that ignores access considerations is a trial that will eventually be re-run. The goal of modern design is to make evidence multidimensional: scientifically rigorous, economically credible, and socially relevant.

The Strategic Role of Design

Trial design is strategy in disguise. Every choice of endpoint, comparator, and patient population sends a message about how the company defines value. These decisions determine not only regulatory approval but also how convincingly the therapy's value can be demonstrated to payers and clinicians.

From an organisational perspective, the design phase is the most powerful moment to influence access. After protocols are finalised, flexibility shrinks, and costs rise. Integrating access thinking at this stage does not slow innovation; it ensures that innovation travels further.

Access-first trial design can be summarised in three principles: relevance, representation, and readiness.

Relevance ensures that endpoints and outcomes are meaningful to those who pay for and use therapies.

Representation ensures that the populations studied reflect those who will receive the therapy in practice.

Readiness ensures that data collection and analysis prepare the organisation for payer, HTA, and clinician scrutiny.

These principles transform trials from scientific exercises into access strategies.

Common Design Errors

Many clinical programmes fail at access because they are built on outdated assumptions. The most common misalignments include:

Endpoints that prove mechanism but not meaning. Regulators accept surrogate endpoints such as tumour shrinkage or biomarker change. Payers and clinicians want evidence of survival, quality of life, or functional improvement.

Comparators that satisfy protocol but not practice. A trial may compare a new therapy against placebo or an outdated standard of care that no longer reflects what doctors actually use. Payers then require additional comparative analyses, delaying access.

Populations that exclude the real-world. Strict inclusion criteria make trials cleaner but less representative. When the therapy reaches broader patient groups, those evidence gaps become visible.

Short time horizons. Trials often measure outcomes for six or twelve months, while payers must forecast cost and benefit over years. The resulting uncertainty slows decision-making.

Each of these errors has the same root cause: delayed and fragmented dialogue between clinical, HEOR, and access teams.

Case Study 1: When PFS Was Not Enough

An oncology company designed a pivotal trial using progression-free survival as its primary endpoint. Regulators accepted it. Payers questioned whether the improvement translated into longer life or better quality of life. When health technology assessment agencies reviewed the dossier, they found the evidence compelling but incomplete. The product was eventually reimbursed, but at a lower price, and only after further data were submitted.

If the trial had included co-primary endpoints for overall survival or validated quality-of-life measures, much of the negotiation could have been avoided. The lesson was simple: clinical significance is not the same as system relevance.

Case Study 2: Designing for Uncertainty in Rare Disease

A biotech company developing a treatment for a rare metabolic condition faced small patient numbers and uncertain endpoints. Instead of designing a traditional single-arm trial, the team co-created a hybrid evidence plan with regulators, payers, and patient groups. They agreed to use a patient-reported outcome developed with the patient community, and to link the trial to a global registry for long-term follow-up.

The result was a smaller but more persuasive dataset. Regulators valued the patient relevance. Payers valued the transparency. Clinicians trusted the findings because they reflected real experience. Access came swiftly. The therapy became a model for future rare disease design.

Framework: The Access-Ready Trial Model

To make access a design principle rather than an afterthought, apply the Access-Ready Trial Model. It consists of four interconnected components:

1. **Define Value Early**
   Begin by defining what "value" means to payers and patients. Is it survival, functionality, independence, or economic relief for health systems? Design endpoints that measure it.
2. **Align Comparators with Practice**
   Use control arms that reflect current clinical standards in target markets, even if regulators allow a different choice. This prevents disputes over relevance later.
3. **Plan for Real-World Continuity**
   Build data systems that allow trial participants to continue contributing outcomes data after the study ends. This smooths the transition from trial to real-world evidence.
4. **Design for Diversity**
   Include patient populations that reflect age, gender, comorbidity, and geography. Broader representation enhances both scientific robustness and payer confidence.

Applying these components early turns a clinical trial into a foundation for adoption. It creates a single evidence narrative that can travel from regulatory submission to reimbursement without contradiction.

Organisational Enablers

Access-optimised trials require organisational alignment before the protocol is locked:

- **Joint Protocol Reviews.** Include HEOR and Market Access representatives in protocol development meetings. Their input anticipates payer questions.

- **Payer Simulation Workshops.** Conduct sessions where internal teams play the role of HTA reviewers to test the strength of the evidence plan.
- **Global Evidence Blueprints.** For multi-country launches, align the trial design with the evidence expectations in major markets. A single global trial rarely fits all. Tailoring is strategic.
- **Evidence Governance Boards.** Establish cross-functional oversight for evidence generation. These boards maintain coherence between trial design, health economics, and post-launch studies.

When these mechanisms are in place, the trial becomes the beginning of access, not a barrier to it.

Evidence that Travels

A well-designed trial should not just prove efficacy. It should also prepare for adoption. The most effective evidence plans are those that travel easily from one audience to another. They move from regulators to payers, from clinicians to patients, and from one country's reimbursement body to another's.

This idea of "evidence that travels" may sound simple, but it requires careful architecture. Each piece of data must serve multiple purposes without losing integrity. For example, a survival curve in oncology is more than a clinical outcome. It can inform health-economic models, quality-adjusted life year calculations, and policy discussions about value for money.

When evidence serves only one purpose, duplication follows. Teams conduct additional studies, repeat analyses, or generate real-world data retrospectively to fill gaps that could have been foreseen. The result is delay, inefficiency, and frustration across stakeholders.

Aligning Endpoints with Real-World Value

Endpoints are the language of value. They define what success looks like. Yet too often, they are chosen for convenience or tradition rather than relevance.

Regulators prioritise safety and efficacy. Payers focus on long-term outcomes, cost, and comparative benefit. Clinicians care about function and usability. Patients care about quality of life and the ability to return to normal activity. A trial that measures only one of these perspectives will inevitably fall short in the others.

Modern endpoint design requires negotiation between these perspectives. It demands clarity on what the therapy is intended to change and how that change, and how that change will be measured in ways that matter scientifically and socially.

For example, in metabolic and neurological disorders, surrogate biomarkers can indicate biological activity but not necessarily clinical improvement. Including patient-reported outcomes, functional scores, or time-to-event data adds human meaning to scientific precision.

Payers also increasingly expect endpoints that connect directly to system value, such as reduced hospital admissions or improved adherence. These may not be regulatory requirements, but they strengthen the overall case for reimbursement.

Data Planning as a Strategic Function

Evidence generation has traditionally been managed as a series of technical tasks. In an access-first model, it becomes a strategic function. Data planning should begin alongside protocol development, defining not only what data will be collected but also how it will be used and by whom.

Effective data planning involves five core steps:

1. **Mapping Stakeholder Requirements**
   Identify the data expectations of regulators, HTA agencies, payers,

and clinicians. Create a consolidated map that highlights overlaps and differences.

2. **Prioritising Reusable Evidence**
   Design data elements that can serve multiple purposes across clinical, economic, and policy domains.
3. **Integrating Real-World Data from the Start**
   Build mechanisms to collect observational data during and after trials. Real-world evidence strengthens both regulatory and payer confidence.
4. **Ensuring Data Quality and Consistency**
   Use uniform data standards and governance frameworks to ensure that trial data and real-world data can be combined without conflict.
5. **Planning for Adaptation**
   Anticipate how data needs may evolve as the therapy moves through different markets and phases of its lifecycle.

When data planning becomes strategic, the organisation moves from reactive analysis to proactive insight. It avoids the common trap of generating impressive but irrelevant evidence.

Case Study: The Protocol That Won Reimbursement

A mid-sized European company developing an immunology treatment adopted an integrated access-first design from the beginning. During protocol development, they involved representatives from clinical, HEOR, and policy teams. Together, they identified key payer concerns: durability of effect, long-term safety, and impact on healthcare utilisation.

The trial incorporated secondary endpoints that captured hospitalisation rates and healthcare resource use alongside standard clinical outcomes. The company also established agreements with national registries to track real-world data after launch.

When the therapy reached submission, the dossier demonstrated not only efficacy but also economic and societal value. HTA bodies across Europe cited the clarity of the evidence narrative as a strength. Reimbursement was approved in record time.

The success was not due to the novelty of the science but to alignment of design, evidence, and access.

Framework: The Access Evidence Lifecycle

To operationalise this approach, apply the Access Evidence Lifecycle framework. It divides the evidence process into four continuous phases that overlap rather than follow one another:

Phase	Core Question	Primary Output	Key Stakeholders
Design	What does value mean for this therapy?	Integrated protocol and evidence plan	R&D, HEOR, Market Access
Generate	How do we prove it?	Trial data and interim analyses	Clinical teams, statisticians
Translate	How do we explain it?	Economic models, value narratives, HTA dossiers	Market Access, Medical Affairs
Sustain	How do we maintain it?	Real-world evidence, post-launch updates	Medical Affairs, policy teams, payers

Table 3.2 The Access Evidence Lifecycle Framework

The framework ensures that evidence remains relevant throughout the product's lifecycle. It keeps every team focused on the same outcome: patient access.

Organisational Examples

Some leading companies are already shifting towards access-integrated design. Global pharmaceutical groups have created "Integrated Evidence Planning Councils" that oversee both clinical and economic evidence across all phases. Others have adopted modular protocol design, where certain trial components can be adapted for regional payer needs without restarting the entire study.

One large oncology company has built an internal "HTA rehearsal" process. Before finalising trial protocols, they simulate national HTA reviews using external experts. The goal is to identify weak points in evidence design before a single patient is enrolled.

These practices represent a practical shift in how trials are conceived. They turn access from a final hurdle into a strategic capability.

Leadership and Culture

Leadership remains the ultimate determinant of whether access-driven design succeeds. It requires leaders to reward integration over speed and collaboration over control. It also requires cultural permission for scientists, economists, and policy experts to question each other constructively.

In an access-first organisation, a protocol is not owned by one department. It is co-authored by the system. Leaders who encourage that behaviour create resilience and agility. They prevent the costly cycle of rework that occurs when access considerations appear too late.

The cultural change can feel uncomfortable. It replaces the neat predictability of linear development with the messier reality of collaboration. Yet it also replaces frustration with foresight.

Key insight

Trial design decisions are among the most powerful determinants of access outcomes. Choices about endpoints, comparators, populations, and duration shape not only regulatory success but also reimbursement credibility and clinical relevance. When trials are designed solely for approval, access barriers are often built in long before launch.

Reflection

Think about a recent trial design decision in your organisation. Whose questions did that decision primarily serve?

Consider which future decision makers were absent from the discussion, and what assumptions were made about how evidence would later be interpreted.

Try this

- Review a current or recent trial protocol and list its primary and secondary endpoints.
- Ask which of those endpoints matter most to payers and clinicians.
- Identify where comparator choice may limit relevance in real-world settings.
- Consider whether trial populations reflect those most likely to be treated.
- Reflect on how early payer or HTA input might have altered the design.

Summary

- Trial design shapes access long before launch.
- Regulatory relevance does not guarantee reimbursement relevance.
- Narrow endpoints create downstream credibility gaps.
- Comparator choice is a strategic access decision.
- Early dialogue reduces late-stage redesign.
- Designing for access requires anticipating multiple decision makers.

If trial design determines what evidence exists, the next question is how that evidence is planned, generated, and used over time. The following chapter examines evidence strategy as a learning system, rather than a static submission exercise.

CHAPTER 5

EARLY EVIDENCE AND HEOR INTEGRATION

"Evidence only becomes strategic when it is generated for the people who will say no."
– Egbert Floppercough

Trial design determines what data exist. Evidence strategy determines how that data will be interpreted and trusted. This chapter reframes evidence generation as a continuous learning process rather than a submission exercise and explains why early integration of economic and outcomes thinking is essential for access.

The Meeting That Measured Everything but Learned Nothing

The call began with optimism. It was an internal joint review between a global development team and health economists from several regional affiliates. Everyone had logged in armed with data. The oncology asset under discussion had just completed Phase II. The clinical lead spoke confidently. "The data speak for themselves," she said, as the last slide appeared, showing clean safety and efficacy curves.

Silence followed.

A senior health economist cleared his throat. "Do they speak to the payers?"

No one answered. The clinical team looked puzzled, then defensive. "We met all the regulatory standards." The economist nodded. "Yes. But not the reimbursement ones."

That meeting revealed a blunt truth: the data that secure approval are not always the data that secure access. The study was technically flawless but strategically incomplete. It proved that the therapy worked, but not that it was affordable, adoptable, or sustainable at scale. Six months later, the drug was approved. Eighteen months later, it was still waiting for reimbursement in several major markets.

The product had achieved regulatory success but entered commercial limbo. Internally, the post-mortem report concluded that "payer expectations evolved faster than planned." The truth was less elegant: the company had measured everything regulators required but learned little that payers valued.

Why Early Evidence Matters

For most of pharmaceutical history, evidence generation has been linear. Discovery came first, trials followed, and economics arrived at the end. Regulators decided whether a drug could be sold. Once that was done, commercial teams would "figure out access."

That sequence no longer works.

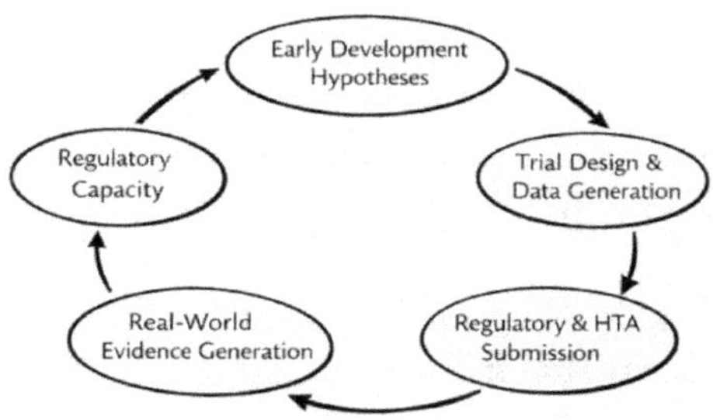

Evidence generation is cyclical rather than linear.

Source: Author framework.

Figure 4.1 Evidence As A Learning Cycle

Health systems now demand evidence that connects clinical outcomes with economic, social, and operational value. Regulators ask if a therapy is safe and effective. Payers ask if it is worth it. Policymakers ask if it can be afforded at scale. Patients ask if it makes a meaningful difference to their daily lives.

Many companies still treat health economics and outcomes research (HEOR) as a compliance exercise rather than a strategic discipline. The result is predictable: therapies that are scientifically approved but commercially stranded.

In Europe, analysis of oncology therapies approved between 2016 and 2021 found a median time from regulatory approval to reimbursement of over 400 days. In many cases, the delay was not driven by disagreement about efficacy, but by disagreement about value. The data collected for regulators did not align with what HTA bodies needed to make coverage decisions.

This is not about speed alone. It is about relevance. If the evidence narrative is not built to answer the questions payers will ask, approval becomes a new starting point for negotiation.

The Evidence Integration Model

The **Evidence Integration Model (EIM)** brings together scientific data, economic reasoning, and operational foresight to make sure innovation and adoption move in step.

It is based on three interlocking elements:

1. **Clinical Relevance**: Designing studies that measure outcomes meaningful to both regulators and payers.
2. **Economic Credibility**: Building cost-effectiveness and value models early so that evidence supports price and policy.
3. **Operational Readiness**: Ensuring systems and partnerships are in place to maintain evidence post-launch.

These elements form a feedback loop rather than a sequence. Trial outcomes shape models, models identify data gaps, and post-launch evidence updates both.

In mature organisations, this loop becomes an engine of learning, a system that evolves with every dataset and every payer discussion.

Clinical Relevance: Measuring What Matters

Regulatory endpoints often fail to capture what payers value most. Regulators look for proof of effect. Payers look for proof of impact.

The distinction matters. For instance, a therapy may improve progression-free survival by four months. This may be statistically impressive, but if it does not reduce hospital admissions, extend overall survival, or improve quality of life, the payer perspective remains sceptical.

A study in respiratory disease illustrates this mismatch. A biologic reduced exacerbation rates but did not demonstrate reduced emergency admissions or improved productivity. Approval came quickly, but reimbursement took over a year. The therapy's economic argument was built after the fact, not before.

Early alignment could have avoided the gap. Designing the trial with endpoints that linked clinical improvement to system savings would have allowed the same data to satisfy both regulators and payers.

Economic Credibility: Building the Value Narrative Early

Economic credibility is not about price justification. It is about evidentiary coherence. The HEOR function must be integrated into development planning, not consulted at the end.

Building economic models early allows teams to test assumptions, identify gaps, and simulate scenarios. These living models evolve with each new data release. They help teams rehearse the value conversation long before negotiations begin.

For example, a mid-sized biotech built a cost-effectiveness model for its rare disease therapy in Phase II. When the pivotal study concluded, the model already contained real-world comparator data and scenario analyses for different pricing corridors. Payers described the submission as "complete and transparent." Reimbursement followed within weeks.

Economic modelling should not be seen as a defensive tool but as a design instrument. It ensures that every data point collected has purpose.

Operational Readiness: Sustaining the Evidence Lifecycle

The third element of integration is operational readiness. Evidence does not end at approval. It matures through use.

Companies that plan for continuous data capture through registries, EHR linkage, and patient-reported outcomes maintain credibility with payers and policymakers. These systems also create learning loops across markets.

A cardiovascular programme in Scandinavia built registry linkage directly into its pivotal study. Real-world effectiveness data became available within months of launch. When reimbursement renewals were due, the updated outcomes validated the model assumptions and secured continued funding without renegotiation.

Continuous data flow transforms post-launch maintenance from an obligation into a strategic advantage.

Case Studies: Lessons from Practice

Case 1: The Oncology Delay

A major oncology therapy achieved approval based on strong progression-free survival data. HTA agencies, however, wanted overall survival and cost-effectiveness evidence. The company had none. It took 18 months to collect real-world follow-up data. Competitors overtook it in reimbursement.

Lesson: Regulatory approval guarantees nothing without payer alignment.

Case 2: The Proactive Immunology Programme

An immunology team integrated HEOR expertise during Phase II. They designed endpoints linking patient outcomes to reduced hospital visits and improved productivity. The resulting model connected science and economics seamlessly.

Lesson: When evidence and economics evolve together, access accelerates.

Case 3: The Gene Therapy That Planned for Uncertainty

Facing uncertainty on durability, one company co-designed a managed entry agreement with payers. Payment was linked to outcomes over five years. The therapy achieved rapid adoption despite its high cost.

Lesson: Early transparency builds trust faster than post-hoc persuasion.

Case 4: The Digital Diabetes Platform

By integrating adherence and outcome tracking directly into its technology, a company turned post-launch evidence into an automatic process. This supported outcome-based reimbursement and patient retention.

Lesson: When real-world data become continuous, value arguments never go out of date.

Case 5: The Adaptive Evidence Pilot

A European consortium involving the EMA, FDA, and several companies tested an adaptive trial-to-HTA pathway. HEOR analysts joined during protocol design. The collaboration defined shared evidence standards and adaptive updates as data matured.

When one participating therapy reached submission, both agencies and payers accepted the evidence package without additional data requests. Time from Phase III readout to reimbursement was reduced by half.

Lesson: Joint evidence planning with regulators and payers reduces redundancy and accelerates trust.

Case 6: The Internal Learning Loop

A global company built an internal platform linking all past HTA outcomes, cost models, and trial data. HEOR, clinical, and policy teams used it to analyse patterns. They examined which endpoints were accepted, which assumptions failed, and how regional evidence expectations differed.

Within two years, the platform transformed how teams designed trials. New protocols included endpoints and comparators aligned with local payer preferences. Reimbursement delays dropped by 30 percent.

Lesson: Organisational learning is the most powerful form of access readiness.

Practical Tools and Applications

The Early Evidence Map

A practical guide for aligning scientific, economic, and operational milestones:

Development Stage	Key Decisions	Evidence Needed	HEOR Contribution	Output
Pre-Phase II	Define value hypothesis	Epidemiology, unmet need, comparator landscape	Identify cost drivers and patient outcomes	Preliminary value proposition
Phase II	Validate clinical signal	Efficacy, safety, quality-of-life data	Model early cost-effectiveness	Draft pricing corridors

Development Stage	**Key Decisions**	**Evidence Needed**	**HEOR Contribution**	**Output**
Phase III	Confirm benefit	Comparative and resource-use data	Refine budget impact analyses	Full value dossier
Pre-Launch	Prepare submissions	Real-world readiness, patient data plans	Test local assumptions	Country-specific HTA packages
Post-Launch	Sustain access	Real-world data and adherence metrics	Update models continuously	Evidence renewal

Table 5.1 The Early Evidence Map

The Value Alignment Checklist

1. Are trial endpoints relevant to both regulators and payers?
2. Is the comparator aligned with real-world clinical practice?
3. Have quality-of-life and resource-use data been integrated?
4. Is the model adaptable to different market conditions?
5. Is post-launch evidence collection already funded and designed?

If two or more answers are "no," access risks delay.

The Evidence Maturity Scale

1. **Reactive** – HEOR joins after Phase III.
2. **Aware** – Dialogue begins during Phase II.
3. **Aligned** – Joint endpoint planning.
4. **Integrated** – Shared KPIs and adaptive models.
5. **Optimised** – Continuous evidence lifecycle across all functions.

Organisations should benchmark themselves annually against this scale.

The Access Intelligence Hub

Forward-thinking companies create a central repository for evidence, economic models, and payer feedback. This "evidence brain" prevents repetition and ensures institutional memory. It also enables analytics, identifying patterns in payer decisions across markets.

Such hubs transform HEOR from a function into an enterprise capability.

Strategic and Organisational Implications

1. **Breaking Functional Silos**

   In most companies, evidence flows vertically. Data are collected by clinical teams, analysed by HEOR, interpreted by access, and communicated by medical affairs. Each handover creates loss of meaning.

   Integrated planning restores coherence. It replaces sequential thinking with systems thinking.

2. **Building Data Ecosystems**

   The next frontier in access strategy is not more trials but smarter integration. Data ecosystems combining clinical trial data, registry inputs, claims records, and patient-generated data allow dynamic evidence refresh.

   When data are connected, models evolve continuously. When models evolve, pricing and reimbursement become adaptive rather than fixed.

3. **Embedding Organisational Learning**

   Every failed submission carries lessons. The best organisations treat those lessons as assets. They store outcomes, assumptions, and payer rationales in central databases. Over time, this creates predictive capability.

   Imagine an internal AI that can predict the likelihood of reimbursement approval in different countries based on past decisions, trial designs, and model parameters. Some companies already use this approach to adjust strategies in real time.

Learning from evidence failures turns them into competitive advantages.

Ethical and Societal Dimensions

Early evidence integration has ethical as well as strategic importance. Every delay caused by inadequate planning represents lost patient time.

Ethical HEOR means designing with empathy, anticipating affordability, transparency, and equity. It also means recognising that evidence itself can perpetuate bias. Models built on narrow datasets risk excluding certain populations.

Responsible evidence planning includes diverse representation, context-specific assumptions, and disclosure of uncertainty. It aligns the moral and scientific case for innovation.

As one patient advocate put it, "Uncertainty is acceptable. Ignorance is not."

Key insight

Evidence generation is most effective when treated as a continuous learning process rather than a one-time submission task. Early integration of health economics and outcomes research helps anticipate payer concerns, manage uncertainty, and build credibility over time. When evidence is planned narrowly, organisations are forced into reactive justification after approval.

Reflection

Think about how evidence is discussed in your organisation. Is it framed as something to be completed, or something to be learned from?

Notice when economic and real-world considerations first enter development conversations, and what that timing signals about priorities.

Try this

- Map the full evidence plan for a single asset across its lifecycle.
- Identify where payer, HTA, and clinician questions are explicitly addressed.
- Review when HEOR expertise was first involved in shaping evidence plans.
- Ask how uncertainty is acknowledged and managed, rather than hidden.
- Consider how post-launch evidence feeds back into earlier assumptions.

Summary

- Evidence is a learning system, not a deliverable.
- Early HEOR integration strengthens access credibility.
- Anticipating questions is more effective than defending answers.
- Transparency about uncertainty builds trust.
- Post-launch evidence should inform future decisions, not just justify past ones.
- Reactive evidence generation increases delay and cost.

If evidence must serve multiple audiences over time, the next challenge is who ensures that evidence is interpreted, translated, and trusted in practice. The following chapter turns to Medical Affairs and its role in bridging science, systems, and society.

CHAPTER 6

MEDICAL AFFAIRS: TRANSLATORS, NOT TOUR GUIDES

"Medical Affairs adds value not by explaining the science, but by explaining what the science means in real life."
– Egbert Floppercough

Evidence alone does not create understanding or trust. This chapter explores the role of Medical Affairs in connecting science with real-world decision making. It shows why access improves when Medical Affairs shapes relevance early rather than explaining decisions late.

The Meeting That Changed the Question

It began as another post-launch review. The company had received reimbursement approval for a breakthrough therapy in a chronic inflammatory disease. The science was solid, the economic models were sound, and the launch materials were polished. Yet the numbers on the screen told a different story. Uptake was slow, clinician awareness was limited, and feedback from patient groups was lukewarm.

The Head of Commercial asked a simple question: "What are we missing?"

The silence that followed was familiar. The marketing team had done its work. The Market Access team had done its work. Regulatory had secured approvals. Then, at the far end of the table, the Medical Affairs lead spoke quietly.

"We are missing understanding," she said. "Clinicians know our data, but they do not yet trust our value story. We told them what the medicine does, not what it means."

That sentence changed the tone of the entire discussion. It revealed something that many in the industry already sensed but rarely said aloud. Success in the new access environment depends not only on evidence or economics but on interpretation. Medical Affairs sits at the centre of that translation.

From Messenger to Interpreter

For years, Medical Affairs was seen as the internal conscience of the company, responsible for scientific accuracy and compliance. The function emerged in the 1990s as a bridge between R&D and the field, ensuring that clinicians received balanced information rather than promotional claims. It played a vital but often reactive role. It explained data, answered queries, and ensured that the science stayed honest.

That model worked in a simpler world, one in which the path from approval to use was linear and predictable. Regulators assessed the evidence, clinicians prescribed the product, and the payer followed. Medical Affairs functioned like a tour guide through the data landscape, pointing out the highlights.

The problem is that the landscape has changed.

Today, health systems expect not just data but interpretation. Clinicians want to understand how new evidence fits into complex treatment pathways. Payers want to know how real-world outcomes will evolve. Patients want clarity on what the data mean for daily life. These are not simple questions of efficacy or safety. They are questions of context, relevance, and value.

Medical Affairs is now the only function with both the credibility and the connectivity to answer them. It sits between discovery and delivery, bridging science, policy, and practice. It has access to clinical data, payer dialogue, and patient insights. When used strategically, it can turn scattered facts into coherent meaning.

The New Mandate of Medical Affairs

The modern Medical Affairs function has three interconnected responsibilities:

1. **Translate Science into Practice.** This means more than presenting data. It means framing data in ways that help clinicians understand when and how to use a therapy effectively, safely, and economically.
2. **Shape Evidence Generation Beyond Approval.** Post-launch data collection, registries, and real-world evidence now define long-term success. Medical Affairs must lead this process, ensuring that evidence remains relevant and credible.
3. **Build Trust and Partnership Across Stakeholders.** Medical Affairs professionals are increasingly the company's most trusted external representatives. Their dialogue with patient groups, policymakers, and medical societies shapes perception more than any press release.

These responsibilities require a shift in skills and mindset. The Medical Affairs professional of the future must think like a scientist, a communicator, and a strategist, all at once.

Case Study 1: The Oncology Launch That Needed Translation

A global oncology company launched an immunotherapy with high expectations. The trial results were impressive, showing significant survival benefits compared to standard care. Within six months of launch, uptake was lower than predicted.

The problem was not efficacy but comprehension. Many oncologists struggled to interpret the survival curves and patient subgroup data. They were unsure which patients would benefit most and how to sequence the new therapy within existing regimens.

The Medical Affairs team recognised this early and initiated a targeted "data interpretation programme." They organised regional workshops led by independent clinicians who had participated in the trials. The sessions focused not on product promotion but on practical interpretation, including patient selection, biomarker relevance, and management of immune-related side effects.

Within a year, clinician confidence grew, treatment adoption increased, and the company established itself as a trusted partner rather than a commercial entity. The therapy's trajectory changed not because of new data but because of better translation.

Case Study 2: The Rare Disease Community That Felt Seen

A small biotech developing a therapy for a rare metabolic disorder faced a different challenge. Awareness of the disease was limited, and patient journeys were fragmented. Before approval, the Medical Affairs team began building a collaborative evidence network with patient organisations, diagnostic centres, and specialist clinicians.

They hosted joint data review meetings, co-authored publications with key opinion leaders, and developed educational materials focused on symptom recognition and early diagnosis. These activities were transparent, evidence-based, and patient-centred.

By the time the therapy was approved, awareness among clinicians had improved dramatically. Diagnosis rates increased, and payers cited the company's educational contribution as a reason for their positive reimbursement stance.

The lesson was clear: Medical Affairs can create value even before launch by building understanding, not just awareness.

The Evidence Continuum: From Trial to Trust

Medical Affairs operates across the entire evidence continuum, from pre-launch trial design to post-launch real-world data collection. Each stage offers opportunities to influence adoption.

1. **Pre-Launch: Shaping the Evidence Narrative**
   At this stage, Medical Affairs should help define what outcomes matter to clinicians and patients. Their early input ensures that trial endpoints and quality-of-life measures are clinically meaningful. They can also support scenario planning with HEOR teams to align evidence with payer expectations.
2. **Launch: Translating Data into Clinical Utility**
   During launch, Medical Affairs becomes the interpreter of trial data for diverse audiences. This involves creating materials that explain clinical relevance, limitations, and real-world applicability. It also means equipping field medical teams to hold informed, balanced discussions with healthcare professionals.
3. **Post-Launch: Sustaining Evidence and Trust**
   After launch, the focus shifts to real-world data. Medical Affairs leads the collection and analysis of outcomes from registries, observational studies, and patient-reported data. This ongoing evidence sustains access and informs updates to treatment guidelines.

When Medical Affairs manages this continuum effectively, they turn the therapy's story into a living narrative rather than a static set of trial results.

The Changing Metrics of Success

Traditional metrics for Medical Affairs often focus on activity: number of publications, advisory boards, or field interactions. These metrics measure output, not impact. In an access-first world, the real indicators of success are behavioural and systemic:

- How has clinician confidence changed?
- Has diagnostic accuracy improved?

- Are payers citing company-generated evidence in their assessments?
- Have patient organisations adopted the same value language in their advocacy?

These are harder to measure but more meaningful. They capture the real influence of Medical Affairs as a strategic partner rather than a compliance function.

A New Kind of Expertise

Modern Medical Affairs professionals require new competencies that blend scientific knowledge with strategic thinking. These include:

- **Systems Understanding:** Awareness of how health systems evaluate and adopt new technologies.
- **Health Economics Literacy:** Ability to interpret cost-effectiveness results and explain them credibly.
- **Data Storytelling:** Skill in turning complex data into clear, relevant insights for non-specialist audiences.
- **Policy Awareness:** Understanding of regulatory, reimbursement, and ethical considerations shaping access.
- **Cultural Intelligence:** Sensitivity to how medical narratives differ across countries and populations.

Companies that invest in developing these skills will find that their Medical Affairs teams become catalysts for both adoption and trust.

The Risk of Staying Static

Some organisations still see Medical Affairs as a reactive function. They measure its value through compliance scores and the number of scientific meetings attended. This narrow view wastes potential.

When Medical Affairs is confined to the role of messenger, it cannot influence trial design, evidence strategy, or access outcomes. The result is a loop of repetition: data are generated, shared, misunderstood, and reinterpreted later, often too late to change practice.

In contrast, companies that treat Medical Affairs as a strategic function integrate it into the earliest stages of planning. They empower it to shape narratives, not just deliver them.

Framework: The Three Dimensions of Translation

To move from information delivery to strategic translation, Medical Affairs must operate across three dimensions: **Scientific**, **Clinical**, and **Societal**.

1. **Scientific Translation**

   This is the traditional strength of Medical Affairs. It involves interpreting trial data, explaining mechanisms of action, and ensuring scientific accuracy. However, the best Medical Affairs teams do more than cite data. They interpret uncertainty honestly, contextualise results within the broader literature, and anticipate the next scientific question clinicians will ask.

For example, when launching a new oncology agent with a novel mechanism, the Medical team should discuss not only trial results but also how biomarker variability affects outcomes and how combination regimens might evolve. The goal is not persuasion but confidence, enabling clinicians to apply data responsibly.

2. **Clinical Translation**

   Here the focus shifts from what the therapy does to how it fits into practice. This includes identifying barriers to use, mapping diagnostic pathways, and engaging multidisciplinary teams. A well-designed clinical translation plan anticipates real-world complexity, such as the availability of testing facilities or co-treatment protocols, and supports clinicians in navigating them.

One European respiratory franchise established a "Clinical Integration Programme" led by Medical Affairs. Instead of promotional campaigns, they ran hospital-based workshops bringing together pulmonologists, nurses, and pharmacists to discuss patient flow and logistical barriers. Adoption rose by 40 per cent within a year because clinicians felt supported rather than sold to.

3. **Societal Translation**
   The final dimension links medical evidence with societal value. Medical Affairs professionals increasingly engage policymakers, payers, and advocacy groups to explain how new therapies contribute to public health priorities. They help shape the narrative from "cost" to "investment."

For instance, in a gene therapy case, the medical team worked with health economists and patient advocates to present data on lifetime care cost avoidance. This shifted payer discussions from budget strain to value creation. By speaking the language of social benefit, Medical Affairs elevated the conversation beyond price.

When these three dimensions align, Medical Affairs becomes the voice that connects innovation to legitimacy.

Case Study 3: The Vaccine Programme That Redefined Engagement

During the rollout of a new adult vaccination, uptake lagged far below expectations. Public confidence was low, and healthcare professionals were uncertain about eligibility and logistics. The company's Medical Affairs team, led by a physician with public health experience, proposed a different approach.

They created a "Community Evidence Forum," inviting clinicians, public health officers, and patient organisations to co-develop educational content. Rather than delivering pre-approved slide decks, they facilitated open discussion about the science, safety concerns, and communication strategies.

The result was a series of evidence-based toolkits adapted for primary care, community clinics, and public campaigns. Uptake improved within months. Local media began citing the forum as an example of transparent engagement.

The case demonstrated that when Medical Affairs operates as a convener rather than a messenger, it can influence both clinical behaviour and public trust.

Framework: The Access Partnership Loop

Medical Affairs sits within a loop of continuous interaction among key stakeholders: R&D, HEOR, Market Access, clinicians, and patients. The function's effectiveness depends on how quickly and clearly it circulates insight through this loop.

Stage	Role of Medical Affairs	Objective	Outcome
Evidence Creation	Advise on endpoints, comparators, and outcomes that reflect clinical practice	Align scientific design with real-world relevance	Trials that generate payer-ready data
Interpretation	Translate data for external and internal audiences	Build understanding and trust	Clear, actionable insights
Dissemination	Support education and dialogue through medical publications, advisory boards, and training	Enable confident use of the therapy	Faster adoption and better outcomes
Feedback	Gather real-world data, safety signals, and clinician feedback	Inform next-generation evidence plans	Continuous improvement of product and policy strategy

Table 6.1 The Access Partnership Loop Framework

This cycle never ends. When managed well, it becomes the foundation of evidence credibility and access sustainability.

Bridging Data and Decision

Data alone rarely change behaviour. Clinicians adopt new therapies when evidence connects with their daily reality, when they see peers using it, and when guidance from medical societies supports it.

Medical Affairs can accelerate this process by ensuring early alignment with professional bodies and academic institutions. Joint symposia, collaborative registries, and peer-authored publications all increase legitimacy. The difference lies not in the quantity of interactions but in their authenticity.

A cardiology company once partnered with an independent medical society to establish a real-world registry for a novel anticoagulant. Medical Affairs managed the protocol design and analysis, ensuring scientific neutrality. The resulting data influenced national guidelines and doubled adoption within two years. The company's credibility rose alongside its market share.

This kind of partnership illustrates that Medical Affairs can achieve both scientific and commercial impact without compromising integrity.

Framework: The Four Pillars of Effective Medical Strategy

To structure Medical Affairs within an access-first organisation, build plans around four pillars: Insight, Evidence, Education, and Engagement.

Insight

Medical Affairs must be the company's radar, detecting emerging questions from clinicians, payers, and patients. This requires structured insight-gathering mechanisms such as field medical reporting systems, advisory boards, and social listening tools. The insights should not sit in databases but feed directly into development and access strategy.

Evidence

Medical Affairs should lead the planning of real-world studies, observational cohorts, and patient-reported outcome research. These complement regulatory data with practical relevance. Clear governance frameworks must ensure transparency, data quality, and ethical integrity.

Education

Effective medical education goes beyond data delivery. It builds confidence through dialogue. Tailored programmes for different audiences, from hospital specialists to nurses to policymakers, help translate science into action.

Engagement

The final pillar is relationship building. This includes sustained partnerships with medical societies, public health bodies, and patient advocacy groups. Trust built here often outlasts individual products.

When these four pillars operate in unison, Medical Affairs becomes an engine of adoption rather than a post-launch accessory.

Leadership and Structure

To deliver on this expanded mandate, Medical Affairs must evolve structurally. The most progressive organisations are creating cross-functional "Integrated Evidence Councils," chaired by senior medical leaders but including HEOR, Market Access, and Clinical representatives. These councils decide what data will be generated, how it will be interpreted, and how it will be shared.

The benefit is coherence. Instead of fragmented messages, one for regulators, another for payers, and another for clinicians, the company speaks with one evidence voice.

Culturally, this requires medical leaders who are comfortable with ambiguity and collaboration. The traditional model of medical compliance specialists must give way to scientific communicators who can engage confidently across disciplines.

Case Study 4: From Compliance Function to Strategic Partner

A multinational firm in immunology once treated its Medical Affairs department as a regulatory buffer between science and sales. Reports were meticulous, but influence was minimal. Uptake of new therapies lagged.

Recognising the need for change, the company redefined Medical Affairs as a strategic partner. They appointed a Chief Medical Officer to the executive team, integrated medical staff into early asset planning, and introduced a global "Evidence to Practice" initiative.

Within two years, the company saw measurable outcomes. Real-world studies doubled in number, clinician engagement scores rose, and HTA bodies began citing company-led publications as evidence sources. Most importantly, employee surveys revealed a stronger sense of purpose. Medical staff felt they were shaping strategy, not policing it.

This transformation showed that Medical Affairs can drive organisational renewal when given authority and respect.

Technology and the Future of Medical Affairs

Digital transformation has expanded the reach and responsibility of Medical Affairs. Real-world evidence platforms, virtual advisory boards, and AI-enabled literature analysis allow medical teams to operate with greater precision and transparency.

Technology is not a substitute for trust. Digital tools amplify both good and poor communication. A poorly contextualised dataset can spread confusion faster than ever. The medical communicator's role remains essential. It ensures that interpretation keeps pace with information.

Several leading companies are experimenting with "digital medical ecosystems," where clinicians can access live evidence dashboards, submit questions, and share anonymised data. These platforms turn Medical Affairs into a living network rather than a static function.

The long-term opportunity lies in using these tools to shorten the feedback loop between clinical reality and scientific development.

Culture: From Authority to Partnership

The most significant transformation is cultural. Medical Affairs must move from authority to partnership. The old model of "educating the market" implied hierarchy: we know, you learn. The new model assumes mutual learning. Clinicians, patients, and payers all hold forms of expertise that can enrich the company's understanding.

In practical terms, this means listening before communicating. It means acknowledging uncertainty and co-designing solutions. When Medical Affairs teams approach engagement with humility, they gain credibility.

In one respiratory therapy launch, the medical team invited patient representatives to review draft materials before release. Their feedback reshaped how side effects and adherence issues were described. The resulting resources were clearer, more empathetic, and better received by both clinicians and patients.

This example illustrates a broader truth: respect builds resonance.

Key insight

Medical Affairs plays a critical role in connecting scientific evidence with real-world decision making. Its value lies not in explaining data after the fact, but in shaping relevance, credibility, and dialogue throughout development and access planning. When Medical Affairs is positioned late or narrowly, opportunities to influence access are lost.

Reflection

Reflect on how Medical Affairs is positioned in your organisation. Is it invited into decisions early, or asked to explain them later?

Consider whether Medical Affairs is expected to translate science outward, or also to bring system and patient realities inward.

Try this

- Review when Medical Affairs becomes involved in a typical development programme.
- Identify decisions where earlier Medical input could have altered direction.

- Examine how Medical Affairs engages with clinicians, payers, and patient groups.
- Ask whether insights from the field systematically influence strategy.
- Consider what would need to change for Medical Affairs to act as a true bridge.

Summary

- Medical Affairs is a strategic access function, not a communications layer.
- Early involvement increases relevance and trust.
- Translation must work in both directions.
- Field insights should shape development, not just messaging.
- Credibility is built through engagement, not explanation.
- Access improves when Medical Affairs operates upstream.

If access depends on judgement as much as evidence, the next challenge is how pricing and value decisions are made under constraint. The following chapter examines pricing not as a calculation, but as a series of explicit trade-offs.

PART III

EXECUTION BY DESIGN

CHAPTER 7

MARKET ACCESS AND PRICING BY DESIGN

"Pricing is never a calculation alone. It is a judgement about what the system will tolerate and trust."
– Egbert Floppercough

Evidence and relevance ultimately converge in pricing decisions. This chapter reframes pricing not as a calculation but as a series of judgements made under constraint. It explains why treating pricing as a downstream commercial task almost guarantees late-stage conflict and delay.

The Meeting That Changed the Mood

The meeting had been running for two hours. The slides had blurred into wallpaper. Charts of survival curves and p-values filled the screen. The room was warm. The air was heavy with frustration.

A health economist leaned forward, tapping a pen against a folder. "So, what is the price?"

Silence.

The clinical lead glanced at the regulatory team. The commercial director looked down at the table. Eventually, someone said, "We have not set it yet. We're still finalising the value story."

Across the table, the payer representative smiled politely. It was the kind of smile that comes just before rejection. "You know we can't fund what we can't justify."

The therapy worked. It improved outcomes, reduced hospital visits, and had generated headlines about a breakthrough. Yet the evidence connecting those benefits to cost was weak. The company had waited until after Phase III to involve pricing and access teams. By then, the trial design was fixed, and the opportunity to collect data that would support the payer perspective was gone.

Six months later, the drug was still not reimbursed. A year later, it was competing against two new entrants. Internally, people blamed bureaucracy. The truth was that the delay had been designed into the process from the start.

That meeting was not an isolated story. It was a mirror of a wider industry habit. Treat price as a conclusion rather than a design principle. Everyone loves innovation until the invoice arrives.

The Core Challenge

For decades, the pharmaceutical industry operated on a simple timeline. Discover the molecule, prove it works, get it approved, and then work out what to charge. The sequence was efficient when budgets were looser and expectations simpler. Regulators were the only real gatekeepers of value.

That world no longer exists.

Today, value is negotiated in committee rooms, not declared in press releases. Payers, HTA agencies, and policymakers all have a say in whether an innovation reaches patients. Approval now grants permission to compete for funding, not a guarantee of use.

In Europe, nearly half of new medicines face reimbursement delays beyond twelve months. Even when approvals come, they often arrive with conditions, caps, or partial coverage. The reason is rarely scientific. It is evidentiary.

The clinical data submitted to regulators often fail to answer the questions payers need resolved. Endpoints such as progression-free survival or biomarker response may prove efficacy but do not show cost-effectiveness. The link between clinical value and economic value is still missing.

The result is predictable: brilliant science trapped in budget limbo.

Pricing, in this context, is not a commercial act. It is a strategic signal. It expresses how a company understands both its product and the system it seeks to serve.

When pricing, access, and evidence evolve together, launches move smoothly, negotiations become collaborative, and adoption follows naturally. When they evolve separately, the therapy becomes a policy problem rather than a solution.

The Value-by-Design Model

The Value-by-Design Model reframes pricing as part of the development architecture. It rests on three principles: define value early, build evidence that matches that definition, and design pricing and access together.

1. *Define Value Early*
   Before a single patient is enrolled, determine what value means in each target market. In Germany, it might mean comparative benefit. In the UK, cost per QALY. In Japan, societal productivity. These definitions vary and guessing them later is expensive.

Teams should build a Value Definition Map early in development. It lists the primary outcome that each payer will consider meaningful. It also identifies which endpoints can be measured during trials and which will require real-world data.

2. *Build Evidence That Matches the Definition*
   Once value is defined, design studies that measure it. If the payer cares about avoided hospital days, measure hospital days. If the payer values quality of life, use validated patient-reported outcome instruments.

Clinical development teams often focus on endpoints that regulators prefer. Access-first design expands that lens to include endpoints that matter economically and socially.

3. *Design Pricing and Access Together*
   Pricing and access should not be downstream calculations. Early economic modelling allows teams to test assumptions about price elasticity, budget impact, and payer tolerance. This information can guide trial design, label strategy, and even indication sequencing.

By aligning scientific data with payer expectations, pricing stops being defensive and becomes strategic.

As one payer commented during a workshop, "We like innovation. We just want to know that the innovators understand the health system they are entering."

Case Studies: Proof in Practice

Case 1: When Pricing Met Late Evidence

A major oncology company developed a promising therapy that improved progression-free survival. The team priced it at a premium, confident in the novelty. Regulators approved it swiftly. But when the dossier reached national HTA agencies, they pushed back. The surrogate endpoint was not accepted as proof of long-term survival.

Nine months passed while analysts rebuilt the economic model. By then, competitors had arrived, and the momentum had gone.

Lesson: Regulatory success does not equal reimbursement readiness. Evidence that satisfies one audience often fails another.

Case 2: When Pricing and Evidence Grew Together

A smaller immunology company worked differently. During Phase II, it convened workshops with payers and clinicians to discuss endpoints and comparators. Health economists helped shape trial design.

The team collected data not only on efficacy but also on healthcare utilisation and productivity. When submission time came, the economic case was already built. Reimbursement followed within three months, a record in that therapeutic area.

Lesson: Early integration of evidence, economics, and pricing converts negotiation into dialogue.

Case 3: The Cost of Coming Late

A rare disease therapy launched with strong clinical data and a seven-figure price tag. Long-term durability was uncertain. HTA bodies refused reimbursement, citing a lack of real-world evidence.

The company spent two years building registries and collecting follow-up data. By the time it resubmitted, the competitive landscape had shifted.

Lesson: Data collected too late cost more than data collected early. The most expensive evidence is the evidence you should already have.

Case 4: The Smart Cardiovascular Launch

A cardiovascular therapy team knew that long-term outcomes were slow to appear. They worked with payers during Phase II to identify cost drivers such as hospital admissions and readmissions.

By including healthcare resource use and economic modelling in their design, they created a data package that spoke directly to payer concerns. When approval arrived, reimbursement followed in parallel across five markets.

Lesson: Payer involvement before Phase III changes the tone from justification to partnership.

Case 5: The Vaccine That Priced for Equity

A global vaccine manufacturer faced the challenge of introducing a new pneumococcal vaccine in both high income and low income countries. Instead of setting a single global price, the team developed a three tier structure based on GDP thresholds and disease burden.

High-income countries paid premium rates tied to innovation. Middle income countries received discounts linked to local cost-effectiveness data. Low income regions were covered through a donor-supported access programme.

Within two years, the vaccine achieved broad global uptake and a strong reputation for ethical leadership.

Lesson: Equitable pricing is not charity. It is a strategic investment in legitimacy.

Case 6: The Digital Therapeutic That Misread Value

A digital health company developed an app-based cognitive therapy with strong clinical trial results. The team assumed that payers would treat it like a medicine. They priced it accordingly.

Payers disagreed. They viewed it as a service, not a product, and demanded usage-based pricing. The mismatch delayed reimbursement by eighteen months.

Lesson: every innovation must align its pricing logic with how payers categorise it. Novel technologies require novel economic models.

Organisational Learning: Building Pricing Intelligence

Pricing by design requires structural change. It demands that companies move from departmental silos to an integrated ecosystem where evidence, economics, and empathy coexist.

1. *Create Cross-Functional Access Councils*
   These councils bring together Clinical Development, HEOR, Medical Affairs, Policy, and Commercial teams. Their purpose is not to coordinate meetings but to design decisions. They review

early value assumptions, test economic models, and ensure that pricing reflects data reality.

2. *Build Feedback Loops from the Field*
After every negotiation or HTA interaction, learn. Capture what worked, what failed, and what evidence was missing. Feed that insight into new programmes. Over time, this creates an organisational memory, a pricing intelligence system that evolves faster than the market.
3. *Embed Access Liaisons in R&D Teams*
Assign access specialists to early development units. Their role is to translate clinical outcomes into health system relevance. When they sit inside project teams rather than at the end of the chain, evidence alignment becomes natural, not bureaucratic.
4. *Use Predictive Modelling*
Modern analytics can simulate payer decisions based on current trends in value thresholds and health policy. Running these simulations early helps teams anticipate objections and adjust evidence plans before they become problems.
5. *Reward Alignment, Not Just Approval*
Most performance systems still reward regulatory milestones. Mature organisations also reward early access readiness, i.e. pricing models completed on time, payer input secured, evidence linked to value.

These practices turn pricing into a core capability rather than an administrative function.

Practical Tools

The Value–Affordability Matrix

Use this tool to map how your therapy's clinical strength aligns with economic feasibility. It reveals whether you are designing for speed or struggle.

The Early Payer Engagement Map

Engage payers at defined milestones. By treating engagement as a structured process rather than a favour, companies build predictability and trust.

Innovative Pricing Models

Outcomes-based, amortised, and managed entry agreements remain the most powerful mechanisms for balancing innovation with affordability. The best organisations master all three and select them dynamically depending on the therapy and market.

The Pricing Playbook Template

Create an internal document that evolves with each project. Include sections for payer segmentation, value assumptions, risk-sharing options, and evidence alignment. Treat it as a living manual, not a compliance form.

The Equity Impact Dashboard

Measure who benefits from your pricing. Track uptake by geography, socioeconomic group, and population health indicators. Equity metrics are now as strategic as sales metrics.

Leadership and Culture for Pricing by Design

Leadership is what turns frameworks into behaviour. The best leaders treat pricing as a strategic narrative, not a tactical conversation.

They talk openly about affordability, not as a constraint but as part of innovation. They see access as a measure of success, not a burden of proof. They empower teams to challenge assumptions about what the market can bear.

Culture is the invisible infrastructure of pricing. It shapes how people perceive risk, value, and fairness. In high-trust organisations, pricing discussions are evidence-driven and collaborative. In low-trust ones, they are political and defensive.

Cultural signals matter. When leaders celebrate early payer dialogue or transparent modelling, they normalise curiosity and humility. When they reward only fast approvals, they reinforce old habits.

A chief access officer at one global company once put it simply: "If the only time you mention payers is after approval, you've already lost the argument."

Organisations that internalise this mindset find that their teams begin to think systemically. Scientists start asking economic questions. Economists start learning the science. The walls begin to disappear.

This integration is the foundation of what might be called "pricing maturity." It is not about clever models but collective intelligence, the ability to link every decision back to the question: how will this help patients receive the therapy sooner and fairer?

Strategic and Ethical Implications

Pricing is not just a spreadsheet. It is a statement of intent. Every price declares who counts and who waits.

Equity and Global Access

Fair pricing builds trust across systems. Tiered models and managed entry agreements demonstrate respect for the economic diversity of nations; they also future-proof access against political volatility.

Sustainability and Trust

When pricing becomes exploitative, policy reacts. Transparency prevents that cycle. Companies that articulate their rationale and share their data are less likely to face regulatory retaliation.

Data Transparency and Digital Proof

In an age of real-world evidence and open data, payers can validate claims independently. The companies that thrive will be those who collaborate on evidence rather than defend it.

Patient Impact and Public Legitimacy

Patients notice delay. Public opinion notices inequity. Reputation in pharma no longer depends on innovation alone but on integrity. Ethical pricing protects both.

Try This:

Run a "value rehearsal." Ask your payer engagement team to challenge your pricing proposal as if they were the HTA committee. Record every objection and identify which ones you can pre-empt with stronger data or alternative payment structures.

Reflection

Pricing will always be an uncomfortable conversation because it touches both hope and cost. But when it is transparent, data-driven, and grounded in empathy, it becomes a form of leadership.

Every therapy tells two stories: one about discovery and one about delivery. The second is the one that counts.

The real question is not "What is the price?" but "What proof have we built that this price makes sense?"

As one payer said at the end of a long negotiation, closing his notebook quietly, "Price isn't the problem. Proof is."

That sentence captures the entire philosophy of market access by design: pricing is not about what a product is worth to a company, but what it is worth to society when it is actually used.

CHAPTER 8

EQUITY, INFRASTRUCTURE, AND THE REAL-WORLD BARRIER COURSE

"Equity collapses fastest where infrastructure is assumed rather than designed."
– Egbert Floppercough

Even when pricing is agreed, access often remains uneven. This chapter examines the non-price barriers that shape who actually receives treatment. It shows why equity depends on infrastructure, system readiness, and deliberate design rather than intent alone.

The Last Mile Problem

It was 8:47 a.m. in a small oncology unit outside Bucharest. The nurses had already rearranged the day's infusion chairs to make room for a shipment of vials that still had not arrived. On the whiteboard, next to the patient list, someone had written in red marker: "Truck delayed. Again." In the capital, company executives were celebrating their twenty-fifth country launch of the same therapy. The slides showed global maps shaded in corporate blue, with "ACCESS ACHIEVED" in bold across the top. The press release had already gone out.

But in this clinic, the story looked different. The only patient scheduled to receive the new drug that day had been fasting since dawn. After waiting four hours, she quietly stood up, gathered her things, and told the nurse she would come back "next week, maybe." The nurse nodded, knowing she probably would not. That is what access failure looks like. Not a decision in a boardroom, but an empty chair in a treatment room that was supposed to be full.

Pharmaceutical companies often treat access as a finish line. Once a therapy wins regulatory approval and reimbursement, the assumption is that patients will automatically receive it. Slide decks confirm "market availability." Success stories circulate internally. Then, a few months later, the data begin to tell another story. Uptake is slower than forecast. Disparities appear between regions. A therapy hailed as transformative reaches only a fraction of those who need it.

Access, in truth, does not end with approval. It begins there. Health systems are not smooth pipelines. They are human networks of hospitals, logistics, and habits. A therapy may be scientifically brilliant and commercially viable but still fail if the infrastructure that connects science to patients is weak.

World Bank data show that in many middle-income countries, fewer than half of hospitals outside urban centres have reliable cold-chain storage. Diagnostic turnaround times for advanced testing can exceed six weeks even in parts of Europe. In high-income systems, geography, literacy, and workforce shortages quietly limit who receives care.

The paradox is clear. We live in an age of extraordinary biomedical progress, yet access gaps are widening. New treatments reach the market faster than the systems that must deliver them can adapt. Regulatory approval opens the door, but the corridor beyond it is a barrier course of logistics, diagnostics, and infrastructure. Until those barriers are addressed, access remains theoretical.

A hospital pharmacist once said with weary precision, "Availability means I can order it. Accessibility means I can actually give it." That distinction defines the entire challenge.

Access in practice requires five gates to open. The first is infrastructure readiness. Are there trained professionals, facilities, and equipment to deliver the therapy safely? A breakthrough that requires high-tech infusion centres will stall if regional hospitals cannot handle it. The second is diagnostic capacity. Can the system identify eligible patients in time? In precision medicine, diagnostics are the passport to treatment. A therapy is useless without a functioning testing network. The third is logistical reach. Can the therapy physically reach patients without disruption? Delayed deliveries, fragile cold chains, or fragmented procurement can break access entirely. The fourth is financial accessibility. Can patients afford the total cost of treatment, including travel, time, and accommodation? Financial friction is one of the most underestimated causes of non-adherence. The fifth is health literacy and trust. Do clinicians and patients understand and believe in the therapy enough to use it properly? Misinformation, cultural barriers, and scepticism often undermine the best science.

Each gate can fail on its own, but in practice they fail together. The industry tends to plan for the first and assume the rest will follow. The result is a recurring pattern: global launch success and local delivery failure. Breaking that cycle requires a mindset shift. Access strategy must evolve from market coverage to system coverage. That means understanding how real patients move through real systems, and what stops them along the way.

A major oncology therapy launched successfully across Europe. Pricing and reimbursement were secured quickly. Awareness campaigns were strong, and analysts celebrated the "speed to market." But a year later, the data revealed sharp inequalities. Uptake was high in capital cities, negligible in rural regions. Smaller hospitals lacked trained staff for the infusion protocol, and regional funding did not cover patient travel or accommodation. The company partnered with local authorities to fund nurse training, create regional hubs, and reimburse travel costs. Within twelve months, rural treatment rates rose by sixty percent. Patient satisfaction improved, and payer confidence increased. Approval creates potential, not practice. Access begins when the system itself becomes capable of delivering care.

A targeted therapy for lung cancer was approved for patients with a specific gene mutation. The science was flawless. The problem was that only a handful of national laboratories could perform the test, and turnaround times stretched to six weeks. The company built a diagnostic partnership programme. It funded new testing sites, trained technicians, and created courier routes for biopsy transport. Within a year, testing capacity tripled, turnaround dropped to ten days, and eligible patient identification doubled. A therapy that depends on diagnostics is only as strong as the weakest lab in the system.

A chronic disease therapy was fully reimbursed, yet adherence was poor. Surveys found that patients were skipping doses not because of scepticism but because of indirect costs such as transport, missed workdays, and childcare. The company collaborated with NGOs to subsidise travel and lodging and encouraged clinics to extend evening hours. Within six months, adherence rose by twenty-five percent. Financial equity extends beyond the drug price. The true cost of access includes time, distance, and dignity.

A diabetes management programme introduced remote monitoring through smartphone apps. Uptake was high in cities but negligible in rural areas, where patients lacked devices, data plans, or confidence using technology. The company simplified the interface, built a paper-based alternative, and trained community nurses to support remote care. Engagement in rural areas quadrupled within a year. Technology can amplify inclusion or exclusion. Inclusion must be designed, not assumed.

A biologic therapy required refrigeration, but clinics in tropical regions had unstable electricity. The result was wasted stock and untreated patients. R&D teams developed a room-temperature formulation. Distribution expanded, wastage dropped by eighty percent, and patient coverage tripled. Sometimes, the most transformative innovation is practical, not scientific.

Access success depends on five interconnected dimensions that determine whether patients can actually receive care. Geographic equity asks whether all patients, not just those near major centres, can reach treatment safely. Diagnostic equity asks whether the system can identify who needs the therapy. Financial equity concerns whether patients can afford the total treatment cost. Knowledge equity focuses on whether clinicians and patients understand and accept the therapy. Systemic equity examines whether the system can sustain delivery over time.

When these indicators flatten across populations, equity is working. When they diverge, you are looking at design failure. As one policymaker joked, "Equity dashboards sound dull until you realise they measure who gets to live another year."

The Value–Barrier Matrix helps teams decide where to focus resources. It maps therapies according to their value and the barriers to delivery. If a therapy scores high on value but faces high barriers, invest in system readiness before launch. If it sits low on both, pause and rethink. This simple grid saves teams from discovering too late that their innovation cannot travel the last mile.

Designing for real-world equity begins with mapping the patient journey early. Follow the path from diagnosis to delivery and identify where patients drop out. Assess system readiness by auditing hospital capacity, logistics, and workforce training. Co-design solutions with local stakeholders so that fixes are realistic, not theoretical. Integrate equity metrics into KPIs and track them with the same seriousness as revenue. Finally, plan for sustainability so that programmes continue when initial funding ends. If a solution requires annual applause to survive, it is not real.

Equity in access is also an organisational discipline. It relies on cross-functional coordination, not charity. R&D, HEOR, Medical Affairs, and Market Access must operate as one continuous feedback system, where information flows both ways. Field insights about logistical challenges, diagnostic delays, and patient behaviours should loop back into development and pricing decisions. The organisations that manage this feedback best are usually those that treat access not as a phase but as a continuous learning process.

Access equity is not philanthropy; it is good engineering. A therapy that cannot be delivered effectively is not innovative, it is incomplete. R&D, Market Access, and Medical Affairs must think like systems designers. The question is no longer "Can it be approved?" but "Can it be delivered responsibly?" Governments and payers share that duty. Approvals without infrastructure funding are hollow victories. As one payer said during a European roundtable, "We do not need more miracles. We need more logistics."

Companies that invest in delivery systems earn credibility that outlasts any product. Installing diagnostic labs, training staff, and improving logistics do not just help one drug; they strengthen the ecosystem for all. A vaccine manufacturer once installed solar-powered cold-chain units across sub-Saharan Africa. Ten years later, those same units supported oncology and insulin distribution. What began as corporate responsibility became market readiness. Infrastructure is not a burden. It is a competitive advantage disguised as compassion.

Every therapy that reaches one group and not another reflects a choice. Sometimes deliberate, often invisible. Designing for equity forces those choices into view. Affordability, education, and logistics are ethical responsibilities as much as scientific ones. A regulator in Asia once said, "Approval is permission to deliver responsibly." That single sentence captures what the future of access demands.

Digital solutions can democratise healthcare or deepen inequality. AI-driven diagnostics, telemedicine, and data platforms are only inclusive if designed for diverse contexts. If algorithms are trained mostly on Western datasets or require high-end devices, they risk excluding those most in need. The best digital innovators test for inclusion from the start. They train algorithms on diverse populations and maintain offline options. Technology should shorten the distance between discovery and delivery, not create new eligibility criteria.

Equity is not only ethical; it is economic. Health systems that exclude populations face higher costs later through preventable illness and lost productivity. Some regulators are adapting accordingly. European HTA agencies now ask for evidence of equity impact. In the

United States, reimbursement frameworks are exploring access-linked outcomes. The message is clear: equity is becoming measurable, not rhetorical.

Equity also requires learning cultures. Companies must create feedback loops from clinics, distributors, and patients to continuously adapt. Data on logistics, patient drop-off points, and diagnostic turnaround should flow back into development and policy teams. Organisations that close this loop gain a new kind of intelligence, one that sees access not as a target but as a living system. Cross-functional Access Readiness Boards can turn insights into action. When access leaders sit alongside R&D and supply chain executives, equity stops being an aspiration and becomes a deliverable. A few pioneering companies already run equity reviews before launch decisions, ensuring that every therapy has a realistic delivery plan. That approach should become industry standard.

Access is not abstract. It is a human experience measured in waiting rooms, phone calls, and long journeys. It is a nurse checking a delivery list, a patient wondering if the medicine will arrive, and a policymaker balancing limited budgets with unlimited need. We often say that science saves lives. In truth, systems do. Designing for equity means remembering that every statistic hides a person who cannot afford to wait. A patient advocate at a global summit once said, "We do not need faster approvals. We need shorter distances." That sentence should be printed on every launch plan. Because access-first innovation is not about more molecules. It is about fewer barriers between discovery and the people who depend on it.

Try This:

Choose one therapy in your portfolio and map the full patient journey from diagnosis to treatment. Mark every step that depends on infrastructure, logistics, or literacy. Count the barriers, and treat each as an opportunity for innovation.

Reflection

This chapter exposes the quiet truth behind "approved but unreachable" medicines. Using practical frameworks and real examples, it reframes access as a systems challenge shaped by infrastructure, diagnostics, logistics, and trust. It shows how the Five Dimensions of Access Equity can turn aspiration into implementation, and why investment in delivery systems is both ethical and strategic. The message is simple: science only saves lives when systems let it.

The empty infusion chair in Bucharest is not just a symbol of logistical failure. It is a reminder that every gap in infrastructure is also a gap in information. What the nurse saw as a missing truck, a strategist should see as a missing data point; one that was never captured, shared, or acted upon in time.

Access fails when learning fails. The next phase of pharmaceutical evolution will depend on how well companies can transform data into foresight, not just hindsight. Every supply chain delay, diagnostic bottleneck, and patient drop-off holds clues to how systems behave. The challenge is to collect, interpret, and act on those signals before they turn into missed treatments.

Artificial intelligence, biomarkers, and real-world analytics promise to close that gap. For the first time, it is becoming possible to trace a medicine's journey from molecule to market to patient outcome in near real time. Algorithms can now detect who will respond best to treatment, when adherence may falter, and how pricing can be tied to measurable value rather than abstract assumptions.

Yet the same technologies that offer precision can also entrench inequity if deployed without context. AI models trained on unrepresentative data can exclude entire populations. Predictive systems built without transparency can erode trust. The tools of the future will succeed only if the lessons of access are carried into their design with fairness, adaptability, and human judgment at the centre.

As one payer remarked after a recent joint advisory with regulators, "We do not fear innovation. We fear innovation that learns nothing from its own consequences."

Designing for equity is only half the story. The other half begins after approval, when the real-world tests every assumption and access depends less on intent and more on execution. The next chapter turns that lens onto the post-approval phase, where strategy meets the practical realities of reimbursement, supply, and patient reach.

CHAPTER 9

THE POST-APPROVAL PLAYBOOK

"Most launches fail not because something went wrong after approval, but because nothing changed after it."
– Egbert Floppercough

Approval and reimbursement change the context, not the challenge. This chapter focuses on what happens after a therapy becomes technically available. It explains why access remains fragile without deliberate execution, learning, and adaptation in real health systems.

Launch Day Minus the Applause

The conference room was full, the coffee was strong, and the banners were up. On the wall, a slide glowed with the words *Launch Success: Approved Across All Major Markets.*
Applause followed. Someone opened a bottle of champagne. A camera flash captured the team smiling beside the slide.

Three months later, the same room felt very different. The lights were dim, the coffee cold, and the tone defensive. A marketing manager spoke softly. "We expected two thousand patients by now. We've reached two hundred."

The access head looked at the line on the graph that refused to rise. "We celebrated approval," she said. "We forgot adoption."

That single remark captured a deeper problem. Post-approval is not victory. It is the start of the hardest phase of innovation, turning approval into use, and use into sustained value.

Every launch teaches the same lesson in its own way: access achieved is not access maintained.

Context and Core Challenge: The Second Development Phase

Pharmaceutical development once ended at approval. Success was defined by the label. Adoption was assumed.

Today, that logic fails. Regulators approve therapies. Health systems decide whether anyone can use them. Patients and clinicians determine whether they actually will.

Across Europe and North America, a growing number of therapies achieve approval but stall after launch. In oncology, median time from regulatory clearance to full reimbursement exceeds a year in several markets. In rare diseases, some therapies remain unfunded for years despite proven benefit.

The reason is rarely lack of innovation. It is lack of readiness, organisational, operational, and evidential.

Post-approval now represents a second development phase. It demands new forms of evidence, new partnerships, and a new kind of corporate rhythm.

Where earlier stages are defined by data generation, the post-approval phase is defined by system navigation. The best companies are those that treat post-approval not as an afterthought but as the central arena of learning.

Framework: The Post-Approval Value Loop

The **Post-Approval Value Loop** describes how innovation, evidence, and access evolve together after approval. It has four phases:

1. **Activation** – Turning approval into practical access.
2. **Observation** – Capturing real-world data and feedback.
3. **Adaptation** – Evolving strategy, evidence, and pricing based on insight.
4. **Renewal** – Institutionalising learning to strengthen future launches.

These stages overlap. The strength of one determines the resilience of the others.

Phase 1: Activation – Turning Approval into Use

Activation is the moment a molecule meets the system. It is where theory confronts reality.

It begins with a simple question: are health systems actually ready?

The checklist is unforgiving. Are clinicians trained? Are diagnostic pathways defined? Are reimbursement codes live? Are logistics prepared?

Most launches that underperform fail this test. Approval opens the door, but activation requires operational alignment.

One European oncology company learned this the hard way. After approval, hospitals lacked staff trained to administer the therapy. Diagnostic tests were delayed. Patients waited. Within six months, uptake was half forecast.

The company responded by creating an *Activation Dashboard* that tracked readiness indicators for every country - centre accreditation, reimbursement status, training completion, and stock availability. Regional gaps triggered rapid response teams. Within a year, uptake variance between countries fell from 60 per cent to 10 per cent.

Lesson: Activation is not an announcement; it is a rehearsal for the real-world.

Phase 2: Observation – Listening to the Real-World

Once a therapy reaches patients, data take on new meaning. The trial tells you what can happen; real-world observation tells you what does happen.

Observation is more than safety reporting. It is structured curiosity. It involves listening to clinicians, pharmacists, patients, and payers, and translating their experiences into evidence.

A chronic disease therapy in Scandinavia discovered through patient feedback that discontinuation had less to do with side effects and more to do with travel time. A small logistical subsidy programme doubled adherence in six months.

The insight was not clinical. It was human. Observation means finding such truths early, before they become statistics.

Lesson: Observation converts outcomes into understanding.

Phase 3: Adaptation – Evolving with the Evidence

The third phase, adaptation, is the mark of maturity. It means acting on what observation reveals.

Adaptation can take many forms — adjusting patient eligibility criteria, revising dosing schedules, re-analysing cost-effectiveness models, or introducing outcomes-based agreements.

A gene therapy team in Southern Europe pioneered a flexible payment structure tied to real-world outcomes. As data confirmed durability, payer confidence grew, leading to faster reimbursement of subsequent therapies in the same class.

Adaptation is not a sign of weakness. It is a demonstration of accountability.

Lesson: The most adaptive organisations are the most trusted.

Phase 4: Renewal – Closing the Learning Loop

Renewal transforms isolated success into sustained capability.

Every post-approval experience becomes a lesson for the next asset. Data from one market inform strategy in another. Insights from one therapy shape trial design for the next.

Companies that formalise renewal create a learning ecosystem. They move from launch events to launch systems.

As one medical affairs leader put it: "Every label gives us data; every patient gives us direction."

Case Studies: Lessons from the Field

Case 1: The Oncology Stall

A high-profile oncology therapy launched with strong regulatory backing. Six months later, uptake was stagnant. Investigations revealed a diagnostic bottleneck — the biomarker test required to identify eligible patients was not reimbursed.

The company established a co-funded diagnostic programme and trained local labs. Within a year, patient access tripled.

Lesson: Access stops where infrastructure ends.

Case 2: The Adaptive Rare Disease Launch

A rare disease therapy with uncertain long-term durability entered markets through conditional reimbursement. The company agreed to share patient-level data annually. When results confirmed sustained benefit, payers renewed funding automatically.

Lesson: Transparency is a faster path to trust than perfection.

Case 3: The Vaccine Coordination Success

A vaccine programme achieved rapid adoption by co-investing in logistics and public awareness. The company partnered with ministries of health to upgrade storage facilities and train nurses.

Lesson: When delivery systems improve, access equity follows.

Case 4: The Digital Dashboard Failure

A company launched a complex post-approval data platform without consulting clinicians. Data entry took too long; engagement collapsed. Payers later criticised the lack of usable real-world information.

Lesson: Technology must serve the user, not the architect.

Case 5: The Continuous Learning Model

A global company built an internal evidence hub linking HEOR, medical affairs, and access data across markets. Each affiliate shared outcomes, payer comments, and pricing adaptations.

AI analytics identified emerging trends and forecasted potential barriers for new launches. Access preparation time dropped by 40 per cent.

Lesson: Knowledge multiplies when shared systemically.

Mini-Case 1: The Germany HEOR Re-alignment Pilot

Germany's AMNOG process is one of the most demanding in the world, often leading to rapid price adjustments after launch. One company facing steep post-launch erosion initiated a *HEOR Re-alignment Pilot* across its European affiliates.

The pilot involved re-analysing cost-effectiveness assumptions with local claims data within the first six months post-launch. The company published the findings jointly with an academic partner, showing more accurate utilisation patterns and real-world adherence.

The reassessment improved the product's incremental cost-effectiveness ratio and strengthened negotiation for price maintenance.

More importantly, it changed internal behaviour. Post-launch HEOR became standard practice rather than crisis response.

Lesson: Informed recalibration is better than defensive justification.

Mini-Case 2: Japan Adaptive Reimbursement Review

In Japan, a large multinational introduced a novel oncology therapy under conditional approval. Payers required periodic evidence reviews to validate long-term cost-effectiveness.

The company established a *Joint Evidence Council* with the National Cancer Centre and payer representatives. They met twice yearly to review registry data, patient outcomes, and health system costs.

When data revealed shorter hospital stays than predicted, the council agreed to extend reimbursement for an expanded indication.

The collaboration demonstrated a new model of adaptive access: evidence and policy evolving together rather than apart.

Lesson: Joint evaluation builds shared ownership of value.

Practical Tools: The Post-Approval Toolkit

1. ***The Access Maturity Ladder***

Level	Description	Organisational Behaviour
1	Reactive	Post-approval seen as administrative clean-up.
2	Aware	Some local data collection and payer contact.
3	Structured	Dedicated real-world evidence and access monitoring.
4	Integrated	Continuous data flow, cross-functional collaboration.
5	Predictive	Insights drive proactive contract renewal and design of future trials.

Table 9.1 The Access Maturity Ladder

Teams can self-assess annually and plan maturity upgrades as part of strategic objectives.

2. ***The Real-World Activation Map***

Dimension	Core Question	Typical Action	Measure of Success
Clinical Infrastructure	Are centres ready to treat?	Training, accreditation, logistics checks	Percentage of eligible sites active
Economic Alignment	Are payers satisfied with current data?	Budget reviews, outcomes contracts	Renewal cycle speed
Data Feedback	Are outcomes captured efficiently?	Registries, EHR linkage, digital tools	Completeness and usability of data
Patient Engagement	Are patients informed and supported?	Education materials, advocacy input	Adherence and satisfaction rates

Table 6.2 The Real-World Activation Map

Each dimension should have clear accountability and KPIs at launch readiness reviews.

3. ***The Launch Learning Review***

Every 12 months, a structured review captures three lessons from each market:

1. What succeeded operationally.
2. What failed in evidence or communication.
3. What should change next time.

Insights are archived in an internal knowledge base and fed back into early development plans.

4. ***The Access Health Check***

A biannual diagnostic of post-approval performance covering:

- Evidence relevance to evolving payer expectations.
- Consistency of messaging across countries.

- Inclusivity metrics (geographic reach, population diversity).
- Readiness for re-appraisal.

If any indicator trends negatively, a joint remediation plan is triggered.

Strategic and Organisational Lessons

From Events to Systems

Most organisations still treat launch as a celebration, not a system. Mature access cultures understand that launch is a transition point in a continuous process.

From Data to Insight

Collecting real-world data is only the first step. Turning it into actionable insight requires integrated analytics, standard definitions, and a shared narrative across functions.

From National to Global Learning

A payer decision in one country contains lessons for many others. Companies that capture and analyse these decisions build predictive capability. Shared intelligence shortens preparation for future submissions and strengthens negotiation confidence.

From Transactional to Relational Access

Access maintenance is not a series of transactions. It is a relationship built on transparency and shared evidence. Regular dialogue with payers and regulators reduces confrontation and increases flexibility when uncertainty arises.

The Role of Digital Infrastructure

The new frontier of post-approval strategy lies in digital integration.

Companies are building *Access Intelligence Centres* that connect HEOR models, registry feeds, and commercial data. These centres run near real-time dashboards that highlight gaps between expected and observed outcomes.

AI systems can now predict the likelihood of payer renewal based on past submissions, utilisation rates, and real-world adherence. Used responsibly, such tools allow proactive engagement before a problem becomes a rejection.

Technology, however, is only as effective as governance. Data quality, transparency, and interoperability remain the hardest challenges. The goal is not more data, but better use of it.

Ethical and Societal Implications

Post-approval performance is where the ethical dimension of access becomes visible. Approval gives a company permission to sell. Sustained access earns permission to matter.

When companies neglect the post-approval phase, the result is silent exclusion. A therapy may exist, but patients cannot reach it.

Ethical post-approval management demands openness. When outcomes differ from predictions, organisations must share findings promptly, even if unfavourable. Honesty builds legitimacy; defensiveness erodes it.

As one payer commented, "We can handle risk. We cannot handle secrecy."

Transparency transforms suspicion into partnership.

Try This:

At your next governance review, replace the usual "launch metrics" with one question: *"How many patients have started treatment?"* Track that number weekly. It will refocus your team faster than any dashboard.

Reflection

Post-approval is where theory meets the human condition. It is where models are tested not by peer reviewers but by people waiting for care.

The organisations that thrive here are those that view every approval not as an end but as a promise. They stay curious, humble, and responsive.

When a therapy succeeds post-approval, it rarely happens because the molecule changed. It happens because the organisation did.

The science of access is no longer about data alone. It is about continuity, empathy, and adaptation.

A senior market access leader once said, "We used to chase approvals. Now we chase understanding." That captures the evolution perfectly.

Even the strongest access strategy can fail inside an organisation that cannot learn or collaborate. Success depends not just on frameworks, but on how people and systems work together across boundaries. The next chapter explores what it takes to lead beyond silos and build organisations that think and act access-first from the inside out.

PART IV

LEADERSHIP AND SYSTEM CHANGE

CHAPTER 10

LEADING BEYOND SILOS: BUILDING ACCESS-FIRST ORGANISATIONS

"Access improves when leadership rewards shared outcomes instead of defended territory."
– Egbert Floppercough

Sustained access cannot be delivered by any single function. This chapter examines the leadership behaviours required when responsibility is distributed across teams. It shows why access succeeds or fails based on how leaders coordinate decisions under pressure.

The Meeting of Perfectly Misaligned Excellence

The conference table was long, the agenda longer.
The R&D lead began with confidence. "Our Phase III data are outstanding — 90 per cent response rate in the target population."

Next came Market Access. "Excellent, but the comparator arm isn't what payers expect. We'll need a new cost-effectiveness model."

Medical Affairs added, "We're building an evidence dissemination plan, but there's no patient-reported outcomes data yet."

Regulatory said, "We can file on current endpoints, but let's not delay submission."

Silence followed. The project manager finally asked, "So, are we aligned?"

Everyone nodded cautiously. No one actually was.

That meeting captured the core paradox of modern pharma: each function can perform brilliantly on its own, yet the organisation still fails collectively. The data can be strong, the team competent, and the market strategy impressive — but if each function optimises its own goal, patients still wait.

Access failure often begins not with science, but with structure.

Context and Core Challenge: The Silo Trap

Pharmaceutical companies are among the most technically sophisticated organisations in the world. Yet they often struggle to act as one.

The industry's success depends on coordination across science, regulation, economics, and policy. Each function brings expertise essential to patient access. But when incentives and reporting lines separate them, information becomes currency rather than collaboration.

A 2023 survey by the Pharmaceutical Executive Network found that 68 per cent of global executives cited "cross-functional misalignment" as the main reason for access delays. Most of these issues were not scientific. They were structural: late communication between clinical development and market access, fragmented data systems, and differing definitions of success.

The traditional model rewards functional excellence including great trials, great dossiers, great negotiations, but rarely systemic performance.

As one European market access head said: "We celebrate milestones, not connections."

To move beyond this, leadership must rethink the organisation itself. Access cannot depend on goodwill alone. It must be designed into the operating model.

Framework: The Access Alignment Model

The **Access Alignment Model** describes how to turn siloed expertise into shared purpose. It rests on three levels of organisational integration:

1. **Strategic Alignment** – A shared definition of value and success.
2. **Operational Alignment** – Cross-functional processes and data systems.
3. **Cultural Alignment** – Leadership behaviour and incentives that reward collaboration.

Each level reinforces the next. When one fails, silos return.

1. ***Strategic Alignment – One Definition of Value***

Most organisations still define success differently by function. Clinical teams chase endpoints, market access teams chase cost-effectiveness, commercial teams chase uptake.

Strategic alignment starts with a single question: *What does access-first success look like for this product?*

The answer should combine three perspectives — clinical, economic, and societal. This is the **New Value Triangle** introduced earlier in the book, but applied to organisational design.

Every major development decision should map against it. If a trial endpoint has no economic relevance, redesign it. If a pricing strategy damages trust, revise it. If a policy engagement plan excludes patients, rebuild it.

Leaders must anchor all planning in this unified definition of value. Only then can execution align.

2. ***Operational Alignment – Shared Systems and Seamless Processes***

Even the best strategies collapse under weak systems.

Operational alignment means connecting information and decision pathways across functions. It includes:

- Shared dashboards where data flow automatically from trials to access planning.
- Cross-functional evidence reviews that include HEOR and payer insights before protocol lock.
- Integrated launch readiness teams where each function reviews dependencies in real time.

A global company introduced a single "Access Readiness Platform" combining trial milestones, pricing models, and payer intelligence. Each function could see dependencies in one view.

Within a year, average launch readiness gaps fell by 35 per cent.

Operational alignment turns transparency into efficiency.

3. ***Cultural Alignment – Leadership and Incentives***

Culture decides whether alignment lasts.

If each leader's promotion depends solely on functional metrics, collaboration will always be secondary.

Access-first organisations redesign incentives. They include shared KPIs for cross-functional outcomes — for example, "time from approval to reimbursement" or "percentage of payers engaged pre-submission."

Cultural alignment also means humility. Scientists must understand policy. Policy experts must respect science. Leadership must model curiosity and collaboration.

As one CEO put it: "Our silos didn't disappear when we drew new org charts. They disappeared when we changed who got thanked."

Case Studies: Breaking the Silo Habit

Case 1: The Cardiovascular Collaboration

A global cardiovascular company created an *Integrated Evidence Council* that met monthly from Phase II onwards. It included clinical, HEOR, regulatory, and payer experts.

The council reviewed data gaps and adjusted trial endpoints to ensure relevance for both approval and reimbursement. When the product launched, every dossier already included health-economic evidence and patient outcomes.

Time to reimbursement was six months faster than the company average.

Lesson: The best access planning begins before the first patient is enrolled.

Case 2: The "No Surprises" Governance Model

A biotech introduced a rule: no function could present new data to payers or regulators without first discussing it in a cross-functional forum.

This eliminated conflicting narratives that had previously delayed reviews. It also built mutual respect across departments.

Lesson: Predictability builds trust, both internally and externally.

Case 3: The Access Accelerator Hub

A major oncology company created a central *Access Accelerator Hub* — a multidisciplinary team reporting directly to the executive committee. The hub coordinated clinical strategy, pricing, and evidence generation across all new assets.

It acted as an internal consultancy, diagnosing barriers before launch and deploying joint taskforces to resolve them.

The result was measurable: two consecutive launches achieved reimbursement within nine months, compared to a historical average of eighteen.

Lesson: Structural empowerment matters as much as cultural aspiration.

Case 4: The Digital Dialogue Project

A European rare disease consortium established a digital workspace linking company teams with regulators and HTA bodies during early development. Secure data exchange and scenario modelling replaced static meetings.

Transparency reduced duplication and improved predictability for all sides.

Lesson: Communication speed is a strategic asset.

Case 5: The One-Voice Initiative

A company struggling with inconsistent payer messages launched the *One-Voice Initiative.* All external communications were reviewed by a cross-functional committee including Medical Affairs and Policy.

The tone shifted from advocacy to partnership, improving the company's reputation among health ministries.

Lesson: Alignment is as much about language as it is about process.

Practical Tools for Access-First Leadership

1. ***The Collaboration Compass***

A diagnostic tool mapping how well teams collaborate across four dimensions: Purpose, Process, People, and Performance.

Dimension	Key Question	Example Indicators
Purpose	Do all teams share a definition of access success?	Alignment of KPIs and project goals

Dimension	Key Question	Example Indicators
Process	Are decisions made jointly or sequentially?	Number of cross-functional checkpoints
People	Are teams co-located or virtually integrated?	Joint training sessions completed
Performance	Are outcomes measured collectively?	Shared access metrics and incentives

Table 10.1 The Collaboration Compass

Scores below 70 per cent indicate structural misalignment.

2. ***The Organisational Access Heatmap***

A visual audit that identifies where access readiness breaks down across functions.

For each stage of the development-to-launch continuum, teams rate performance on evidence, communication, and collaboration.

Heat zones reveal systemic bottlenecks — often invisible until displayed visually.

This simple exercise frequently sparks uncomfortable but productive conversations.

3. ***The Decision Clarity Framework***

Defines decision ownership, timing, and escalation for every major access-related choice. It prevents ambiguity and ensures that cross-functional decisions do not drift.

The framework has three rules:

1. Every decision must have a named owner and a visible timestamp.
2. No decision can proceed without documented input from all affected functions.
3. Disagreements are escalated to an Access Governance Board within one week.

The aim is not bureaucracy but clarity.

4. ***The Access-First Operating Rhythm***

A schedule of recurring cross-functional events — evidence reviews, payer scenario simulations, and stakeholder feedback sessions — aligned to development milestones.

This rhythm keeps dialogue constant. Teams no longer "loop in" others; they move together.

Organisational Learning: From Functions to Systems

Access-first organisations behave more like ecosystems than hierarchies. They adapt through feedback, share knowledge across boundaries, and learn collectively from success and failure.

1. ***Feedback Loops***

   Every major launch should trigger a structured debrief involving all functions. Lessons feed into an institutional learning database.

2. ***Knowledge Portability***

   Insights from one therapy inform the next. Access-first cultures avoid "project amnesia." They document, codify, and reuse learning through living playbooks.

3. ***Data Ecosystems***

   Organisational learning depends on shared data visibility. A single evidence platform accessible to all functions replaces fragmented spreadsheets. When everyone works from the same truth, collaboration accelerates naturally.

4. ***Leadership Modelling***

   Leaders who share credit across functions set the tone for systemic performance. When executives celebrate collaboration rather than control, culture follows.

Mini-Case 1: The Scandinavian Alignment Pilot

A Scandinavian affiliate introduced a joint planning process linking clinical and market access teams from Phase II. Each decision included a short "Access Impact Note" summarising downstream implications.

The pilot reduced late-stage protocol changes by 40 per cent and improved payer dialogue. It was later adopted globally.

Lesson: Small habits of transparency scale into culture.

Mini-Case 2: The Leadership Shadow Programme

A large multinational launched a "Leadership Shadow" scheme. Senior executives were paired with leaders from different functions for two months, attending each other's meetings to observe priorities and pressures.

The programme revealed how often decisions were made in isolation. Within a year, joint goal-setting sessions became standard practice.

Lesson: Understanding precedes integration.

Ethical and Strategic Implications

Cross-functional alignment is not just operational — it is ethical. Every delay caused by internal miscommunication translates into delayed patient benefit.

Access-first organisations view collaboration as an ethical obligation, not a management trend. They measure success by collective impact, not departmental achievement.

Strategically, alignment reduces waste, speeds launches, and strengthens payer credibility. Health systems increasingly expect companies to demonstrate internal coordination as a proxy for reliability.

As one regulator noted, "When your internal story is consistent, our confidence grows."

Cultural Levers of Change

1. ***Language***

   Words shape identity. Replace "handover" with "collaboration," "sign-off" with "alignment," and "my project" with "our programme."

2. ***Incentives***

   Reward teams for cross-functional results such as patient reach, reimbursement speed, or joint publications.

3. ***Visibility***

   Make success stories of collaboration visible — feature them in town halls, newsletters, and performance reviews.

4. ***Time***

   Build time for collaboration. Alignment cannot occur in diaries already full of functional meetings.

Try This:

List three critical decisions in your organisation that require input from at least two functions. For each, identify whether those functions collaborate proactively or reactively. True integration starts when those decisions are made together, not passed along.

Reflection

The opposite of a silo is not a department merger. It is a mindset of shared responsibility.

When a therapy succeeds, no single function owns the victory. Science provided the possibility. Policy made it affordable. Communication made it trusted.

Leadership beyond silos means designing organisations that think and act as one. It is not about removing expertise, but connecting it — through clarity, curiosity, and purpose.

A senior leader once said, "We used to ask who's accountable. Now we ask who's involved." That is the sound of culture evolving.

Access-first organisations are not born; they are built, one conversation at a time.

Once organisations learn to align internally, the next challenge is to harness technology intelligently. Data, biomarkers, and AI now shape decisions as profoundly as clinical trials once did. The following chapter looks ahead to this new era, where precision in science must be matched by precision in policy.

CHAPTER 11

THE FUTURE: AI, BIOMARKERS, AND PRECISION POLICY

"New technologies accelerate old problems when governance stays exactly the same."
– Egbert Floppercough

New technologies promise better decisions, but they also magnify existing structures. This chapter explores how tools such as AI and biomarkers interact with governance, incentives, and judgement. It explains why technology alone cannot fix access problems and may reinforce them if poorly governed.

The Algorithm That Waited for Approval

The meeting took place in a glass-walled room at a European regulatory agency. On the agenda was an unusual file: a new oncology companion algorithm designed to predict patient response in real time. The company's presentation opened with promise. The AI model could analyse genomic data, imaging scans, and patient history within seconds to recommend the most effective treatment plan.

The regulators were intrigued. The clinicians were impressed. The payers were cautious.

A health technology assessor asked quietly, "Who's accountable if the algorithm is wrong?"

The company's AI lead hesitated. "Technically, it's not a product. It's a process."

The payer replied, "And yet it drives clinical decisions. Our policies weren't built for this."

By the end of the meeting, everyone agreed the technology was extraordinary — and no one knew how to pay for it. The file was left "under review," caught between the rules of the past and the realities of the future.

That exchange captures the challenge at the heart of modern access: science is moving faster than policy. Artificial intelligence, digital biomarkers, and precision medicine are reshaping how we discover, test, and deliver therapies. Yet the systems that govern approval and reimbursement still operate on linear models designed for a simpler world.

Innovation no longer stops at the molecule. It now extends into algorithms, data, and decisions — and access must evolve with it.

Context and Core Challenge: When Precision Outpaces Policy

For decades, medicine has been designed around populations. Trials measured averages, payers priced for groups, and approvals applied to all. Precision medicine reverses that logic. It targets subgroups defined by molecular markers, genetic signatures, or algorithmic predictions.

This shift changes everything — trial design, evidence requirements, manufacturing, pricing, and equity. It also introduces new questions. How should value be measured when effectiveness differs by genotype? How can AI tools be validated when they learn continuously? How do payers budget for treatments that may apply to only a few hundred people but deliver life-changing benefit?

The challenge is not scientific potential but systemic readiness. Health systems were built for static evidence, predictable pricing, and centralised expertise. Precision medicine depends on dynamic evidence, distributed data, and cross-sector collaboration.

A 2024 OECD review of personalised medicine policies found that while 80 per cent of member countries had launched national genomics initiatives, fewer than 25 per cent had aligned reimbursement frameworks. The result is uneven access, delayed adoption, and growing frustration among innovators and patients alike.

We are entering an era where policy precision will matter as much as scientific precision.

Framework: The Precision Access Model

The **Precision Access Model** links three evolving domains that must now work in concert:

1. **Predictive Science** – The tools that identify who benefits (AI, biomarkers, digital diagnostics).
2. **Adaptive Policy** – The frameworks that evaluate and pay for those benefits.
3. **Equitable Implementation** – The systems that ensure those benefits reach all populations.

These three pillars form a triangle of dependency. Each strengthens or weakens the others. Precision without adaptive policy creates stagnation. Policy without infrastructure creates inequity. Equity without evidence creates inefficiency.

1. ***Predictive Science: The Rise of Intelligent Evidence***

AI and biomarkers are redefining what counts as evidence. Instead of relying solely on trial averages, they generate probabilistic insights about individual patients.

Machine learning models can now identify treatment responders in oncology or predict adverse reactions in metabolic disorders. Digital biomarkers — physiological data captured via sensors or wearables — offer continuous, real-world measurement.

These tools expand the data universe beyond the clinic. But they also create challenges of validation, bias, and accountability. If an algorithm predicts risk using incomplete or biased data, inequity becomes encoded in code.

Predictive science must therefore be governed as carefully as it is developed.

2. ***Adaptive Policy: From Assessment to Co-Evolution***

Traditional HTA models assume static evidence. AI and biomarker-driven therapies evolve through use. Policies must therefore shift from assessment to co-evolution — a living partnership between innovators, regulators, and payers.

Several regulators are already experimenting. The UK's *Innovative Licensing and Access Pathway* (ILAP) and the EMA's *Adaptive Pathways* allow rolling evidence submissions. In the United States, the FDA's *Real-Time Oncology Review* evaluates data as they emerge.

These approaches reduce lag between discovery and decision, but they also require new governance. Evidence can no longer be frozen in a dossier; it must be continuously curated and shared.

Adaptive policy turns payers and regulators into learning partners rather than final judges.

3. ***Equitable Implementation: The Infrastructure Test***

Precision therapies demand precision systems. Genetic testing, data analytics, and patient navigation must all work together. Yet many health systems still lack the diagnostic infrastructure or workforce to deliver these innovations fairly.

In Europe, access to genomic sequencing varies more than tenfold between countries. In low- and middle-income regions, the gap is far wider. Even within high-income nations, patients in rural areas are less likely to receive biomarker tests than those near academic centres.

Precision without equity risks creating a two-speed health system — one for those who can access diagnostics, another for those who cannot.

Real-world access therefore depends as much on logistics and literacy as on science.

Case Studies: The Future in Practice

Case 1: AI in Oncology – The Diagnostic Shortcut

Challenge:

An AI tool designed to detect lung cancer from CT scans promised earlier diagnosis and better outcomes.

Action:

The company partnered with a public health authority to validate the model across multiple hospitals using retrospective data. Payers were included from the start to define what "improved outcomes" meant economically.

Outcome:

When launched, the AI system reduced diagnostic time by 30 per cent and improved stage-at-diagnosis distribution. Payers approved reimbursement under a performance-linked agreement based on continued accuracy monitoring.

Lesson:

AI adoption accelerates when validation, evidence, and value are co-designed.

Case 2: Biomarker-Based Reimbursement – Paying for Proof

Challenge:

A targeted oncology therapy was approved for a genetic subset representing only 5 per cent of patients. The high unit cost triggered payer resistance.

Action:

The company proposed a tiered pricing model. Full price applied to confirmed biomarker-positive cases, while a discounted price applied during screening programmes. Data from each treatment cycle fed into an outcomes registry.

Outcome:

The hybrid model improved affordability and enabled real-time learning about biomarker prevalence and response.

Lesson:

Precision pricing creates economic precision.

Case 3: National Genomics Infrastructure – The French Model

Challenge:

France sought to integrate genomics into routine care through its *France Médecine Génomique 2025* initiative. The vision required both sequencing capacity and equitable access.

Action:

The programme established regional sequencing hubs, a national data platform, and reimbursement codes for genomic testing. It also created a transparent governance system involving patients and policymakers.

Outcome:

By 2026, more than 300,000 patients had been sequenced, with turnaround times dropping to under ten days. Integration of genomic data into reimbursement decisions improved both efficiency and fairness.

Lesson:

National precision requires national planning — data, policy, and access must evolve together.

Case 4: The Ethics of AI in Rare Disease Prediction

Challenge:

An AI-driven platform claimed to predict undiagnosed rare diseases by analysing electronic health records. Early tests showed promise but also raised privacy and bias concerns.

Action:

Regulators and patient groups co-developed ethical guidelines requiring transparency of algorithms, explainability of predictions, and patient opt-in.

Outcome:

The model gained regulatory acceptance and payer confidence once accountability was clear.

Lesson:

Trust is the currency of precision. Transparency is its exchange rate.

Practical Tools and Applications

1. ***The AI-to-Access Map***

A practical roadmap linking data maturity to policy readiness.

Stage	Data Characteristics	Policy Needs	Recommended Action
Prototype	Limited, high bias risk	Regulatory sandbox	Early dialogue with agencies
Validated Model	Multisite data	Evidence framework	Joint payer-regulator evaluation
Operational Model	Integrated in care	Pricing and accountability model	Define outcome metrics
Adaptive Model	Learning algorithm	Continuous oversight	Real-time performance audit

Table 11.1 The AI To Access Map

This map helps organisations gauge when their innovation is scientifically ready and when it is policy-ready.

2. ***The Biomarker Value Ladder***

A structured approach for linking biomarker discovery to payer evidence.

Level	Biomarker Type	Evidence Requirement	Value Proof
1	Exploratory	Analytical validity	Hypothesis only
2	Validated	Clinical association	Risk stratification
3	Companion	Predictive response	Treatment selection
4	Surrogate	Outcome substitution	Pricing linkage

Table 11.2 The Bio Marker Value Ladder

Climbing the ladder requires increasing evidence strength and policy alignment. It ensures that reimbursement follows validation, not speculation.

3. ***The Precision Policy Radar***

Tracks how regulators and payers adapt globally.

Key observation points:

- **Regulatory innovation:** adaptive approvals, algorithm oversight.
- **HTA reform:** flexible cost-effectiveness thresholds for rare subgroups.
- **Payment innovation:** outcome-based contracts tied to biomarker validation.
- **Equity safeguards:** mandates for diagnostic availability.

Companies use the radar to anticipate policy shifts and prepare submissions accordingly.

Organisational Strategy: Building Precision Readiness

Adopting AI and biomarker-driven approaches requires organisational learning, cross-functional governance, and investment in data infrastructure.

1. ***Governance***

   Create multidisciplinary *Precision Access Councils* linking R&D, Data Science, Regulatory, and Access teams. Their role is to synchronise scientific, ethical, and economic perspectives from early development.

2. ***Data Strategy***

   Move from isolated studies to federated data ecosystems. These systems allow secure collaboration across hospitals, geographies, and regulators without moving raw data.

3. ***Capability Building***

   Train access leaders to speak both algorithm and economics. New roles such as *AI Policy Liaison* or *Digital Health Economist* are emerging.

4. ***Ethical Culture***

   Transparency about data sources, algorithmic logic, and potential bias must become standard. An honest conversation about limitations is more valuable than an ambitious claim that cannot be explained.

The Strategic and Ethical Horizon

1. ***Algorithmic Equity***

   AI can widen or narrow disparities. Algorithms trained on Western populations risk misclassifying patients from under-represented groups. Ensuring data diversity and fairness testing becomes a moral as well as technical obligation.

2. ***Data Ownership and Consent***

   Patients increasingly expect control over their data. Future policies will likely require dynamic consent — allowing patients to decide, in real time, how their data can be used.

3. ***Policy Convergence***

   International harmonisation will become crucial. Divergent AI and biomarker regulations increase costs and delay global access. Joint frameworks like ICMRA's *AI in Medicines Initiative* are early signs of convergence.

4. ***The Future of Evidence***

   Evidence itself is evolving from static to streaming. Real-world data, digital twins, and predictive analytics will supplement or even replace traditional trial designs. This will demand new forms of peer review, validation, and payer dialogue.

If You Remember One Thing

1. Precision medicine and AI are rewriting the rules of access.
2. Success depends on three aligned forces — predictive science, adaptive policy, and equitable implementation.
3. AI and biomarkers expand the evidence base but challenge validation and governance.
4. Adaptive policy models must evolve toward continuous learning and shared accountability.
5. Infrastructure determines equity. Precision without capacity creates inequality.
6. Trust, transparency, and fairness will define the next generation of leadership in access.

Try This:

Identify one process in your organisation that could be improved through data automation or predictive modelling. Then, before investing, define the access question it must answer. Technology that doesn't advance access is just noise.

Reflection

Every revolution begins with confusion. AI and precision medicine promise a world where treatment is tailored, waste reduced, and outcomes improved. But the transition will test our discipline, humility, and ethics.

The future of access will not be determined by who builds the smartest algorithm, but by who builds the fairest system.

As one regulator said at a recent roundtable, "Innovation without inclusion is just another form of inefficiency."

Access-first innovation in the era of AI and biomarkers means designing technology not just for speed, but for solidarity, making precision equitable and intelligence accountable.

CHAPTER 12
THE ACCESS-FIRST MANIFESTO

"What an organisation declares matters less than what it repeatedly chooses to tolerate."
– Egbert Floppercough

After exploring design, evidence, leadership, and tools, this chapter consolidates the core principles of access-first thinking. It sets out a coherent operating philosophy to guide decisions when data are incomplete and trade-offs unavoidable. This manifesto provides a shared language for consistent practice.

The Room Where the Question Finally Landed

The quarterly launch review was nearly over. The graphs looked good, the KPIs glowed green, and the global access map was impressively shaded in company blue. Then the CEO, who had been silent through most of the meeting, leaned forward and asked quietly, "How many patients have we actually reached?"

The slide deck froze. Someone began to speak, stopped, and glanced at the others. A market access lead offered an estimate. The regulatory director added that national approvals were on track. The commercial lead pointed to "potential reach" in the next quarter.

The CEO asked again. "No. How many people are actually on treatment right now?"

The silence that followed lasted longer than anyone expected. It was not a silence of failure, but of realisation.

For years, the company had celebrated approvals, launches, and label extensions as milestones of success. Yet the only number that mattered — lives improved — was absent. That moment changed the conversation. It was the day the leadership team decided that innovation alone was not enough.

That question — *How many patients have we actually reached?* — became the first line of their new access strategy.

It is also the first line of this manifesto.

Context: Why a Manifesto Is Needed

The pharmaceutical industry stands at a paradox. It has never been more inventive, more data-driven, or more globally connected. Yet access gaps are widening. Therapies win approvals faster than ever, but adoption stalls. Science advances at speed, while systems crawl under the weight of complexity, cost, and fragmentation.

Over decades, companies have mastered the art of discovery and regulatory navigation. What they have not mastered — at least not fully — is the art of delivery. The structures, incentives, and metrics that once rewarded speed to approval now hinder speed to access.

A generation of professionals has been trained to celebrate the wrong finish line. The culture of the industry often prizes precision in data over empathy in design, and compliance in process over coherence in purpose.

The result is a widening innovation–access gap. It is not a moral failing so much as an organisational design flaw. Processes that once worked in the blockbuster era now fail in the age of precision, affordability, and accountability.

This manifesto is not a slogan. It is a framework for rethinking how organisations, systems, and leaders define success. It calls for an alignment of science, value, and humanity — a system where access is not an afterthought but an organising principle.

The Core Argument: What Access-First Innovation Really Means

Access-first innovation means designing every part of the system — from molecule to market — around the question: *Can patients actually use this?*

It is not about lowering standards or ignoring commercial realities. It is about building evidence, pricing, and delivery structures that make innovation sustainable and inclusive.

It rests on four truths that have echoed through every chapter of this book.

1. *Innovation is only real when used.*

   A therapy that exists only on paper, in warehouses, or in a select few hospitals is not a success. It is a missed opportunity disguised as progress.

2. *Access is not charity; it is design.*

   Equity cannot be retrofitted after launch. It must be engineered into the development plan — through endpoints, pricing models, and distribution strategies.

3. *Equity is not a side project; it is strategy.*

   Sustainable access is not an ESG initiative. It is the core of long-term market viability and public trust.

4. *Collaboration is not a value; it is a system.*

   True innovation happens when regulators, payers, policymakers, and patients share accountability for outcomes.

Access-first innovation replaces the old linear pipeline with a living network of continuous feedback — where data, dialogue, and decisions flow in both directions. It demands humility from companies, flexibility from regulators, and openness from payers. Above all, it demands leadership that measures impact not by approval letters, but by lives reached.

The Access-First Leadership Code

The manifesto rests on ten guiding principles — the Access-First Leadership Code. They are written not as aspirations but as operating rules for organisations that wish to lead the next era of healthcare.

1. ***Start with the Patient, Not the Product***

   Design development, evidence, and pricing from the lived experience outward. Every dataset represents someone's story, and every delay represents someone's wait.

   Action: Include patient journeys in early development reviews, not only in launch communications.

2. ***Align Science with System Reality***

   Innovation that ignores the delivery environment will fail in translation. Design trials, endpoints, and logistics that reflect real-world capacity, not theoretical perfection.

   Action: Use system-readiness audits before Phase III.

3. ***Make Access Measurable***

   If you can't measure access, you can't manage it. Develop KPIs that track reach, equity, and speed to treatment alongside revenue and share of voice.

   Action: Create an Access Dashboard reviewed at every executive meeting.

4. ***Integrate Evidence and Economics***

   Evidence without cost insight creates argument; cost without evidence creates rejection. Build the two together.

   Action: Require HEOR input at every major scientific milestone.

5. ***Price for Partnership, Not Confrontation***

   Payers are not obstacles; they are co-investors in outcomes. Price based on proof, not aspiration.

   Action: Conduct value rehearsals with payers before launch.

6. ***Treat Infrastructure as Strategy***

   A therapy cannot succeed where systems cannot deliver it. Supporting diagnostics, cold-chain, and workforce capacity is not philanthropy — it is risk mitigation.

   Action: Include delivery infrastructure in business cases for every major launch.

7. ***Build Organisations That Learn, Not Just Report***

   Continuous evidence generation should inform continuous improvement. Use data not only to justify but to adapt.

   Action: Create real-world evidence loops between market access, medical, and development functions.

8. ***Lead with Transparency***

   Trust grows in sunlight. Share assumptions, evidence limitations, and rationales openly. Silence and secrecy cost more than disclosure.

   Action: Publish value frameworks and rationale summaries for major pricing decisions.

9. ***Redefine Success as Shared Impact***

   A therapy's true performance is measured not by units sold but by outcomes achieved collectively — by industry, system, and society.

   Action: Establish shared metrics with payer and policy partners.

10. ***Close the Loop with Humanity***

    Every chart, model, and policy ends with a human consequence. The work is not about perfect systems but fairer outcomes.

Action: Begin every leadership offsite with a patient story, not a forecast.

These principles are not abstract ideals. They are the architecture of future leadership — a structure where science, ethics, and economics reinforce rather than contradict one another.

Organisational Manifesto: From Function to Purpose

Access-first thinking requires cultural redesign. It turns each function from a specialist unit into a contributor to a shared purpose.

R&D must shift from proving efficacy to designing relevance. Trials should measure endpoints that resonate with payers and patients.

Regulatory Affairs must evolve from gatekeeping to guidance — anticipating policy shifts and co-creating pathways with agencies.

HEOR and Market Access must stop being late-stage translators and become early-stage architects. They hold the language that connects innovation to affordability.

Medical Affairs must bridge science and society, ensuring that information is truthful, contextual, and usable.

Commercial Teams must replace volume-based targets with value-based engagement, focusing on sustainability and trust.

Leadership must model humility — recognising that power in this ecosystem comes not from control, but from coordination.

In an access-first organisation, meetings sound different. People talk less about share of market and more about share of impact. The scoreboard expands from revenue and reach to include fairness, inclusion, and time to patient benefit.

The best companies will no longer ask, "How do we win?" but "How do we work better with others to make the system win?"

Systems Manifesto: Beyond the Company

Access-first innovation extends beyond corporate walls. It depends on alignment between industry, regulators, payers, and policymakers. The manifesto therefore also speaks to the system itself.

Regulators must adapt from certainty-seekers to uncertainty managers. Adaptive approvals, real-world evidence pilots, and algorithmic validation must become mainstream tools.

Payers must evolve from cost controllers to outcome partners. Contracts should reward sustained value, not short-term price cuts.

Policymakers must view access as investment, not expenditure. Funding infrastructure, data platforms, and workforce capacity multiplies the value of every new therapy.

Academia and Patients must be recognised as equal contributors to evidence generation and decision-making. Their insights complete the data picture that models alone cannot see.

Global Agencies must harmonise definitions of value, affordability, and evidence. Fragmented standards waste time, money, and lives.

A functioning access ecosystem requires mutual accountability. Each player must commit to transparency, proportionality, and shared learning.

An aligned system doesn't mean uniformity; it means direction. Everyone rowing toward the same outcome — more patients treated, sooner, and fairly.

Case Vignettes: The Manifesto in Action

Case 1: The Company That Made Access a KPI

A global biopharma company redefined its success dashboard. Alongside sales, it added "patients reached within 90 days of approval." The number was publicly reported. Within two years, process redesigns shortened internal timelines by 40 per cent.

Lesson: What gets measured moves.

Case 2: The Joint Evidence Platform

Three competing firms in rare diseases pooled anonymised registry data under independent governance. Payers gained confidence in real-world performance, enabling outcome-based contracts across all participants.

Lesson: Collaboration can be competitive advantage.

Case 3: The Regulator Who Invited the Payers In

An early scientific advice session in the EU brought regulators, payers, and patient advocates into the same room. Disagreement was fierce, but the result was a single aligned evidence plan.

Lesson: Friction early prevents paralysis later.

Case 4: The Country That Funded Delivery First

A middle-income nation tied approval of a gene therapy to parallel investment in cold-chain and workforce capacity. Within a year, treatment uptake matched that of high-income peers.

Lesson: Access follows infrastructure.

Case 5: The Patient Boardroom Seat

A major company created a "Patient Impact Chair" at its executive committee, giving direct input on launch priorities and equity measures. The chair's questions became cultural checkpoints.

Lesson: Representation is not symbolism; it is governance.

Try This:

Write your own team's Access Manifesto. In five sentences, describe what access-first means for your function. Post it where decisions happen. Shared principles turn slogans into culture.

The Human Closing: The Real Finish Line

A few months after the CEO's fateful question, the same company held another review meeting. This time, the first slide looked different. It showed no bar charts, no market forecasts, no brand colours. It showed photographs — patients from different countries holding handwritten cards with one word each: "Here."

The global access lead explained quietly, "These are the first 10,000 patients who have started treatment." The room fell silent again, but it was a different silence — not one of uncertainty, but of pride.

That is what access-first innovation looks like when it becomes real. It is not a new department or an initiative. It is a way of thinking that reconnects the science of healing with the purpose of serving.

Approvals will still matter. KPIs will still matter. But they will now be steps on the path, not the destination.

As one nurse once said during a patient roundtable, "We don't need more miracles. We just need the ones we already have to reach us."

The future of pharma belongs to those who understand that sentence.

The next section turns reflection into practice. It provides real-world scenarios, exercises, and team discussion prompts to test and apply the principles of this manifesto. Because access-first thinking only matters when it changes how people work — not just what they believe.

PART V

THE PRACTITIONER'S TOOLKIT

CHAPTER 13

SCENARIO-BASED LEARNING WORKBOOK

"Access thinking becomes real when a scenario makes hesitation visible."
– Egbert Floppercough

Principles only change behaviour when they are tested under realistic conditions. This chapter introduces scenario-based learning as a way to rehearse judgement, surface assumptions, and build access capability. It shifts the focus from knowing what to do to practising how decisions are made.

Introduction – Turning Principles into Practice

Ideas change nothing until they change behaviour. That is why this chapter exists. The previous chapters have laid out the logic and the frameworks of Access-First Innovation. This one takes them into the room where decisions happen: the portfolio meeting, the cross-functional review, the pricing debate, and the payer negotiation.

These scenarios are not case studies in hindsight. They are designed as live exercises that test judgement, coordination, and courage. Each is drawn from real patterns seen across the industry, reconstructed so that the reader can engage actively rather than observe passively.

The goal is simple. By working through each exercise, you and your team will learn to spot access risks earlier, align faster, and act with clearer intent.

Use this workbook during leadership offsites, functional training, or pipeline planning sessions. Treat it as rehearsal for the conversations that matter most — the ones that determine whether a therapy reaches patients or remains a line on a spreadsheet.

You will not find perfect answers here. Only better questions. Because Access-First leadership begins when people learn to ask the right questions at the right time.

How to Use This Chapter

Each scenario follows the same structure:

1. **Context** – a brief description of the situation.
2. **The Dilemma** – the decision point or conflict.
3. **Discussion Prompts** – questions to stimulate team dialogue.
4. **Analysis** – insights drawn from real-world experience.
5. **Practical Reflection** – what leaders should take away.

You can run each as a 45-minute discussion or expand them into half-day workshops. Keep the tone open and critical. The value lies not in agreement but in debate.

Scenario 1: The Oncology Bottleneck – The Early Payer Engagement Dilemma

Context

A global oncology team is developing a targeted therapy for a common cancer subtype. The Phase II results are promising, and senior management is eager to accelerate regulatory submission. The science team believes early engagement with payers might slow momentum or create misaligned expectations.

The Dilemma

Do you approach payers and HTA agencies before Phase III design is locked, or wait until the data are final and risk potential misalignment later?

Discussion Prompts

1. What are the possible benefits of early engagement with payers?
2. What risks or misconceptions might delay that engagement?
3. How could you balance regulatory speed with evidence alignment?
4. Who inside your organisation should own the first dialogue?

Analysis

Teams often fear that payers will "move the goalposts," but experience shows the opposite. Early dialogue reduces uncertainty, identifies data gaps, and strengthens credibility. In one real example, a company that engaged early avoided a one-year reimbursement delay because its trial already contained endpoints that matched HTA expectations.

The best organisations treat payers not as post-launch gatekeepers but as co-designers of relevance. A simple rule applies: if your Phase III endpoints surprise the payer, you have already lost a year.

Practical Reflection

Access alignment is not a detour from innovation; it is the road that ensures the innovation arrives.

Scenario 2: The Equity Blind Spot – Global Launch Prioritisation

Context

You lead the launch planning team for a rare-disease therapy. Manufacturing capacity limits the first-year supply. Senior management wants to prioritise markets with the highest price potential to recover R&D costs quickly. Regional access teams argue that middle-income countries have the highest unmet need.

The Dilemma

How do you balance commercial imperatives with equity and reputation?

Discussion Prompts

1. What criteria should guide market sequencing?
2. How might different choices affect long-term trust and policy access?
3. What infrastructure or data investments could offset short-term loss?
4. What message will your first-wave launch send to the world?

Analysis

Access leaders increasingly face this tension: optimise revenue first or optimise legitimacy. Companies that select launch countries purely by GDP often encounter reputational backlash that later limits market expansion. A measured approach combines tiered pricing, staggered entry, and shared evidence platforms that allow lower-income markets to participate early without destabilising revenue.

Practical Reflection

The sequence of your launches tells the world who you believe deserves innovation first. Equity strategy is brand strategy.

Scenario 3: The Adaptive Pricing Challenge

Context

Your company has developed a one-time curative gene therapy for a chronic condition. Payers admire the science but cannot afford the upfront cost. Finance insists on maintaining list price to protect global reference pricing.

The Dilemma

Should you offer outcomes-based or amortised payment models that reduce immediate revenue but increase adoption, or protect the headline price and risk limited uptake?

Discussion Prompts

1. What economic models could align payer and company incentives?
2. How might the accounting treatment of revenue influence your decision?
3. What governance and data systems are required to track outcomes reliably?
4. How can you communicate flexibility without undermining value?

Analysis

In practice, flexible models strengthen credibility. Companies that pilot outcomes-based agreements often secure faster coverage and stronger partnerships. The critical enabler is trust in data. Without transparent real-world evidence, even the best contract fails.

Practical Reflection

Pricing innovation is not financial creativity; it is access engineering.

Scenario 4: The Real-World Evidence Dilemma

Context

A therapy has achieved rapid regulatory approval under accelerated pathways, but the post-marketing data infrastructure is weak. Real-world evidence collection is fragmented across regions, and leadership is hesitant to invest in a global registry.

The Dilemma

Should the company invest heavily in a unified evidence platform now or rely on national data partnerships later?

Discussion Prompts

1. What are the risks of fragmented post-launch data collection?
2. How could shared evidence infrastructure serve multiple assets?
3. What governance or privacy safeguards are essential for credibility?
4. How might real-world evidence improve payer confidence over time?

Analysis

Companies that treat post-approval evidence as optional usually face renewal challenges within three years. Investment in a coherent data ecosystem turns compliance into competitive advantage. It reduces uncertainty, accelerates label expansion, and supports adaptive pricing discussions.

Practical Reflection

Evidence is not a report to regulators; it is the language of trust with society.

Scenario 5: The Cross-Functional Gridlock

Context

A late-stage development asset is approaching submission. Market Access requests changes to trial endpoints to meet HTA needs. Regulatory Affairs objects, fearing delays. Medical Affairs sits in the middle, translating but not deciding.

The Dilemma

How can leadership break the gridlock and ensure scientific and access goals align?

Discussion Prompts

1. Where does decision authority truly sit in your organisation?
2. How might shared KPIs prevent silo conflict?
3. What is the cost of internal delay compared with regulatory delay?
4. How could scenario planning help resolve this earlier next time?

Analysis

Most gridlocks result from incentive misalignment. When R&D success is measured by submission speed and Market Access success by payer approval, conflict is inevitable. Companies that establish shared outcome KPIs — such as "time to first reimbursement" — align effort across functions.

Practical Reflection

Leadership alignment is not achieved through structure but through shared consequence.

Scenario 6: The Transparency Test

Context

A Phase III trial shows strong efficacy but a small safety signal that may concern payers and clinicians. Communications teams propose minimising discussion until formal review. Medical Affairs argues for full transparency with stakeholders.

The Dilemma

How open should you be about uncertainty?

Discussion Prompts

1. What are the ethical and strategic costs of selective disclosure?
2. How can transparency strengthen rather than weaken credibility?
3. How might patient advocacy groups respond to different approaches?
4. What long-term effects could short-term silence create?

Analysis

The reflex to control information is understandable but counterproductive. Every data gap will surface eventually, and owning the narrative early builds trust. Companies that proactively discuss uncertainty often find payers more willing to negotiate adaptive reimbursement or conditional approvals.

Practical Reflection

Transparency is not risk exposure; it is risk insurance.

Scenario 7: The Infrastructure Investment Debate

Context

A new biologic therapy requires cold-chain logistics that smaller hospitals cannot maintain. Operations teams propose funding refrigeration units, but Finance questions the return on investment.

The Dilemma

Should you fund delivery infrastructure that lies outside your legal responsibility but inside your moral one?

Discussion Prompts

1. How can infrastructure investment influence long-term access and brand trust?
2. What partnerships could share the cost?
3. How might delayed adoption offset any short-term savings?
4. When does "not our problem" become everyone's problem?

Analysis

Companies that invest in infrastructure rarely regret it. Beyond immediate access benefits, they build goodwill that accelerates subsequent launches. Infrastructure is the silent multiplier of access success.

Practical Reflection

System capacity is part of product design.

Scenario 8: The Cultural Reset

Context

A cross-functional survey reveals that most employees equate success with regulatory approval, not with patient reach. Leadership wants to shift culture toward access metrics but worries about morale and measurement complexity.

The Dilemma

How can an organisation re-anchor its sense of achievement without eroding motivation?

Discussion Prompts

1. What stories does your organisation celebrate publicly?
2. How could you visualise access impact internally?
3. Which incentive structures reinforce the wrong behaviour?
4. How can you make patient reach emotionally visible?

Analysis

Culture changes through symbols and repetition, not slogans. When teams see their work translated into lives improved, purpose strengthens. Some companies now publish internal "Patients Reached Today" dashboards. Others invite patients to speak at milestone celebrations.

Practical Reflection

Access culture grows when success feels human again.

Scenario 9: The Policy Partnering Challenge

Context

A government health ministry wants to pilot a shared-risk fund for high-cost therapies but demands joint governance over data and outcome measurement. Legal and compliance teams hesitate, fearing loss of control.

The Dilemma

Should you accept shared governance or insist on company-owned metrics?

Discussion Prompts

1. What are the benefits of genuine partnership versus transactional contracts?
2. How can you ensure data integrity while sharing oversight?
3. What governance models have succeeded in similar settings?
4. How might joint ownership reshape public perception?

Analysis

The most durable agreements are built on co-ownership of outcomes. Transparency transforms suspicion into collaboration. Accepting joint governance signals maturity and earns policy credibility that no marketing campaign can match.

Practical Reflection

Partnership begins where control ends.

Scenario 10: The Launch That Learns

Context

A therapy has been launched in ten markets. Uptake is uneven. Instead of waiting for year-end analysis, you propose a rolling "Access Learning Review" to capture and act on real-time feedback.

The Dilemma

Can large organisations adapt fast enough to learn while launching?

Discussion Prompts

1. What systems could support continuous learning across regions?
2. How might local insights feed global strategy without chaos?
3. What incentives encourage teams to share early failures?
4. How can leadership model curiosity rather than defensiveness?

Analysis

Learning organisations treat every launch as an experiment, not an event. They capture weekly access metrics, share insights openly, and iterate quickly. Over time, this discipline compounds into structural agility.

Practical Reflection

The opposite of failure is not success; it is learning.

Facilitator's Guide – Running the Scenarios

To turn these scenarios into practice:

1. **Form mixed groups** – include Clinical, HEOR, Medical, Regulatory, and Commercial participants.
2. **Assign roles** – one acts as payer, one as regulator, one as company lead.
3. **Debrief** – focus on reasoning, not on who "won."
4. **Capture lessons** – identify systemic barriers and convert them into organisational actions.

Encourage challenge. The objective is to surface blind spots and rehearse cross-functional decision-making under pressure.

Leadership Application – Embedding Scenario Thinking

Scenario-based learning only works when it shapes real processes. To embed it:

- Integrate one scenario exercise into every major governance meeting each quarter.
- Link insights to actual KPI revisions or SOP updates.
- Capture scenarios in digital playbooks accessible company-wide.
- Encourage country affiliates to submit new scenarios for global sharing.

Over time, this builds an organisational habit of reflection and anticipation. Teams stop asking "what went wrong?" and start asking "what could go wrong next?"

Try This:

After each scenario, run a short team debrief: What assumption was exposed? What cross-functional dependency was missed? Capture the lesson in one sentence. Over time, those sentences form your organisation's learning manual.

Closing Reflection – The Real Test of Learning

Access leadership is not measured by the number of workshops held but by the quality of decisions made when no one is watching.

If this workbook achieves anything, let it be this: that the next time a team faces an ambiguous decision — when evidence is incomplete, time is short, and the patient is waiting — someone in the room pauses and says, "Let's run the scenario."

Because that single moment of reflection is how systems evolve.

Access is not delivered by frameworks alone. It is delivered by people who think ahead, act together, and learn continuously.

The next chapter looks forward. It examines how technology — from artificial intelligence to predictive biomarkers — is reshaping evidence, pricing, and policy alignment. Where this chapter trained leaders to think adaptively, the next explores how new tools can make adaptive systems real.

CHAPTER 14

PATIENT-CENTRICITY AND EQUITY IN ACCESS DESIGN

"Patient-centricity only becomes real when it changes who gets treated, not just how decisions are described."
– Egbert Floppercough

Scenarios reveal that patient-centricity is rarely straightforward. This chapter examines how access decisions balance equity, efficiency, and feasibility in practice. It reframes patient focus as a decision lens rather than a slogan and makes trade-offs explicit.

The Meeting That Forgot the Patient

It was a late afternoon in a glass-walled conference room at headquarters. The topic was an upcoming launch for a rare neuromuscular therapy. The agenda listed forty-three slides. None of them mentioned a patient.

The team discussed reimbursement hurdles, stakeholder mapping, and risk mitigation. They debated whether to include new biomarkers in the follow-up study. The patient advocacy lead, seated near the back, finally raised her hand.

"Can I ask," she said quietly, "how many of these plans involve speaking directly to the people who will actually live with this treatment?"

The room paused. The project manager looked uncomfortable. The medical lead offered a polite assurance that patient interviews had been conducted two years ago during Phase II. The meeting moved on.

Three months later, when the therapy was launched, uptake lagged. Patients were hesitant, clinicians uncertain, and reimbursement decisions slow. Feedback showed that the treatment regimen was too burdensome. The dosing schedule required travel to distant centres, and few patients could manage it. The team had built a plan for efficiency, not empathy.

That moment, unremarkable at the time, became a lesson that echoed across the organisation. The science had been flawless. The patient experience had been invisible.

The Core Challenge – When Patients Become Data Points

For decades, the pharmaceutical industry has spoken about being "patient-centric." The phrase appears in mission statements, corporate reports, and conference slogans. Yet too often, it stops there.

True patient-centred design goes far beyond listening sessions or advisory boards. It means structuring development, evidence, and access strategies around the lived realities of patients — how they navigate diagnosis, treatment, cost, and care systems.

The problem is not intent; it is translation. Organisations still interpret patient-centricity through the lens of compliance or marketing. The result is empathy expressed in PowerPoint form, not in process.

In practice, most patients encounter the industry only after everything is decided — after the trials are designed, the price set, and the submission filed. By that point, their role is symbolic.

This chapter argues for a different model: patient-centricity as an organising principle for access. When patients are part of evidence design, reimbursement planning, and delivery logistics, the entire system performs better.

Patient insight is not soft data. It is operational intelligence.

Why Patient-Centricity Matters for Access

Patient-centred access design is not an act of kindness; it is a strategic advantage. There are three reasons why.

1. **It strengthens evidence relevance**

   Patients identify endpoints that matter in daily life, not just in clinical charts. When those outcomes are measured, payers see real-world benefit, and regulators gain confidence in external validity.

2. **It accelerates adoption**

   Therapies designed with patient convenience and comprehension in mind are used more quickly and consistently. Adherence improves, reducing downstream cost.

3. **It builds legitimacy**

   Public trust in the industry remains fragile. When patients see themselves reflected in decision-making, confidence grows. That legitimacy converts into political and payer goodwill.

A senior policymaker once put it succinctly: "If patients are not at the table, payers will assume you are hiding something."

In short, patient inclusion is not a reputational gesture. It is a precondition for sustainable access.

Framework – The Patient Access Integration Model

To operationalise patient-centric access, organisations can use a five-layer framework called the **Patient Access Integration Model**. It connects insight, design, and measurement into one coherent process.

Layer	Key Question	Primary Responsibility	Example in Practice
1. Discovery and Insight	What do patients experience before diagnosis and treatment?	Medical Affairs and Patient Engagement Teams	Mapping diagnostic delay, emotional burden, and treatment fatigue.
2. Development and Design	How can trial design reflect real-world use?	Clinical Development	Flexible scheduling, decentralised sites, home dosing feasibility.
3. Evidence and Evaluation	Which outcomes matter to patients and payers alike?	HEOR and Clinical Teams	Combining survival data with patient-reported outcomes and quality-of-life indices.
4. Access and Affordability	What are the hidden costs beyond drug price?	Market Access and Policy	Analysing travel, time off work, and caregiver support.
5. Adoption and Experience	How can real-world delivery maintain dignity and equity?	Commercial, Operations, and Medical Affairs	Patient support programmes, digital education, community outreach.

Table 14.1 The Patient Access Integration Model Framework

This model aligns scientific, economic, and ethical value. It transforms patient feedback from anecdote into evidence.

One access director described it as "the difference between designing for patients and designing with them."

Case Studies – Lessons from Practice

Case 1: The Rare Disease That Redefined Evidence

Context

A biotech developing a therapy for a paediatric rare disease discovered that conventional endpoints — enzyme levels and MRI changes — did not reflect what families cared about most: mobility, speech, and independence.

Action

The team partnered with patient groups to co-design a new composite outcome that combined functional metrics with caregiver-reported data. They secured regulatory agreement to include it as a key secondary endpoint.

Outcome

When the therapy reached HTA review, payers commended the dataset for capturing "meaningful benefit." The result was faster reimbursement and a more compelling value story.

Lesson

Relevance is the new currency of evidence.

Case 2: The Clinical Trial That Went Home

Context

A global oncology company noticed high dropout rates in its Phase II trial due to travel burden. Many patients lived far from treatment centres.

Action

They piloted a decentralised trial design. Home-based blood draws and remote consultations replaced some clinic visits. Patient adherence increased dramatically.

Outcome

Completion rates rose from 68 to 92 percent. Data quality improved because patients were less fatigued. Regulators later cited the design as a model for future studies.

Lesson

Convenience is not a luxury; it is data integrity.

Case 3: Affordability Beyond the Price Tag

Context

A chronic therapy in Southeast Asia had full reimbursement yet low uptake. Investigations revealed that patients could not afford transport to clinics or the cost of missing work.

Action

The company collaborated with local NGOs to fund travel vouchers and flexible appointment schedules.

Outcome

Adherence increased by 30 percent, and discontinuation rates halved. The therapy's reputation with local payers improved, leading to inclusion in national programmes.

Lesson

Access is shaped as much by time and geography as by money.

Case 4: Listening Early, Saving Late

Context

A European cardiovascular trial faced delays after an ethics committee questioned its patient burden. The original design required weekly site visits.

Action

The company convened a patient advisory board before restarting recruitment. Patients proposed remote monitoring options and simplified consent forms.

Outcome

The redesigned trial cut visit frequency by half and regained momentum. Regulators approved the modifications quickly.

Lesson

Patient feedback is a free form of risk mitigation.

Case 5: The Digital Divide in Real Time

Context

A multinational launched an app-based adherence programme for diabetes management. Uptake in urban areas was strong; in rural regions, negligible.

Action

Local affiliates introduced a call-centre alternative and distributed low-cost phones through clinics.

Outcome

Engagement equalised across demographics. The hybrid model became a template for other markets.

Lesson

Digital innovation must include analogue empathy.

Practical Tools for Patient-Centred Access

Tool 1: The Patient-Informed Value Framework

To link clinical benefit to perceived value, map every outcome through three lenses:

1. **Clinical relevance** – measurable improvement in health status.
2. **Practical relevance** – effect on daily life and self-management.
3. **Emotional relevance** – meaning, motivation, and dignity.

When all three align, you have a defensible and human value story.

Tool 2: The Equity Impact Assessment

Before launch, run an internal audit of equity implications.

Ask:

- Who cannot access this therapy under current logistics?
- Which groups might be disadvantaged by eligibility criteria or technology requirements?
- How can support programmes close those gaps?

Score each factor by likelihood and severity. This simple exercise often reveals the most overlooked barriers.

Tool 3: Patient Partnership Charter

Formalise the role of patients in evidence design through a clear charter:

- Involve at least two patient representatives in protocol review.
- Share summary results in plain language.
- Provide feedback on how input shaped decisions.

Charters turn promises into accountability.

Tool 4: Patient Journey Mapping

Visualise the steps from symptom onset to sustained treatment. Identify friction points — diagnosis delay, referral loops, affordability, side effects, follow-up gaps.

Use this map to plan support interventions that make each step navigable.

Tool 5: Real-World Experience Dashboards

Beyond safety and efficacy, track qualitative indicators such as travel time, satisfaction, and adherence patterns. Feed these into monthly access performance reviews.

Data without empathy is incomplete; empathy without data is unconvincing.

Strategic and Ethical Implications

Patient-centred access design reshapes both responsibility and reward. It requires leaders to think differently about where value originates.

1. **From Products to Experiences**

   Pharma once sold molecules. Now it delivers experiences. That includes diagnosis, delivery, adherence, and long-term follow-up. Each is a determinant of access success.

2. **From Compliance to Collaboration**

   Traditional patient involvement was framed as regulatory expectation. True collaboration begins when patients help define success metrics.

3. **From Equity as Ideal to Equity as Design**

   Equity cannot remain a policy aspiration. It must be measurable. Companies that embed equity metrics into performance indicators demonstrate both ethical integrity and operational maturity.

   A regulator once remarked, "Show me your metrics, and I will tell you your values."

4. **From Transactional Trust to Shared Purpose**

   Trust is built not through messaging but through reciprocity. When patients see transparency in data, affordability, and delivery, trust grows organically.

5. **From Marketing to Meaning**

   The most credible brand story is not told in adverts but in access reports that show who was reached and who was not — and what the company is doing about it.

Embedding Patient Voice in Organisational DNA

Building a patient-centred organisation takes more than a department. It requires structural commitment.

Leadership Signals

Executives should speak about patients not as "stakeholders" but as partners. Small linguistic shifts influence culture.

Governance

Include patient engagement metrics in board reporting. Require annual reviews of patient involvement across trials and access programmes.

Training

Equip staff to translate medical complexity into human language. Emotional literacy is as important as data literacy.

Feedback Loops

Create continuous dialogue with patient groups through digital forums or advisory panels. Close the loop by showing how feedback changes policy or design.

Celebration of Impact

Highlight stories of real patients whose access improved through company initiatives. Visibility reinforces purpose.

Case Reflection – The Oncology Summit

At a European oncology summit, several companies presented innovations. Amid the technical discussions, a patient advocate stepped to the microphone.

She said, "I have read all your posters and listened to your presentations. You talk about hazard ratios, progression-free survival, and incremental cost-effectiveness. But in my world, the question is simple: can I get to the hospital on Tuesday, and will the nurse have the time to talk to me?"

The room fell silent. Later, several executives said it was the most valuable session of the conference. Not because it offered data, but because it restored perspective.

That is what patient-centric access really means — restoring perspective to complexity.

The Business Case for Patient-Centric Access

Executives sometimes ask, "How do we justify patient engagement to shareholders?" The answer is evidence.

Studies have shown that therapies co-developed with patients achieve faster uptake, lower discontinuation rates, and longer market longevity. Access delays decrease because value stories resonate with payers.

In financial terms, investment in patient engagement pays back through efficiency, reputation, and risk reduction. In human terms, it pays back in lives reached.

A global health economist described it simply: "Patient-centricity is not about being nice. It is about being effective."

Future Directions – Digital Empowerment and Data Ethics

As health systems digitise, patient voice will increasingly manifest through data. Wearables, home diagnostics, and mobile health apps generate unprecedented insight into real-world experience.

However, the power of data brings ethical responsibility. Consent must be informed, privacy protected, and algorithms transparent. Otherwise, patient-centricity becomes surveillance.

The future lies in partnership models where patients own and share their data for mutual benefit. Blockchain-enabled consent, open-source registries, and federated data networks can make this possible.

The principle remains the same: the patient is not the subject of data; the patient is the source of knowledge.

Try This:

Invite a patient advocate to review your trial materials or value messages. Ask them to explain, in their own words, what they think the therapy does. Their response will tell you more about clarity and trust than any internal review ever will.

Reflective Closing – The Human Constant

Science evolves. Technology accelerates. But one constant remains: the person waiting at the centre of the system.

Every form, every policy, every data field ultimately traces back to someone sitting in a clinic chair, hoping that the medicine arrives, that the side effects are manageable, that the process respects their time and dignity.

Patient-centred access design is the bridge between innovation and that moment of care. It is the discipline of seeing the human first and the data second.

As one clinician told a room full of executives, “When we remember who we are doing this for, everything else makes sense.”

That sentence is the quiet truth of Access-First Innovation.

The next chapter explores the moral dimension that underpins access-first thinking. It looks at how ethics and transparency shape credibility, sustainability, and trust — the foundations on which all access strategies ultimately rest.

CHAPTER 15
ETHICS AND TRANSPARENCY IN INNOVATION ACCESS

"Ethics rarely fail at the level of principle.
They fail at the point where a difficult trade-off is quietly avoided."
– Egbert Floppercough

When trade-offs are unavoidable, legitimacy depends on how they are justified. This chapter explores ethics and transparency as practical disciplines rather than abstract ideals. It explains why making reasoning visible strengthens trust even when decisions remain contested.

The Email That Changed the Meeting

The meeting was supposed to be routine: a cross-functional review before a major market access submission. The slides were ready, the talking points rehearsed, the regulatory timeline mapped to the hour.

Ten minutes before the call began, an email arrived. It was from a medical liaison in one of the company's Eastern European affiliates. The message was short.

"Local clinicians are reporting patient dropouts due to travel distance and affordability. If this goes unaddressed, the therapy will be reimbursed but unused. I think this needs to be raised."

The regional lead hesitated. Including the note might derail the discussion. The agenda was already tight, and senior executives were focused on approval deadlines. The message was quietly filed away under "to review later."

A month after launch, the same problem surfaced in national media: "Life-changing therapy available but out of reach." The company's stock dipped, and the CEO demanded an investigation.

In the follow-up meeting, someone finally said what everyone was thinking: "We didn't lack data. We lacked honesty."

That moment encapsulated the heart of this chapter — the recognition that access without ethics is a hollow victory.

Why Ethics Matters in Access

Pharmaceutical innovation exists in a permanent tension between two imperatives: profit and purpose. Without the first, the system collapses. Without the second, it loses legitimacy. Ethics is the bridge that keeps those imperatives aligned.

In theory, everyone agrees on this. In practice, ethical compromise often begins quietly. It might be a decision to delay disclosure of side-effect data until "the full picture is clear," or to withhold pricing details to preserve negotiation leverage, or to approve promotional material that implies broader benefit than evidence supports. Each act feels small. Cumulatively, they erode the trust on which access depends.

Ethics in access is not about personal virtue; it is about institutional discipline. It asks three questions that every company must answer:

1. **Who benefits first?**
2. **Who bears the risk?**
3. **Who decides what is fair?**

When those questions are left unanswered, policies fill the void. Regulation tightens, reputations fade, and collaboration with payers turns defensive rather than productive.

Ethical clarity, by contrast, creates freedom. When an organisation acts transparently, payers and regulators engage as partners, not adversaries.

The Moral Contract of Innovation

Every medicine carries an unspoken social contract: society funds research through taxes, universities, or public infrastructure; in return, companies deliver treatments that improve lives within fair economic boundaries.

When that contract breaks, backlash follows — not because people dislike profit, but because they perceive imbalance.

Consider the public reaction to high-priced curative therapies. Few object to rewarding innovation. What triggers outrage is opacity. When companies fail to explain cost structures or value rationale, public debate fills the gap with suspicion.

Transparency, then, is not an act of generosity. It is a defence against misunderstanding.

An experienced payer once remarked, "We don't expect cheap drugs. We expect clear logic."

That is the moral baseline of modern market access.

Framework – The Ethical Access Model

To operationalise ethics, organisations can apply a structured approach known as the Ethical Access Model. It translates principles into actions across four dimensions.

Dimension	Core Question	Examples of Good Practice	Indicators of Integrity
1. Transparency	What information are we willing to share, and when?	Publish clinical protocols, pricing rationale, and real-world outcomes.	Public trust, policy stability, reduced conflict.

Dimension	Core Question	Examples of Good Practice	Indicators of Integrity
2. Fairness	Are benefits and burdens distributed equitably?	Use tiered pricing, equitable trial recruitment, and affordability measures.	Balanced access across income and geography.
3. Accountability	Who owns the consequences of delay or inequity?	Define responsibility for post-approval follow-up and access monitoring.	Clear governance and public reporting.
4. Respect	Are patients and partners treated as equals, not subjects?	Co-create evidence, acknowledge feedback, and protect data privacy.	Sustained engagement and advocacy support.

Table 15.1 The Ethical Access Model Framework

Ethics cannot be outsourced to compliance. It must live in strategy, operations, and communication alike.

Transparency in Evidence

1. *Trial Design and Disclosure*

   Ethical evidence generation begins before the first patient enrols. Protocols should be registered publicly, and outcome measures defined transparently. Selective publication remains one of the industry's most persistent credibility gaps.

   Companies that disclose both positive and negative results earn long-term trust with regulators and payers. The short-term discomfort of openness is outweighed by reputational resilience.

2. *Real-World Evidence and Data Sharing*

   Post-launch, transparency extends to real-world data. When outcome registries are proprietary, scepticism grows. Shared registries and independent data audits increase credibility.

An oncology company once invited national HTA agencies to co-govern its real-world evidence platform. The decision slowed initial setup but accelerated subsequent approvals because payers trusted the data source.

Transparency, in this context, is not public relations. It is verification.

Transparency in Pricing

The most contentious form of transparency concerns price. Few topics generate more heat or less light.

Pharmaceutical pricing is complex by design: multiple intermediaries, confidential discounts, managed entry schemes, and international reference systems. The opacity may protect negotiation flexibility, but it also fuels suspicion.

Principles for Transparent Pricing

- **Explain value clearly.** Break down cost components — R&D, manufacturing, distribution, and reinvestment — in simple terms.
- **Align pricing with outcome risk.** If uncertainty is high, link payment to performance.
- **Disclose rationale, not just numbers.** Payers respect clarity even when they disagree on price.

A rare-disease company once published a public "value letter" outlining how its price was derived. Critics remained, but the tone of debate shifted from accusation to discussion.

Transparency turns confrontation into collaboration.

Fairness and Global Equity

Ethical access cannot be confined to high-income markets. Global equity remains one of the defining moral tests of the industry.

When breakthrough therapies launch exclusively in wealthy countries, innovation reinforces inequality. The argument that "affordability varies" is factually true but ethically incomplete.

Fairness demands proportionality — adjusting expectations, prices, and support according to need. Tiered pricing, local manufacturing partnerships, and voluntary licensing can reconcile profit and purpose.

The success of global HIV programmes demonstrated this decades ago: open licensing, generic competition, and international funding turned scarcity into scale. The same logic now applies to oncology, rare diseases, and gene therapy.

An African regulator once said, "We don't need donations. We need inclusion."

Ethical access delivers inclusion as strategy, not charity.

Accountability – The Courage to Own Consequences

Accountability in access means recognising that delay is not a neutral event. Every month lost between approval and delivery represents patients untreated and lives constrained.

Too often, accountability dissolves in complexity. Teams blame regulators for slow review, regulators blame companies for incomplete dossiers, and patients fall through the gap.

To counter this, leading organisations establish **Access Accountability Boards** — cross-functional groups that monitor time-to-reimbursement, regional disparities, and patient reach. Their mandate is not punitive but corrective.

A company in Scandinavia created such a board after repeated reimbursement delays. Within two years, average time to access dropped by 40 percent. The difference was not new policy but shared responsibility.

Ethics begins when someone says, "This is our delay, and we will fix it."

Respect – The Everyday Expression of Ethics

Respect is the most visible form of ethics and the easiest to neglect. It manifests in how companies communicate, engage, and respond.

Respect means answering questions without jargon. It means acknowledging uncertainty instead of concealing it. It means treating every partner — regulator, payer, clinician, or patient — as capable of reasoning.

A patient group once described its most valued corporate partner as "the one that tells us the bad news early." That is respect in action.

Internally, respect also shapes culture. When teams feel safe raising ethical concerns, they do so. When fear dominates, silence follows. Psychological safety is therefore an access enabler.

Case Studies – Ethics in Action

Case 1: The Pricing Disclosure Debate

A European company debated whether to disclose its net prices during a government investigation into drug affordability. Legal advisers warned against it. The CEO decided otherwise, publishing the figures along with an explanation of rebate structures and reinvestment plans.

The result surprised many. Public opinion softened, and policymakers praised the transparency. Although margins narrowed slightly, the company gained reputational strength and faster policy dialogue.

Lesson: Courageous openness often yields pragmatic benefit.

Case 2: The Trial Diversity Commitment

An oncology trial in North America initially enrolled patients almost exclusively from urban centres. Advocacy groups criticised the lack of diversity. The company paused recruitment, added rural sites, and partnered with community clinics.

The decision cost six months of delay but produced richer data and improved regulatory confidence.

Lesson: Fair evidence is better than fast evidence.

Case 3: Post-Launch Silence

A metabolic therapy showed excellent early results but later generated reports of side effects. Corporate communications delayed acknowledgement pending internal review. By the time a statement was issued, trust was gone.

A competitor that had faced similar issues earlier but communicated openly retained support.

Lesson: Delay in transparency costs more than disclosure ever will.

Case 4: Shared Governance in Data

A global vaccine manufacturer invited the World Health Organization and national health ministries to co-own post-market surveillance data. The shared oversight prevented allegations of bias and enabled faster response to safety signals.

Lesson: Shared data ownership converts suspicion into partnership.

Case 5: The Honest Apology

After a supply chain failure caused regional shortages, a company issued an immediate apology, explained the cause, and outlined corrective measures. Instead of regulatory sanctions, it received public commendation for responsibility.

Lesson: Accountability is the shortest route to forgiveness.

Tools for Ethical Access Leadership

1. *The Transparency Ladder*
   A diagnostic tool that rates organisational openness across five levels:

- Minimal disclosure (reactive)
- Compliance disclosure (required only)

- Strategic transparency (selected insights shared)
- Collaborative transparency (shared governance)
- Radical transparency (open data and rationale)

Teams should aim for level 4 wherever confidentiality allows.

2. *The Ethical Decision Checklist*
Before major access decisions, ask:

- Who benefits and who might be excluded?
- What would happen if this decision were public tomorrow?
- Have we tested our assumptions with external stakeholders?
- Are we proud of the reasoning, not just the result?

If any answer feels defensive, the decision is not ready.

3. *The Integrity Dashboard*
Integrate ethical indicators into performance reviews:

- Percentage of disclosed trials.
- Time between safety signal and public notification.
- Proportion of equitable access initiatives funded.
- Independent stakeholder trust scores.

What gets measured gets maintained.

The Role of Leadership

Ethical cultures start with visible leadership. Senior executives must model openness even when inconvenient. When a CEO publicly acknowledges uncertainty or complexity, it signals permission for the rest of the organisation to do the same.

One multinational began every quarterly town hall with a section titled "What we got wrong." It quickly became the most popular part of the meeting. Staff reported greater confidence in raising concerns, and external partners noticed the change.

Ethical leadership is not about perfection; it is about credibility under pressure.

Cultural Challenges

Many ethical lapses stem from good intentions constrained by bad systems. Targets, incentives, and hierarchies can unintentionally reward opacity.

To counter this, companies can:

- Align bonuses with long-term access outcomes, not quarterly revenue.
- Train managers to recognise ethical stress and provide support.
- Establish safe channels for reporting and discussing dilemmas.

Ethical maturity is achieved when transparency feels natural, not risky.

Policy and Industry Trends

Regulators and payers are formalising transparency expectations.

- The European Medicines Agency now mandates public lay summaries for clinical results.
- HTA agencies increasingly request access impact assessments.
- Public procurement frameworks reward data openness.

These shifts mean that ethical leadership is no longer voluntary; it is a market requirement.

Companies that act early shape the rules instead of reacting to them.

The Economics of Ethics

Ethical behaviour is often portrayed as costly. In reality, it reduces systemic friction. Transparency shortens negotiations, prevents litigation, and builds goodwill.

A review of European reimbursement timelines showed that companies rated "high trust" by payers achieved access an average of nine months faster. The correlation was not coincidental. Ethics pays dividends in efficiency.

The cost of opacity, by contrast, is delay, scrutiny, and regulatory constraint — a slow tax on secrecy.

Ethics in the Age of AI and Data

Artificial intelligence introduces new moral questions: algorithmic bias, consent, and explainability. When predictive models determine eligibility or pricing, transparency must extend to code and logic.

Ethical AI requires three commitments:

1. **Traceability** – every decision must be explainable.
2. **Equity** – algorithms must be tested for demographic bias.
3. **Consent** – patients must understand and control data use.

Technology amplifies values; it does not replace them. A transparent system with flawed ethics will fail faster.

Reflections from the Field

During a workshop on access ethics, a regulator asked participants to define transparency in one sentence. A market access director replied, "It's when I tell you everything you'll find out eventually, just earlier."

Everyone laughed, but the truth landed. Transparency is not revelation; it is timing. Ethical companies choose to be early.

Another participant, a patient advocate, added, "Transparency without humility feels like advertising." The comment reminded everyone that tone matters as much as data.

Reflective Closing – The Mirror Test

Ethics and transparency are not academic ideals; they are daily habits. They appear in how teams respond to pressure, how leaders handle bad news, and how organisations tell their stories.

Every company faces moments when the easy path and the right path diverge. The mirror test is simple: if you had to explain your decision to a patient tomorrow, would you feel proud?

If the answer is no, the decision is not ethical enough for access.

Transparency is the mirror that keeps the system honest.

As one veteran policymaker concluded at the end of a long roundtable: "In the end, trust is cheaper than secrecy, and faster too."

The next chapter turns ethics into measurement. It explores how to design dashboards that capture not only commercial and clinical metrics but also equity, transparency, and trust. Because what leaders choose to measure is what their organisations learn to value.

CHAPTER 16

METRICS AND DATA VISUALISATION TECHNIQUES FOR ACCESS LEADERSHIP DASHBOARDS

"What gets measured does not merely report behaviour.
It teaches people what the organisation truly values."
– Egbert Floppercough

Ethical intentions and good judgement fade without feedback. This chapter examines how metrics and dashboards shape behaviour over time. It reframes measurement as an active influence on future access options rather than a retrospective reporting exercise.

The Dashboard That Missed the Point

The executive meeting began with confidence. A massive dashboard filled the wall screen, glowing with colours and charts. Green indicators everywhere: market share up, time-to-approval on track, budget within tolerance.

The Market Access head watched silently as the performance summary rolled by. Then she asked one question that froze the room.

"How many patients have actually started treatment?"

Silence. The dashboard could not answer.

After a pause, a junior analyst said, "We can estimate, but the data are fragmented."

The CEO leaned forward. "So, we know how fast we're working, but not who we're reaching."

That single question turned the meeting into a reckoning. The company had built a reporting system that measured activity, not impact. It tracked progress against internal milestones, not patient outcomes or equity.

By the end of the quarter, a new instruction was issued: build a dashboard that measures what matters, not what flatters.

This chapter explains how.

Why Access Metrics Matter

Metrics define reality. What organisations choose to measure becomes what people strive to achieve.

If a company measures submission timelines, teams will optimise for speed. If it measures approval numbers, teams will focus on regulatory success. If it measures patient reach and time-to-treatment, teams will prioritise access and equity.

The difference lies in intent. Access-first metrics reorient an organisation from outputs to outcomes. They make invisible gaps visible.

Traditional performance systems were designed for commercial success. Access-first systems must be designed for societal success. They do not replace financial metrics; they complete them.

As one payer observed, "We judge companies by what they measure. It tells us whether they care about patients or only about profit."

The Evolution of Access Measurement

Historically, pharmaceutical metrics have fallen into three categories:

1. **Scientific Metrics** – trial timelines, regulatory submissions, publications.
2. **Commercial Metrics** – market share, price, revenue growth.
3. **Operational Metrics** – manufacturing efficiency, cost control, logistics.

These remain essential but insufficient. They describe motion, not meaning.

Access-first organisations add a fourth dimension: **Impact Metrics** — indicators that measure reach, equity, trust, and sustainability.

The shift mirrors what happened in other sectors when environmental and social governance emerged. Just as ESG made sustainability measurable, access metrics make fairness measurable.

The challenge is not data scarcity but data selection. Every organisation already collects more numbers than it can use. The question is which ones tell the real story.

Framework – The Access Metrics Compass

The **Access Metrics Compass** provides a structured way to balance four key dimensions of performance: Reach, Readiness, Equity, and Trust.

Dimension	Guiding Question	Example Metrics	Leadership Use
Reach	Are eligible patients actually receiving treatment?	Number of patients treated per month; time from approval to first patient; treatment initiation rate.	Measures real impact and speed of access.

Dimension	Guiding Question	Example Metrics	Leadership Use
Readiness	Are systems prepared to deliver at scale?	Diagnostic capacity, site readiness, supply chain uptime, clinician training completion.	Identifies bottlenecks and infrastructure needs.
Equity	Are all populations benefiting equally?	Geographic variation, gender and ethnicity representation, affordability metrics.	Reveals disparities and guides resource allocation.
Trust	Do stakeholders believe in the company's integrity and transparency?	Payer satisfaction index, patient group trust score, publication timeliness.	Tracks legitimacy and ethical credibility.

Table 16.1 The Access Metrics Compass Framework

The compass ensures balance. A company with strong reach but low equity still fails in purpose. A company trusted but slow to deliver lacks impact.

Access performance is therefore multidimensional by design.

Designing an Access Dashboard

An effective Access Leadership Dashboard is not an IT project; it is an alignment tool. Its purpose is to make access visible, actionable, and shared.

Principles for Design

1. **Start from purpose, not data availability.**

   Decide what impact you want to demonstrate — then find or build the data to prove it.

2. **Keep it human.**

   Each metric should correspond to a real-world experience: a patient reached, a system strengthened, a barrier removed.

3. **Prioritise clarity over complexity.**

   Executives have minutes, not hours. The most powerful dashboards answer one question clearly: Are we delivering access fairly and fast enough?

4. **Integrate, don't duplicate.**

   Align access metrics with existing systems like commercial reporting and regulatory timelines. Integration prevents isolation.

5. **Visualise stories, not spreadsheets.**

   Charts should invite insight. Use heatmaps, timelines, and progress arcs to make patterns visible at a glance.

A well-designed dashboard makes leaders ask better questions, not just approve better numbers.

The Access Metrics Pyramid

Data should cascade logically from system-level outcomes to operational inputs. The **Access Metrics Pyramid** defines three layers of measurement.

Level	Focus	Example Metrics	Frequency
Strategic Outcomes	What impact are we having on patients and systems?	Patients reached, equity index, time to reimbursement, payer satisfaction, public trust index.	Quarterly to annual.
Tactical Enablers	How effectively are we preparing systems for access?	Diagnostic readiness, site capacity, affordability programme reach.	Monthly to quarterly.
Operational Drivers	What daily activities support access?	Training sessions completed, data registry entries, partnership agreements signed.	Weekly to monthly.

Table 16.2 The Access Metrics Pyramid

By aligning each level, leaders can trace how operational choices influence real outcomes.

As one country manager remarked, "When my dashboard connects training sessions to patient reach, I finally understand why every action matters."

Examples of Access Metrics in Practice

1. ***Time-to-Access (TTA)***

Measures the number of days between regulatory approval and first patient treated.

- *Why it matters:* Quantifies efficiency of launch readiness and payer engagement.
- *How to use it:* Benchmark across markets to identify process gaps.

2. **Equity Coverage Index (ECI)**

Assesses distribution of therapy across geography, income, and demographic variables.

- *Why it matters:* Reveals hidden inequities before they become scandals.
- *How to use it:* Track percentage of eligible population reached by region.

3. ***Payer Confidence Score (PCS)***

Derived from structured feedback surveys post-reimbursement negotiation.

- *Why it matters:* Correlates with renewal rates and future collaboration.
- *How to use it:* Include qualitative comments for context.

4. ***Diagnostic Readiness Ratio (DRR)***

Percentage of patients who can be accurately identified through existing diagnostic capacity.

- *Why it matters:* Determines potential patient flow and bottlenecks.
- *How to use it:* Pair with investment data on laboratory expansion.

5. ***Patient Experience Index (PEI)***

Aggregates satisfaction, adherence, and burden-of-treatment data.

- *Why it matters:* Links access to sustained usage.
- *How to use it:* Combine PROs, digital feedback, and hotline data.

6. ***Transparency Timeliness Metric (TTM)***

Measures how quickly new data (positive or negative) are disclosed publicly.

- *Why it matters:* Operationalises ethical transparency.
- *How to use it:* Report lag time between internal discovery and disclosure.

7. ***Health System Strengthening Contribution (HSSC)***

Quantifies infrastructure, training, or diagnostic investments supporting access.

- *Why it matters:* Demonstrates partnership and sustainability.
- *How to use it:* Value contributions in both financial and outcome terms.

Together, these metrics create a 360-degree view of access performance.

Visualising Access Data Effectively

Visualisation is not decoration; it is cognition. The way data is presented determines whether leaders see signal or noise.

1. *Heatmaps for Equity*

   Display regional patient reach, colour-coded by access density. Hot zones show saturation; cold zones expose neglect. Simple, immediate, and morally powerful.

2. *Timeline Arcs for Time-to-Access*

   Plot key events from regulatory approval to first treatment. Use vertical markers for policy milestones. The visual narrative shows not just delay but cause.

3. *Layered Dashboards*

   Combine four panels: Reach, Readiness, Equity, Trust. Each panel uses the same traffic-light logic for quick comprehension.

4. *Rolling Trend Lines*

   Show month-to-month improvement or regression. Continuous trends motivate teams more than static snapshots.

5. *Qualitative Insight Cards*

   Next to each chart, include one quote from a patient, payer, or clinician. It reminds users that data represent people, not numbers.

As a medical director said after his first access dashboard review, "Once you see a heatmap of inequality, you can't unsee it."

From Data to Dialogue

A dashboard only becomes valuable when it changes behaviour. That requires conversation, not just presentation.

Monthly Access Reviews

Dedicate part of executive reviews to discuss the dashboard insights. Ask:

- What is working and why?
- Where are we falling behind?
- What can we change immediately?

Country Comparisons

Encourage friendly benchmarking between affiliates. Reward innovation in data use, not just good results.

Public Reporting

Share summarised indicators externally through annual Access Reports. Transparency strengthens legitimacy and invites collaboration.

Learning Loops

Feed new findings back into process design. Metrics are not judgement; they are feedback.

Case Studies – Dashboards in Action

Case 1: The European Access Dashboard

A European biopharma company created a real-time dashboard showing time-to-access across fifteen countries. Initially, the leadership assumed variation was regulatory. The data revealed internal submission delays were the main cause.

They introduced a pre-launch readiness checklist tied to dashboard updates. Within a year, average access time dropped by 30 percent.

Lesson: Measurement turns excuses into evidence.

Case 2: Equity Visualisation in Latin America

A multinational plotted therapy uptake by region and income bracket. The map revealed stark inequities within the same country.

The company launched a targeted support programme for underserved regions, improving national equity index scores by 25 percent.

Lesson: Equity only improves once you can see it.

Case 3: Patient Experience Dashboard

A rare-disease unit created a digital feedback platform where patients rated treatment experience monthly. The aggregated results fed into the executive dashboard.

Negative trends triggered cross-functional task forces to fix root causes. Satisfaction scores improved consistently.

Lesson: Listening can be operationalised.

Case 4: Trust Metrics in Policy Engagement

A global vaccine manufacturer tracked "policy confidence" through sentiment analysis of government communications and media tone. Spikes of negativity often predicted reimbursement challenges.

The dashboard allowed early engagement and corrective transparency.

Lesson: Trust has leading indicators; watch them.

Linking Metrics to Incentives

Metrics shape behaviour only when they influence rewards.

- **Leadership KPIs:** Tie executive bonuses partly to patient reach and equity outcomes.
- **Cross-functional goals:** Share success indicators across R&D, HEOR, Market Access, and Medical Affairs.
- **Country-level scorecards:** Publish comparative metrics internally to promote accountability.

When access becomes part of performance evaluation, it becomes part of culture.

One executive summarised the logic neatly: "People follow the numbers that follow the money."

Ethics and Accuracy in Metrics

Numbers can mislead as easily as they inform. Ethical measurement demands rigour.

Common Pitfalls

- Over-aggregation hides disparities. Always disaggregate by region, gender, or socioeconomic status.

- Selective framing exaggerates success. Display full context.
- Vanity metrics prioritise optics over impact. Drop them.

An access metric that feels uncomfortable is probably the right one.

Transparency extends to measurement itself. Publish methodologies and data sources. Allow external validation. Trust thrives in sunlight.

Technology Enablers

Modern analytics platforms make sophisticated dashboards achievable with modest investment. Key enablers include:

- **Integrated data lakes** combining regulatory, clinical, and market datasets.
- **APIs** connecting field reporting to central dashboards.
- **Natural language processing** for analysing patient feedback at scale.
- **Cloud-based collaboration** allowing affiliates to input data in real time.

However, technology alone does not guarantee insight. Human interpretation remains the decisive factor.

As one data scientist said, "A good dashboard tells you what's happening. A great dashboard tells you what to talk about next."

From Metrics to Mindset

Metrics are mirrors of culture. When an organisation measures access seriously, people start to think access-first.

Visual dashboards become moral instruments — not because they enforce rules, but because they make reality unavoidable.

A head of R&D once commented, "For years, I saw our success in charts of approvals. Now I see it in maps of patients reached. It changed how I lead."

That shift — from metrics as compliance to metrics as conscience — marks the arrival of Access-First maturity.

Reflective Closing – Measuring What Matters

The ultimate purpose of access dashboards is not to impress investors or regulators. It is to ensure that innovation achieves its reason for existing.

Every green light on a dashboard should represent a life improved, a delay shortened, or a barrier removed.

Measurement is not the end of accountability; it is the beginning.

As one policymaker said at a recent summit, "Data will not save patients. But without data, no one will know who was saved."

That sentence captures the paradox of access leadership: metrics are both mirror and compass — reflecting where you are and pointing to where you must go next.

The next chapter examines the regulatory environment that surrounds access. It explores how global agencies are beginning to harmonise evidence standards and accelerate pathways that prioritise patient access without compromising rigour. Metrics measure progress; policy determines pace. The two now move together.

CHAPTER 17

REGULATORY HARMONISATION AND ACCESS: GLOBAL INITIATIVES TRANSFORMING THE PHARMA LANDSCAPE IN 2026

"Harmonisation matters most when it shortens waiting, not when it standardises paperwork."
– Egbert Floppercough

Access outcomes are shaped by how systems interact, not just how organisations perform. This chapter explores regulatory harmonisation as a structural access issue rather than a technical one. It explains why misalignment across jurisdictions perpetuates delay and inequity.

The Joint Advice Session

The virtual room filled with muted anticipation. On one side of the screen sat the company's regulatory and market access teams. On the other side were representatives from the European Medicines Agency, the US Food and Drug Administration, and three national health technology assessment bodies.

This was not a standard scientific advice meeting. It was a pilot joint advice session — part of a new global initiative designed to bring regulators, payers, and companies together long before submission.

The molecule under discussion was a novel gene therapy for a paediatric metabolic disorder. The science was strong, but the evidence plan was ambitious and expensive. In the old world, the company would have sought regulatory advice first, payer feedback later, and then discovered that the two disagreed.

This time, the process was different.

The EMA official spoke first. "We agree with your primary endpoints but recommend broader post-market data collection."

The payer representative nodded. "If you collect that data, it will also satisfy our long-term uncertainty concerns."

The company's access lead typed a quiet message to the team: "We just saved two years of negotiation."

That is the power of regulatory harmonisation — alignment that turns friction into flow.

The Context – A System Built for a Simpler Era

For decades, global pharmaceutical regulation evolved in parallel tracks. The FDA, EMA, and national authorities each built frameworks for safety, efficacy, and quality. HTA agencies, meanwhile, developed methods for cost-effectiveness and real-world relevance.

Both systems worked, but they rarely spoke to each other.

Regulators asked, "Does it work safely?"
Payers asked, "Does it work affordably?"
Patients asked, "Can I actually get it?"

The answers arrived on different timelines, using different data, and filtered through different languages of evidence.

This fragmentation was tolerable when innovation moved slowly. It is untenable now. Gene therapies, cell therapies, and AI-driven diagnostics blur the line between research and care. By the time traditional evaluation concludes, the science has moved on.

The old sequence — trial, approval, reimbursement, access — has become a bottleneck. Each gatekeeper waits for the last one to act. Patients wait longest of all.

Regulatory harmonisation is not about lowering standards; it is about synchronising them. It recognises that value and safety are two sides of the same decision.

Why Harmonisation Matters

There are three reasons why harmonisation defines the future of access.

1. **The Acceleration Imperative**

   Innovation cycles are shortening. Traditional review processes cannot keep pace without cooperation. Harmonisation eliminates duplication and compresses timelines.

2. **The Evidence Integration Challenge**

   Modern therapies generate complex, multidimensional data — clinical, genomic, economic, and real-world. No single agency can interpret it all in isolation. Collaboration ensures coherence.

3. **The Trust Dividend**

   When regulators and payers speak with one voice, public confidence grows. Transparency improves, and industry gains a predictable environment.

As one senior EMA official said at a 2024 summit, "The problem is not a lack of standards. It is too many standards pretending to be different."

Framework – The Global Access Alignment Model

To navigate this evolving landscape, companies can use a structure called the **Global Access Alignment Model (GAAM)**. It maps how scientific, regulatory, and economic evidence align through five stages of coordination.

Stage	**Objective**	**Key Stakeholders**	**Example Outcome**
1. Early Dialogue	Identify shared expectations on endpoints, comparators, and uncertainty.	Regulators, HTA bodies, patient groups.	Joint advice meeting with aligned evidence requirements.
2. Integrated Evidence Plan	Develop a single plan that satisfies both regulatory and payer needs.	Clinical, HEOR, RWE, access teams.	Unified evidence submission.
3. Parallel Review	Enable simultaneous regulatory and HTA assessments.	EMA, FDA, national HTAs.	Reduced time-to-reimbursement.
4. Linked Post-Approval Commitments	Coordinate post-market data collection for both safety and value.	Regulators, payers, companies.	Shared real-world evidence registries.
5. Continuous Dialogue	Maintain ongoing transparency between all parties.	All stakeholders.	Adaptive licensing and managed entry schemes.

Table 17.1 The Global Access Alignment Model Framework

This model converts linear approval into a continuous, collaborative ecosystem.

One executive described it simply: "The goal is not faster approval. It is smarter alignment."

Global Initiatives Reshaping the Landscape

1. ***The EMA–EUnetHTA 21 Collaboration***

   The European Medicines Agency and EUnetHTA have been building a joint framework for early dialogue, now fully operational across EU member states. Companies can submit a single request to receive consolidated feedback from regulators and HTA bodies.

   This means that evidence packages designed for clinical efficacy can also meet payer needs. It reduces the risk of post-approval surprises and redundant studies.

   Results from the first 50 joint consultations show an average six-month reduction in time-to-reimbursement.

   The principle is simple: one conversation, multiple approvals.

2. ***The FDA–EMA Parallel Scientific Advice Programme***

   The FDA and EMA have expanded their long-standing collaboration to include early payer input from US and European stakeholders. This is a quiet revolution. It allows multinational programmes to align endpoints and statistical plans across regions, reducing duplication and increasing credibility.

   A US oncology company participating in the scheme described it as "two continents, one learning curve."

3. ***Project Orbis and the Access Cluster***

   Project Orbis, coordinated by the FDA's Oncology Center of Excellence, brings together multiple regulators — including those in the UK, Canada, Australia, Singapore, and Switzerland — to review oncology submissions concurrently.

   It transforms approval from a serial to a parallel process. In 2024, Project Orbis reduced average oncology approval lag between the US and Europe from 12 months to under 3.

   Building on its success, a new **Access Cluster** initiative has been proposed to integrate HTA perspectives into the same process, turning regulatory synchronisation into true access alignment.

As one Canadian official remarked, "Patients do not care which agency approves first. They care who works together fastest."

4. ***The WHO Collaborative Registration Procedure***

   In low- and middle-income countries, the World Health Organization's Collaborative Registration Procedure (CRP) has become a lifeline for timely access. National regulators can rely on WHO-prequalified assessments to expedite local authorisations.

   Between 2017 and 2024, this procedure shortened average approval timelines by 40 percent across participating countries.

   Its next evolution includes integration with pooled procurement systems to align approval with supply readiness — an access-first model for global equity.

5. ***International Coalition of Medicines Regulatory Authorities (ICMRA)***

   ICMRA functions as the coordination table for the world's leading regulators. Its recent Access and Equity Task Force focuses on harmonising digital evidence standards, AI validation, and data ethics.

   This work underpins the next frontier: real-time regulatory collaboration built on shared analytics platforms rather than documents.

   One task force leader summarised it neatly: "The future of harmonisation is not paper alignment but data alignment."

Case Studies – Harmonisation in Practice

Case 1: The Parallel Pathway in Oncology

A European biotech developing an immunotherapy joined a parallel scientific advice session with EMA and several HTA bodies.

The feedback revealed a misalignment between clinical endpoints (progression-free survival) and payer expectations (overall survival and quality-of-life impact).

The company adjusted its evidence plan to include real-world follow-up and cost-effectiveness modelling.

Result: approval and reimbursement were achieved within four months of each other — a milestone previously unheard of.

Lesson: Harmonisation saves years of delay when pursued early.

Case 2: The Orbis Ripple Effect

A US-based oncology firm submitted its therapy through Project Orbis, receiving near-simultaneous approval in six countries.

When the company later applied for HTA review in Europe, the existing joint regulatory dossier served as a foundation. Data consistency accelerated acceptance.

Lesson: Consistent evidence builds cumulative trust.

Case 3: The African Access Partnership

A consortium of African regulators implemented a regional joint review system supported by the WHO and African Union Development Agency. Companies could file once for multiple markets.

As a result, time-to-market dropped from an average of 24 months to less than 8.

Lesson: Harmonisation is not a privilege of high-income systems; it is a catalyst for global equity.

Barriers to Harmonisation

Despite progress, full harmonisation remains elusive. The main barriers include:

1. *Legal Sovereignty*

   National regulators remain bound by domestic legislation. Aligning methods does not mean surrendering authority.

2. *Data Privacy and Security*

   Cross-border data sharing raises ethical and legal questions. Data localisation laws complicate joint registries.

3. *Resource Disparity*

   Not all agencies have equal capacity. Smaller regulators struggle to participate fully without funding and digital infrastructure.

4. *Cultural and Political Resistance*

   Institutional pride and historical independence can slow cooperation. As one senior regulator quipped, "We all want alignment, as long as it happens our way."

   Overcoming these barriers requires diplomacy as much as data.

Tools for Access Teams – Navigating the Harmonised Environment

1. *The Regulatory Mapping Grid*

   Create a matrix listing each target market, its regulatory authority, HTA body, and current collaboration channels. Update quarterly. This ensures visibility of alignment opportunities.

2. *The Early Advice Tracker*

   Record outcomes of joint advice sessions, noting alignment gaps between regulatory and payer expectations. Use this to refine development plans.

3. *The Evidence Convergence Map*

   Visualise where data requirements overlap. Highlight shared evidence and identify additional needs unique to each agency. This avoids duplication.

4. *The Harmonisation Readiness Checklist*

   Before submission, confirm:

   - Have we sought parallel advice?
   - Are our endpoints and comparators accepted across regions?
   - Do our real-world evidence plans satisfy both regulators and payers?
   - Are we ready to share data transparently post-approval?

5. *The Collaborative Data Room*

   Create a secure digital platform where regulators, payers, and company teams can review evidence in real time. It reduces lag and builds trust through openness.

Strategic Implications for Companies

1. **Evidence Planning as Diplomacy**

   Regulatory harmonisation is as much relationship management as science. Building credibility through consistent quality and early engagement earns long-term advantage.

2. **Data Infrastructure as Competitive Edge**

   Companies that can generate, curate, and share real-world data across markets become preferred partners. Data agility equals access agility.

3. **Policy Engagement as Strategic Investment**

   Participation in pilot programmes, public consultations, and regulatory working groups allows companies to shape standards rather than chase them.

4. **Cultural Shift to Co-Development**

   Teams must evolve from seeing regulators as gatekeepers to seeing them as collaborators. The most successful companies view harmonisation not as compliance but as co-creation.

Ethical and Equity Dimensions

Harmonisation is not only a technical exercise. It is an ethical commitment to fairness.

When approval speed depends on geography, patients in smaller or poorer markets are disadvantaged. Harmonisation corrects that imbalance by sharing expertise and workload.

It also promotes transparency. Joint assessments reduce the temptation for selective disclosure and promote consistent public information.

An African health minister described harmonisation as "the quiet form of justice — the kind that ensures our patients wait no longer than others."

That phrase captures its deeper moral meaning.

Technology and the Future of Regulatory Science

Digital transformation is accelerating harmonisation.

1. **Cloud-Based Regulatory Portals**

   Shared platforms allow simultaneous dossier review, eliminating the need for sequential submissions.

2. **Artificial Intelligence for Data Analysis**

   Machine learning tools identify safety signals and predictive efficacy trends across jurisdictions.

3. **Blockchain for Data Integrity**

   Immutable records ensure that evidence cannot be altered post-submission, building trust.

4. **Real-World Evidence Networks**

   Federated databases allow regulators and payers to assess outcomes continuously.

These innovations make the dream of "real-time regulation" increasingly feasible.

The goal is not faster paperwork but adaptive oversight that mirrors the pace of modern science.

Case Reflection – The Global Oncology Alliance

In 2025, a cross-continental alliance of regulators and payers established a shared review mechanism for oncology drugs. For the first time, HTA and regulatory experts evaluated the same evidence simultaneously.

The outcome was transformative: median time-to-access fell below 120 days across participating markets.

A senior EMA official concluded, "We did not change the rules. We changed the rhythm."

That rhythm — coordinated, transparent, and humane — defines the direction of regulatory science for the next decade.

The Role of Leadership in the Harmonisation Era

Corporate leaders must now think in multilateral terms. Strategic planning must integrate policy foresight.

Actions to consider:

- Embed regulatory affairs and market access under a shared governance structure.
- Establish global evidence steering committees to ensure alignment from Phase II onwards.
- Train teams in international policy literacy, not just compliance.
- Recognise and reward participation in harmonisation initiatives.

Leadership in this new era means contributing to the system, not just navigating it.

Key insight

Regulatory fragmentation is not simply a policy inconvenience. It is a structural contributor to access delay and inequity. Harmonisation does not require uniformity, but it does require alignment of expectations, evidence standards, and timelines across systems. Without this, access remains uneven regardless of scientific quality.

Reflection

Behind every acronym and framework lies a simple truth: regulatory harmonisation exists to shorten the distance between discovery and delivery.

Each day saved in approval is a day gained for a patient.

At a recent joint meeting, a patient representative addressed the room of regulators, payers, and executives.

She said, "You all speak about alignment and data standards. To me, those are just ways of saying you are trying to agree on how soon I can start living again."

The room went quiet. It was a reminder that beyond procedure lies purpose.

Try this

- Identify one product facing divergent regulatory or HTA requirements across regions.
- Map where evidence expectations differ and where they overlap.
- Ask which differences are scientifically necessary and which are procedural.
- Reflect on how early alignment could have reduced duplication or delay.
- Consider where collaboration across agencies could realistically be encouraged.

Summary

- Regulatory fragmentation delays access.
- Harmonisation is about alignment, not sameness.

- Divergent evidence standards increase inefficiency.
- Early coordination reduces downstream complexity.
- System-level alignment improves equity.
- Access depends on how systems interact, not just how products perform.

If access challenges span systems and jurisdictions, the next question is how organisations work across institutional boundaries. The following chapter explores cross-sector collaboration as a practical requirement for sustained access.

CHAPTER 18

CROSS-SECTOR COLLABORATION MODELS BEYOND PHARMA

"Collaboration fails less from lack of goodwill than from disagreement about what success actually means."
– Egbert Floppercough

Many access challenges sit between institutions rather than within them. This chapter examines collaboration across industry, payers, regulators, clinicians, and patient groups. It shows why durable access requires shared incentives and coordinated action across boundaries.

The Unexpected Partnership

The press conference in Geneva looked ordinary enough. Rows of journalists, coffee cups balanced on laps, polite applause as executives took their seats. What caught attention was not the announcement itself but the logos on the screen behind them.

A global pharmaceutical company stood beside a telecommunications provider, a logistics giant, and a patient advocacy coalition. Together, they unveiled a partnership to deliver oncology therapies and digital diagnostics across sub-Saharan Africa.

Reporters asked the usual questions about funding and timelines. But one journalist, a veteran of global health coverage, asked something different: "What does a telecom company have to do with cancer?"

The CEO smiled. "Connectivity is care," he replied. "Without digital links, diagnostics don't work, follow-up fails, and patients disappear. Access needs signal strength as much as science."

The comment captured a quiet revolution. The future of access is no longer defined by molecules alone but by the ecosystems that carry them.

The Context – Why Pharma Cannot Do It Alone

Pharmaceutical innovation has reached extraordinary heights. Yet access gaps remain persistent and predictable. Therapies are discovered, approved, and reimbursed but fail to reach those who need them most.

This is not purely a scientific problem. It is structural. Healthcare systems are complex networks of infrastructure, information, and incentives. No single actor can fix them.

Historically, pharmaceutical companies operated within a closed model: research, manufacture, distribute, and negotiate. Every challenge outside that chain—digital records, logistics, diagnostics, education—was someone else's responsibility.

That model is breaking down. Access now depends on systems that extend far beyond pharma's traditional reach. Delivering precision therapies requires digital platforms, genomic databases, and interoperable patient records. Ensuring affordability demands financial innovation, insurance design, and public-private partnerships.

Access is now a team sport. The companies that recognise this early will redefine not just their markets but their mission.

The Collaboration Spectrum

Cross-sector collaboration is not one thing. It spans a spectrum of depth and purpose.

Level	Type	Objective	Example
1. Transactional Partnerships	Time-limited agreements to deliver a specific service.	Logistics, data sharing, training.	Pharma and courier company managing cold-chain delivery.
2. Strategic Alliances	Long-term collaborations built around shared objectives.	Digital monitoring, diagnostic access, affordability programmes.	Pharma and telecom company co-developing patient tracking apps.
3. Ecosystem Platforms	Multi-stakeholder systems integrating public, private, and non-profit actors.	Sustainable access models across sectors.	Global vaccine distribution alliances or health-data collaboratives.

Table 18.1 The Collaboration Spectrum

Understanding where a partnership sits on this spectrum helps determine governance, investment, and accountability.

The most successful collaborations evolve from transactional to transformational—moving from "help us deliver" to "let's redesign the system."

Framework – The Access Partnership Model

Effective collaboration can be guided by the **Access Partnership Model (APM)**, which defines five critical dimensions for design and governance.

Dimension	Core Question	Example Practices	Indicators of Success
Alignment	Do all partners share the same access objective?	Co-create measurable goals and equity metrics.	Unified success indicators.
Complementarity	Does each partner bring distinct, necessary value?	Leverage technical, logistical, or financial strengths.	No duplication, clear role clarity.
Governance	Are decisions transparent and accountable?	Create joint steering committees and open reporting.	Shared decision logs, conflict resolution mechanism.
Sustainability	Will the partnership outlast funding cycles?	Design models with local ownership and scalable design.	Continued operation after initial phase.
Equity	Do all partners and beneficiaries have voice and agency?	Include patient groups, regional authorities, and local entrepreneurs.	Representation in governance bodies.

Table 18.2 The Access Partnership Model Framework

This framework transforms collaboration from a public-relations exercise into an operational discipline.

Case Studies – Collaboration in Action

Case 1: The Diagnostic Connectivity Network

A European pharmaceutical company partnered with a telecom operator to connect pathology labs in East Africa. The goal was to enable remote diagnosis for oncology patients.

The telecom firm provided cloud infrastructure and training; the pharma company supplied reagents and diagnostic protocols. Local universities managed data governance.

Outcome: turnaround time for test results dropped from three weeks to three days. Patient eligibility for targeted therapies increased fourfold.

Lesson: A therapy is only as accessible as the data network that supports it.

Case 2: The Cold-Chain Consortium

A logistics company, a pharmaceutical manufacturer, and a renewable energy start-up formed a joint venture to install solar-powered vaccine storage units across remote regions of India.

The model was simple: the logistics company managed distribution, the start-up supplied energy systems, and the pharmaceutical company funded infrastructure through advance market commitments.

Within two years, vaccine wastage dropped by 80 percent, and coverage expanded to rural populations previously excluded.

Lesson: Infrastructure is innovation when shared.

Case 3: The Affordability Alliance

A pharmaceutical company collaborated with a global bank and a social enterprise to design microfinance schemes that helped families pay for chronic disease treatment.

Loans were structured with flexible repayment linked to treatment milestones, reducing default risk and improving adherence.

Lesson: Financial engineering can be as powerful as molecular engineering for access.

Case 4: The Digital Therapeutics Ecosystem

A multinational partnered with a software company, an insurer, and a patient advocacy group to launch an integrated digital platform for diabetes management.

Patients could track medication, diet, and glucose levels through a single app. The insurer offered premium discounts for consistent adherence, while the advocacy group provided education.

Within one year, adherence improved by 30 percent, and claims for complications decreased significantly.

Lesson: Access is sustained through engagement, not just entry.

Case 5: The City Health Sandbox

In Singapore, a public-private initiative created a "sandbox city" for testing urban health innovations. Pharmaceutical, technology, and government partners piloted integrated systems linking pharmacy data, hospital records, and wearable devices.

Insights from the project informed national digital health strategies and accelerated regulatory approval for data-driven therapies.

Lesson: Collaboration can generate not just outcomes but policy.

How to Build an Effective Cross-Sector Partnership

1. ***Define a Shared Vision***

   The most common cause of failure in partnerships is misaligned purpose. Begin by defining a vision statement that answers one question clearly: "What patient problem are we solving together?"

   Clarity of purpose prevents dilution of effort and helps partners measure value beyond financial returns.

2. ***Establish a Governance Charter***

   Design a governance structure before signing any contracts. Define who decides what, how disagreements will be resolved, and how results will be communicated.

Transparent governance prevents mistrust later. The best collaborations operate like joint ventures, not loose coalitions.

3. ***Invest in Relationship Capital***

   Partnerships succeed through trust, not transactions. Allocate time for relationship-building and shared learning before major milestones.

   Include cultural induction sessions where partners learn each other's values, vocabulary, and constraints.

   As one executive noted, "We discovered that our tech partner thought in weeks, our legal team in months, and our regulator in years. The first collaboration was synchronising calendars."

4. ***Co-Fund and Co-Own Data***

   Joint ownership of data and outcomes builds accountability. Establish shared platforms for monitoring progress and measuring impact.

   If one partner controls the data, the relationship remains transactional. When data are shared, so is success.

5. ***Plan for Exit and Legacy***

   Every partnership should include a sustainability plan that defines how the model will continue without perpetual corporate funding.

   The best exit strategy is empowerment: local institutions capable of sustaining the system independently.

Emerging Models of Collaboration

1. **Health-Tech Convergence**

   The boundary between pharma and technology is dissolving. AI diagnostics, wearable devices, and digital biomarkers are redefining treatment delivery.

   Companies like Roche and Google Health, or Sanofi and Verily, are building hybrid ecosystems that blend pharmaceutical science with digital analytics.

These models depend on data interoperability, patient consent, and shared value frameworks.

Principle: Whoever owns the insight, not the data, controls the value.

2. **Social Impact Coalitions**

   Non-profits, donors, and industry increasingly collaborate under impact investment models. Rather than donating medicines, companies co-invest in system strengthening.

   An example is the Global Fund's new co-financing mechanism, where private partners contribute not only funds but also logistics, analytics, and training.

   This approach transforms philanthropy into co-creation.

3. **Community-Led Micro Ecosystems**

   In emerging markets, community-based entrepreneurs are designing last-mile delivery models. Pharmaceutical companies supply medicines; local operators provide reach and trust.

   This decentralised model mirrors the logic of microfinance: small, distributed networks solving local problems sustainably.

4. **Financial Innovation Partnerships**

   Access bottlenecks often stem from payment delays and affordability gaps. Financial institutions are now entering health partnerships to design outcome-based bonds, subscription models, and dynamic pricing mechanisms.

   A Latin American example saw a national insurer, a biotech, and a development bank launch a "Cure Bond" that paid returns based on disease eradication rates.

   Lesson: Money can be made moral through design.

Framework – The Collaboration Value Map

To evaluate cross-sector partnerships, organisations can use the **Collaboration Value Map (CVM)**.

Value Type	Description	Measurement Example
Patient Value	Improved access, affordability, or outcomes.	Patients treated, quality-of-life gains.
System Value	Strengthened infrastructure or efficiency.	Reduction in turnaround times, lower logistics cost.
Corporate Value	Enhanced reputation, policy influence, innovation learning.	Stakeholder trust index, new data assets.
Societal Value	Broader benefits such as employment, education, and resilience.	Jobs created, local training programmes.

Table 18.3 The Collaboration Value Map

Plotting each value on the map helps determine balance and ensure mutual benefit.

Sustainable collaborations create value in all four quadrants.

Risks and How to Manage Them

1. **Mission Drift**

   When partners pursue divergent priorities, coherence collapses. Prevent it through periodic alignment reviews and transparent communication.

2. **Data Governance Conflicts**

   Cross-sector data sharing raises privacy and intellectual property issues. Agree on principles upfront and involve legal experts early.

3. **Power Imbalance**

   Large corporations can dominate smaller partners. Mitigate through equitable governance, shared decision-making, and capacity-building.

4. **Reputational Risk**

   Partners' actions reflect on each other. Vet collaborators carefully and include ethics clauses in agreements.

5. **Sustainability Gaps**

   Projects often fade after pilot funding. Build in local ownership and business models from the start.

The Role of Government and Policy

Governments act as both regulators and conveners. Public-private partnerships succeed when policy frameworks enable experimentation.

Key enablers include:

- Fast-track approval for collaborative pilots.
- Data-sharing legislation that protects privacy but encourages interoperability.
- Fiscal incentives for impact investment.
- Procurement models that reward system strengthening, not just lowest price.

Public policy sets the tempo. Collaboration thrives where governments act as facilitators, not merely enforcers.

Cultural and Organisational Shifts

For pharmaceutical companies, effective cross-sector collaboration requires cultural evolution.

From Competition to Co-Creation

Competitors can cooperate on infrastructure and data while still competing on science.

From Ownership to Stewardship

Access-first leadership sees knowledge and infrastructure as public goods, not proprietary assets.

From Compliance to Curiosity

Partnerships work best when teams are trained to ask questions rather than defend positions.

The mindset shift is as strategic as any molecule.

Case Reflection – The Pandemic Legacy

The COVID-19 pandemic proved that cross-sector collaboration is not idealism but survival. Vaccine development, distribution, and monitoring required coordination among pharma, governments, logistics providers, and digital platforms.

That experience rewired expectations. What was once exceptional became precedent. Regulators, payers, and the public now assume that collaboration is part of good practice.

As one policymaker observed, "The world saw what happens when industries stop protecting turf and start sharing purpose."

The Future – Access Ecosystems

The next stage of evolution is the **Access Ecosystem** — a dynamic network where pharma, tech, finance, and civil society operate as co-developers of health solutions.

Characteristics of mature ecosystems include:

- **Data unity** – shared standards and ethical frameworks.
- **Financial integration** – outcome-based funding.
- **Local empowerment** – community-led implementation.
- **Adaptive governance** – continuous feedback and shared learning.

In this model, access becomes not a pipeline but a platform — one that learns, evolves, and scales with society's needs.

Key insight

Access problems rarely sit within a single organisation's control. They emerge at the intersections between industry, regulators, payers, providers, and patient groups. Cross-sector collaboration is therefore not optional. It is a core access capability. Without it, solutions remain partial and fragile.

Reflection

Think about a collaboration you have been involved in. Was it transactional or genuinely joint?

Notice whether incentives were aligned, or whether cooperation relied on goodwill and personal relationships.

Try this

- Identify one access challenge that spans organisational boundaries.
- Map the stakeholders involved and their incentives.
- Ask where collaboration breaks down and why.
- Reflect on what information or authority is missing at the interface.
- Consider one concrete step that would make collaboration more durable.

Summary

- Access challenges cross organisational boundaries.
- Collaboration must be designed, not assumed.
- Misaligned incentives weaken partnerships.
- Durable collaboration requires shared outcomes.
- Trust is built through consistency, not rhetoric.
- Access improves when systems work together.

If collaboration is essential, the next challenge is how value and risk are shared in practice. The following chapter examines advanced payment models as mechanisms for aligning incentives and managing uncertainty.

CHAPTER 19

ADVANCED PAYMENT MODELS AND CONTRACTING INNOVATIONS

"Payment models break down when certainty is protected at the expense of learning."
– Egbert Floppercough

As therapies become more complex and costly, traditional payment models struggle. This chapter explores advanced payment mechanisms as tools for sharing uncertainty and aligning incentives. It explains why trust and governance matter more than technical design.

The Meeting That Changed the Price Tag

The negotiation had reached its ninth hour. Around the table sat the usual mix of finance directors, market access leads, and payer representatives. The drug in question was a one-time gene therapy priced at nearly a million pounds per patient.

The payer looked weary. "We can't commit that much up front," she said. "The clinical results are impressive, but we need proof it lasts."

The company's market access lead leaned back. "What if we link payment to performance?"

The room went quiet.

She continued, "You pay half at treatment, and the rest only if the therapy continues to work over five years. If outcomes fall short, you pay less."

The payer raised an eyebrow. "You're suggesting an instalment plan for a cure?"

"Think of it as outcome insurance," the company lead replied.

A week later, the agreement was signed. The therapy reached patients within months instead of years. The headlines celebrated "a new era of performance-based medicine."

The truth was simpler. It was the first time both sides agreed that price and proof should travel together.

Why Traditional Pricing No Longer Works

Pharmaceutical pricing used to be straightforward. Companies developed drugs, calculated production costs, added margins, benchmarked against competitors, and negotiated rebates.

That world is disappearing.

Modern therapies challenge every assumption of traditional pricing. Gene and cell therapies offer potential cures but carry unprecedented upfront costs. Digital therapeutics require ongoing support and updates. Personalised medicines target small populations with high research expenses.

Meanwhile, payers face shrinking budgets and increasing public scrutiny. Health systems must choose between funding many incremental therapies or a few transformative ones.

The result is a structural tension between innovation and affordability.

In high-income markets, that tension delays reimbursement. In middle-income markets, it blocks access altogether.

Advanced payment models emerged to solve this tension — not by reducing prices but by redistributing risk. They align payment with performance, affordability with accountability.

The Framework – The Value-Linked Payment Continuum

Modern payment models exist along a continuum. The **Value-Linked Payment Continuum (VLPC)** maps five key approaches to managing uncertainty and affordability.

Model Type	Mechanism	Risk Shared	Ideal Use Case	Example
Traditional Payment	Single upfront payment.	None.	Low-cost, low-uncertainty drugs.	Generic medicines.
Outcomes-Based Agreements (OBA)	Payment contingent on predefined clinical outcomes.	Clinical performance risk.	High-cost, measurable outcomes (e.g. gene therapies).	Oncology, rare diseases.
Amortised or Instalment Models	Payment spread over time.	Financial timing risk.	Curative therapies with long-term benefit.	Cell and gene therapies.
Managed Entry Agreements (MEA)	Conditional reimbursement while collecting more data.	Evidence uncertainty risk.	Therapies with limited data at launch.	Oncology, rare diseases.
Subscription and Access Models	Fixed payment for unlimited or population-level use.	Volume and uncertainty risk.	Public health interventions, infectious disease.	Hepatitis C elimination programmes.

Table 19.1 The Value-Linked Payment Continuum

Each model balances clinical, financial, and ethical dimensions differently. The goal is not to choose one model but to design the right combination for each therapy and context.

Case Studies – Payment Innovation in Practice

Case 1: The Outcomes-Based Oncology Agreement

A global oncology company faced payer resistance for a new immunotherapy priced at £250,000 per patient. The therapy worked spectacularly for some but not for all.

The solution was an outcomes-based agreement. The company agreed to reimburse partial costs for patients who discontinued treatment within six months due to lack of response.

Result: payer confidence increased, negotiations accelerated, and patient access improved by 30 percent.

Lesson: Sharing performance risk builds credibility and trust.

Case 2: The Gene Therapy Instalment Plan

A gene therapy for spinal muscular atrophy cost £1.8 million per treatment. National health systems balked.

The manufacturer proposed a five-year amortisation model, with annual payments tied to sustained motor function milestones.

Result: therapy approved within six months. The budget impact became manageable, and public support grew.

Lesson: Time is a form of affordability.

Case 3: The Subscription Model That Beat Hepatitis C

Australia and several European countries pioneered "Netflix-style" subscription models for hepatitis C antivirals. Governments paid a fixed annual fee for unlimited access, incentivising them to treat as many patients as possible.

Within five years, infection rates plummeted, and total system costs declined.

Lesson: When payment aligns with population health goals, everyone wins.

Case 4: The Managed Entry Pilot

A rare disease drug with limited trial data entered the market through a managed entry agreement. The company committed to collecting real-world outcomes data through a national registry.

After three years, evidence confirmed durable benefit, and reimbursement became permanent.

Lesson: Access need not wait for perfect data; it requires credible intent.

Case 5: The Outcome Bond in Latin America

A development bank partnered with a national payer and a biotech company to launch an outcome-based financing instrument for diabetes care. Investors funded treatment expansion; repayments were linked to verified reductions in hospital admissions.

Lesson: Capital markets can fund health outcomes when incentives align.

Designing an Outcomes-Based Agreement

An effective outcomes-based contract rests on four foundations.

1. **Clear, Measurable Outcomes**

   Agree on specific, objective metrics before launch. Use endpoints that reflect meaningful patient benefits such as survival, hospitalisation rates, or quality-of-life improvements.

2. **Robust Data Infrastructure**

   Reliable outcome tracking requires shared registries or electronic health records. Without credible data, the model collapses into dispute.

3. **Proportionate Payment Triggers**

   Define how payments adjust based on results. Avoid all-or-nothing schemes; use graduated tiers that reflect real-world variability.

4. **Transparent Governance**

   Create an independent oversight committee to audit results and arbitrate disagreements. Trust is built through shared verification.

When designed correctly, outcomes-based models turn uncertainty into partnership.

The Economics of Affordability

Advanced payment models do more than manage budgets; they redefine how value is created.

Traditional models treat value as static — a price fixed at launch. Value-linked models treat it as dynamic — verified and refined over time.

For payers, this means lower upfront risk. For manufacturers, it means evidence becomes a revenue driver. The more the product proves itself, the more value it captures.

Economically, these models shift healthcare from one-off transactions to ongoing service relationships. The boundary between therapy and platform begins to blur.

The Role of Real-World Evidence

Real-world evidence (RWE) is the currency of advanced contracting. Without credible post-launch data, outcomes-based and managed entry models cannot function.

Successful systems integrate RWE from multiple sources:

- Patient registries and hospital records.
- Digital health apps and wearable sensors.

- Claims databases and public health datasets.

Regulators and payers are increasingly open to RWE as a complement to trial data. In 2024, over 60 percent of new reimbursement decisions in Europe included real-world evidence components.

The implication is clear: the ability to collect, interpret, and share real-world data is now a commercial competency.

Framework – The Access Financing Matrix

To select appropriate payment models, companies can apply the **Access Financing Matrix (AFM)**, which matches uncertainty type with the right financial design.

Uncertainty Type	Primary Risk	Financial Solution	Example
Clinical Durability	Long-term outcomes unclear.	Outcomes-based instalment model.	Gene therapies.
Budget Impact	High upfront cost.	Amortisation or subscription model.	Vaccines, curative therapies.
Data Limitations	Limited evidence at launch.	Managed entry agreement with registry.	Rare diseases.
Population Variability	Uneven response or small subgroups.	Tiered pricing or adaptive rebate.	Oncology, immunology.

Table 19.2 The Access Financing Matrix

This framework helps align payment logic with the nature of the evidence gap.

Technology Enablers

Digital tools are transforming how payment models operate.

- **Blockchain systems** ensure data integrity and transparent payment triggers.

- **Smart contracts** automate reimbursement once outcomes are verified.
- **AI analytics** identify patient subgroups with differential response, allowing adaptive pricing.
- **Cloud registries** provide real-time access to results across stakeholders.

Technology does not replace trust but scales it. The more automatic the verification, the less adversarial the negotiation.

Barriers to Implementation

Despite enthusiasm, advanced payment models face practical hurdles.

1. **Data Fragmentation**

   Health systems often lack integrated data to track long-term outcomes reliably.

2. **Administrative Complexity**

   Negotiating, monitoring, and auditing performance-based contracts requires new skill sets and resources.

3. **Legal Constraints**

   Procurement laws may restrict multi-year or outcome-linked agreements.

4. **Cultural Resistance**

   Some stakeholders still view payment innovation as riskier than the status quo.

Overcoming these barriers requires policy support, training, and standardised templates.

Policy and System Implications

Governments and regulators are gradually adapting frameworks to enable innovative contracting.

In Europe, the **EU Pharmaceutical Strategy** promotes flexible pricing and outcome-based models to improve affordability.

In the United States, the **CMS Innovation Center** has piloted value-based purchasing for gene therapies, integrating state Medicaid systems into multi-year contracts.

At the global level, the **WHO Fair Pricing Forum** encourages transparency and shared risk models to balance innovation with access.

Policy evolution lags behind science, but momentum is clear. Advanced payment models are no longer experiments; they are emerging norms.

Ethical Dimensions – Fairness and Transparency

Advanced contracting raises ethical questions. Who decides what outcome is worth paying for? How do we ensure fairness between early adopters and late entrants?

Ethical contracting requires three safeguards.

- **Inclusivity:** patient voices in defining outcomes.
- **Transparency:** public disclosure of payment frameworks.
- **Proportionality:** ensuring savings benefit the health system, not just the balance sheet.

One health economist summarised it well: "The goal is not cheap miracles but justifiable hope."

The Future – Adaptive Contracting and Continuous Value

The next evolution in payment models is **adaptive contracting** — agreements that evolve as evidence accumulates.

Imagine a five-year framework where price, access conditions, and outcome thresholds adjust dynamically based on new data.

In this model, pricing becomes a living reflection of evidence, not a frozen number.

Continuous learning systems, powered by digital registries and AI analytics, will make this possible.

The ultimate aim is not complex contracts but sustainable simplicity — systems where payment naturally follows performance.

Key insight

Traditional payment models struggle to accommodate uncertainty, especially for high-cost and transformative therapies. Advanced payment models offer a way to share risk, align incentives, and sustain access over time. Their success depends less on technical design and more on trust, data, and governance.

Reflection

Reflect on how risk is currently distributed between developers and payers in your context. Who carries the greatest uncertainty?

Notice whether payment structures encourage learning and adaptation, or reinforce defensiveness.

Try this

- Identify a therapy where traditional pricing created access friction.
- Explore which uncertainties could be shared rather than transferred.
- Ask what data would be needed to support outcome-linked payment.
- Reflect on governance requirements for managing long-term agreements.
- Consider how earlier discussion could have expanded feasible options.

Summary

- Payment models shape access sustainability.
- Sharing risk enables faster adoption.
- Data and governance are prerequisites for flexibility.
- Trust determines whether models work in practice.
- Advanced payments require long-term commitment.
- Access improves when incentives are aligned.

If payment models shape access in well-resourced systems, the next question is how access plays out globally. The following chapter turns to low- and middle-income countries, where constraints are sharper and trade-offs more visible.

CHAPTER 20

GLOBAL ACCESS CHALLENGES AND SUCCESS STORIES IN LOW- AND MIDDLE-INCOME COUNTRIES

"Global access efforts fail when affordability is discussed without equal attention to delivery."
– Egbert Floppercough

Access challenges are most visible where constraints are greatest. This chapter examines global inequities in access and the structural factors that sustain them. It argues that access-first thinking must operate at global scale, not only in wealthy systems.

The Hospital Without a Cold Chain

The hospital stood on the outskirts of Accra, Ghana. Its walls were painted a hopeful shade of blue, though the power flickered every few hours. The paediatric ward had a refrigerator meant for storing vaccines and biologics, but it ran only when the generator worked — and fuel was expensive.

When the shipment finally arrived, a box of temperature-sensitive vials, the nurse on duty placed them inside the fridge and said quietly, "Let's hope the lights stay on tonight."

Two thousand miles away, in a London office, a launch team celebrated the same product's successful "regional rollout across Africa."

On paper, access had been achieved. In practice, the hospital had enough usable vials for only half its scheduled patients.

This is what access looks like in much of the world: a map coloured in optimism, overlaid on a reality drawn in logistics, inequality, and endurance.

The Global Inequality in Access

Pharmaceutical access is not distributed evenly. The gap between high-income and low- and middle-income countries (LMICs) is both predictable and persistent.

According to WHO data, one-third of the world's population lacks regular access to essential medicines. In sub-Saharan Africa, that figure rises to nearly half. The same pattern holds for diagnostics, oncology treatments, and novel biologics.

This disparity is not just economic. It is structural. Health systems in many LMICs face a combination of weak supply chains, limited diagnostic capacity, inconsistent funding, and complex regulatory barriers.

At the same time, LMICs represent nearly 80 percent of the global disease burden and the fastest-growing pharmaceutical markets by population.

The challenge is clear: innovation is global, but access remains local.

The industry cannot claim to be access-first until it works in the settings where access is hardest.

The Structural Barriers to Access

While contexts differ, the same five barriers appear repeatedly across LMIC settings.

1. **Regulatory Fragmentation**

   Each country maintains its own approval process, often under-resourced and slow. For smaller markets, duplication of effort creates unnecessary delay.

2. **Infrastructure Gaps**

   Cold-chain logistics, diagnostic facilities, and healthcare workforce shortages restrict delivery even after approval.

3. **Financing Constraints**

   Public budgets are stretched. Out-of-pocket payments remain the dominant model in many countries, pushing households into poverty.

4. **Information and Data Scarcity**

   Lack of real-world data makes it hard to demonstrate value or plan effective interventions.

5. **Equity and Geography**

   Urban-rural divides mean that even when a product is listed, it may not be available where most patients live.

Each barrier represents not a failure of will but of system design. The solutions that work best are those that match local context with global collaboration.

The Framework – The Global Access Maturity Model

To navigate this complexity, global access teams can use the **Global Access Maturity Model (GAMM)**. It describes four progressive levels of capability in national or regional systems.

Stage	Description	Key Features	Example
1. Basic Availability	Medicines listed but inconsistently supplied.	Fragmented procurement, limited regulation.	Early vaccine access in low-income countries pre-Gavi.

Stage	Description	Key Features	Example
2. Structured Procurement	Pooled purchasing and donor coordination.	Regional tenders, global partnerships.	African Vaccine Acquisition Trust (AVAT).
3. Local Adaptation	National manufacturing, tiered pricing, digital logistics.	Infrastructure investment, outcome monitoring.	India's local vaccine manufacturing and digital supply tracking.
4. Sustainable Access Ecosystem	Fully integrated, equitable system linking production, regulation, and care delivery.	Joint regulation, outcome-based financing, digital monitoring.	Brazil's Unified Health System partnerships.

Table 20.1 The Global Access Maturity Model

Most countries sit somewhere between Stage 2 and 3. The goal is not to copy high-income systems but to build adaptive ones that fit local realities.

Case Studies – Success Born from Constraint

Case 1: Rwanda's Digital Health Backbone

Rwanda faced the challenge of healthcare access after decades of rebuilding its national systems. Instead of expanding physical infrastructure alone, it built a digital backbone.

Through partnerships with private telecom companies, every district hospital was connected via mobile networks. Electronic medical records, vaccine tracking, and real-time reporting became standard.

When COVID-19 struck, the same network supported rapid vaccine rollout and pharmacovigilance.

Lesson: Digital infrastructure can leapfrog physical barriers when governance is strong.

Case 2: Nigeria's Pooled Procurement Revolution

Nigeria's state-by-state procurement once led to inefficiency, corruption, and stockouts. In 2018, the government piloted pooled procurement for essential medicines with donor support.

By aggregating demand and negotiating as one buyer, prices fell by 30 percent, and medicine availability increased dramatically.

Lesson: Market efficiency can serve equity when scale and transparency align.

Case 3: Brazil's Local Manufacturing Strategy

Brazil's Unified Health System (SUS) established a long-term strategy of local production through "Technology Transfer Partnerships."

International companies licensing products were required to collaborate with domestic public manufacturers. Over time, Brazil built self-sufficiency in vaccines, insulin, and oncology drugs.

Lesson: Local manufacturing is not protectionism; it is sustainable independence.

Case 4: The Gavi Vaccine Alliance

Perhaps the most successful access collaboration in history, Gavi transformed vaccine availability for LMICs. By pooling donor funds and negotiating with manufacturers, it made life-saving vaccines affordable and widely distributed.

Since 2000, Gavi has supported the immunisation of over 1 billion children, preventing more than 17 million deaths.

Lesson: Pooled funding and guaranteed demand create predictability for both sides.

Case 5: The AMR Subscription Model in the UK and Beyond

Although not an LMIC case, the UK's antimicrobial resistance (AMR) subscription model inspired adaptations in India and Thailand. Governments pay a fixed annual fee to ensure access to critical antibiotics, regardless of usage volume.

In India, this model was repurposed to fund tuberculosis diagnostics and ensure supply continuity.

Lesson: Innovation can move both ways. The South now adapts models from the North creatively and rapidly.

Local Innovation: The Underestimated Frontier

LMICs are not passive recipients of global innovation. They are laboratories of access creativity.

India pioneered low-cost generic manufacturing and global supply of vaccines.

Kenya built one of the world's most sophisticated mobile health payment systems through M-PESA integration.

Bangladesh developed community-based pharmaceutical franchises for maternal care.

Vietnam applied AI for antibiotic stewardship before most high-income countries did.

These examples show that access-first innovation is not about technology transfer; it is about learning transfer.

Design Principles – Building Access in Emerging Systems

Drawing from successful cases, five design principles emerge.

1. **Co-Ownership, Not Charity**

   Sustainable access requires shared investment. Donor dependency creates fragility. Programmes succeed when countries co-finance and co-govern.

2. **Infrastructure Before Innovation**

   A therapy without storage, diagnostics, or workforce readiness is an empty promise. Infrastructure must evolve in parallel.

3. **Local Data, Local Decisions**

   Each country needs its own evidence base to prioritise interventions and justify reimbursement.

4. **Partnership as Policy**

   Governments should institutionalise collaboration with industry, academia, and civil society.

5. **Equity as Efficiency**

   Reaching the poorest populations often delivers the highest return in public health outcomes.

Access-first systems understand that inclusion is not philanthropy; it is strategy.

The Role of Global Partnerships

The access challenge in LMICs has given rise to a new ecosystem of partnerships linking donors, multilateral institutions, and industry.

The Global Fund integrates financing for HIV, tuberculosis, and malaria with supply chain reform.

UNICEF provides last-mile delivery capacity unmatched by any commercial network.

The World Bank supports results-based financing for universal health coverage.

CEPI co-develops pandemic vaccines with local manufacturers.

Unitaid invests in market-shaping to reduce the cost of novel diagnostics and treatments.

These partnerships operate as intermediaries between innovation and implementation. They coordinate, de-risk, and catalyse action where national systems alone cannot.

Framework – The Access Partnership Triangle

A practical way to visualise these dynamics is the **Access Partnership Triangle**, which aligns three forces: innovation, financing, and delivery.

Vertex	Role	Example Actors	Objective
Innovation	Develop safe, effective, context-fit products.	Pharma, biotech, academia.	Create adaptable solutions.
Financing	Pool and channel funds sustainably.	Donors, governments, banks.	Make innovation affordable.
Delivery	Ensure reach and continuity of use.	Health systems, NGOs, logistics partners.	Translate innovation into access.

Table 20.2 The Access Partnership Triangle

When these three elements operate in balance, access becomes self-sustaining. When one is weak, the triangle collapses.

Case Reflection – The COVAX Experience

The COVAX Facility, launched during the COVID-19 pandemic, embodied both the promise and the tension of global access coordination.

It delivered over 1.7 billion vaccine doses to 146 countries. Yet inequities persisted — not because of failure in design, but in power. Wealthy nations secured early supply, leaving poorer countries waiting.

COVAX remains a milestone in global cooperation, but also a warning: global access is not only about logistics; it is about justice.

As one African health minister remarked, "Solidarity delayed is solidarity denied."

Sustainability and Local Capacity Building

True access transformation occurs when local capacity replaces dependency.

This requires investment in:

- **Regulatory strengthening**, to enable reliance and mutual recognition.
- **Workforce development**, ensuring local expertise in manufacturing and clinical delivery.
- **Regional manufacturing hubs**, reducing supply vulnerability.
- **Digital infrastructure**, supporting traceability and pharmacovigilance.

Examples are already emerging. The African Medicines Agency (AMA), established in 2021, is building regional regulatory harmonisation. South Africa and Senegal have invested in mRNA vaccine facilities. These are not aid stories; they are independence stories.

Economic and Ethical Imperatives

Expanding access in LMICs is not only moral; it is economic.

The World Bank estimates that every dollar invested in essential health interventions yields at least ten dollars in social and economic returns through productivity and reduced poverty.

The ethical dimension is equally clear. Diseases of poverty persist not because they are incurable, but because they are unprofitable. Aligning incentives through global financing and tiered pricing can close that moral gap.

Ethical access requires transparency in pricing, inclusive trial participation, and equitable benefit-sharing from research conducted in the Global South.

Technology as the Great Equaliser

Digital transformation is reshaping access landscapes faster than any traditional reform.

- **Telemedicine** connects rural patients to urban specialists.
- **AI-driven diagnostics** allow low-cost screening at primary care level.
- **Drone delivery** ensures last-mile distribution in remote areas.
- **Mobile payment systems** integrate microinsurance with treatment adherence.

The challenge is not adoption but adaptation. Technology succeeds when designed for low-bandwidth environments and local literacy.

In Kenya, AI-assisted ultrasound now helps rural clinics diagnose maternal complications with accuracy rivaling city hospitals. In India, smartphone-based diagnostic apps are used by community health workers to screen for diabetes and anaemia.

Technology does not erase inequality, but it can shorten the distance between discovery and delivery.

Practical Tools – How to Build an LMIC Access Strategy

1. **Map the System**

   Understand where bottlenecks lie — regulation, logistics, financing, or awareness.

2. **Co-Design with Local Partners**

   Collaborate with ministries, patient groups, and NGOs from the start.

3. **Design Tiered Pricing Frameworks**

   Set prices based on affordability and GDP thresholds, not just parity.

4. **Invest in Data Infrastructure**

   Support registries and digital tracking to demonstrate outcomes.

5. **Embed Local Ownership**

   Ensure that programmes are led and sustained by local institutions.

Access designed from within lasts longer than access imposed from outside.

Key insight

Global access inequity is not an unintended side effect of innovation. It is the result of how affordability, infrastructure, and prioritisation are addressed. Improving access in low- and middle-income countries requires deliberate strategies that recognise different constraints while maintaining shared ethical responsibility.

Reflection

Consider how global access is discussed in your organisation. Is it framed as philanthropy, compliance, or strategy?

Notice whether equity across geographies is treated as a core responsibility or an optional add-on.

Try this

- Identify one product with limited reach in low- or middle-income settings.
- Map the non-price barriers to access, including infrastructure and delivery.
- Ask how pricing, partnerships, or tiered approaches could change reach.
- Reflect on how early global planning might have altered outcomes.
- Consider how success would be defined from a global patient perspective.

Summary

- Global access inequity reflects design choices.
- Affordability is necessary but insufficient.
- Infrastructure and readiness shape adoption.
- Equity requires differentiated strategies.
- Global responsibility extends beyond approval.
- Access-first thinking must operate at global scale.

If access must be sustained across systems, sectors, and geographies, the final challenge is how these pressures will intensify in the future. The following chapter looks ahead to access under growing strain, and what it will take to remain credible and resilient.

CHAPTER 21

POST-2026 OUTLOOK: ACCESS UNDER PRESSURE, ACCESS UNDER CONSTRUCTION

"Pressure does not create access problems. It reveals the ones that were already built in."
– Egbert Floppercough

Looking ahead, access will be shaped by intensifying pressure rather than expanding opportunity. This chapter examines how fiscal, political, and demographic forces are narrowing room for manoeuvre. It focuses on resilience and long-term credibility rather than short-term optimisation.

The Budget Hearing

It was a grey morning in Brussels. Inside a government conference room, a national health minister faced a line of journalists after announcing a new austerity plan. "Our goal," she said, "is not to cut healthcare, but to make it sustainable."

A few kilometres away, in the headquarters of a major pharmaceutical company, the Access and Policy team watched the press conference live. Their upcoming oncology launch depended on that same national budget.

By noon, emails began circulating. Reimbursement timelines would likely extend. Health technology assessment committees would demand new evidence of "societal value." The company's CEO, once confident about Europe's stability, called an emergency meeting.

The conversation was not about clinical data or regulatory pathways. It was about survival in a world where access was being rebuilt under pressure — financial, political, and moral.

That meeting, like thousands happening worldwide, captured the essence of the post-2026 era: access is no longer guaranteed by innovation. It must now be earned through legitimacy.

The Context – The End of Automatic Access

For decades, the pharmaceutical industry operated under a stable social contract: innovation justified price, and approval implied access. That contract is breaking down.

By 2026, global health systems face three simultaneous pressures:

1. **Demographic Shifts** – Ageing populations increasing chronic disease burden.
2. **Economic Constraint** – Post-pandemic debt, inflation, and limited public budgets.
3. **Expectation Inflation** – Patients, payers, and policymakers demanding faster, fairer, more transparent access.

These forces collide in the same place: the health system's capacity to absorb innovation.

Payers are no longer passive buyers; they are active co-developers of value. Regulators are evolving from gatekeepers to system architects. Patients are moving from recipients to advocates.

In this new order, access is not a one-time event but a continuous negotiation — between science, affordability, and legitimacy.

The Structural Shifts in Global Access

Three fundamental shifts define the post-2026 access landscape.

1. **From Volume to Value**

   The global move toward outcome-based reimbursement is accelerating. Payers increasingly demand measurable results rather than promises.

   Health systems are investing in value-based procurement, population health contracts, and real-world performance dashboards.

   For industry, this means commercial success will depend less on volume of sales and more on verified patient benefit over time.

2. **From Product to Platform**

   Pharmaceutical innovation is merging with technology. A therapy is now part of a data ecosystem — linked to diagnostics, monitoring devices, and AI-driven analytics.

   Regulators and payers expect companies to demonstrate not only product efficacy but system interoperability.

   The future blockbuster may not be a molecule but a platform that delivers measurable, adaptive outcomes.

3. **From Competition to Collaboration**

   Cross-sector partnerships are becoming the norm. Pharma, insurers, governments, and tech firms now co-design access solutions.

   Shared data, joint governance, and public-private innovation platforms are replacing traditional silos.

   The competitive advantage of the next decade will not come from proprietary control, but from collaborative legitimacy.

Framework – The Access Pressure Matrix

To navigate the post-2026 environment, companies can use the **Access Pressure Matrix (APM)** — a tool that maps external pressures against internal responses.

Pressure Type	Description	Industry Response	Strategic Opportunity
Financial Pressure	Fiscal constraint, slower reimbursement, tighter cost-effectiveness thresholds.	Shift to outcomes-based and amortised models.	Build adaptive payment infrastructure.
Regulatory Pressure	More demanding evidence and accelerated review timelines.	Invest in integrated RWE and lifecycle data strategies.	Position as trusted data partner.
Societal Pressure	Equity, transparency, and environmental sustainability expectations.	Embed ESG and access metrics into leadership KPIs.	Differentiate through credibility and trust.
Technological Pressure	AI, data ethics, and interoperability requirements.	Develop platform-based therapies and digital value layers.	Create data-driven ecosystems.

Table 21.1 The Access Pressure Matrix

By anticipating these pressures, organisations can move from defensive adaptation to proactive leadership.

The Economics of Constraint

Global health expenditure is projected to grow at less than 3 percent annually, far below the rate of innovation-driven cost increases.

This imbalance means that not every innovation can or will be funded. Payers will prioritise therapies that deliver demonstrable, system-level value — reducing hospitalisations, enabling prevention, or supporting population health management.

For pharmaceutical companies, the implication is profound. The question shifts from "Can we prove this drug works?" to "Can we prove it saves the system money or improves sustainability?"

In this environment, economic narratives become ethical narratives. Demonstrating affordability and efficiency is no longer financial prudence; it is moral accountability.

Case Studies – Systems Under Construction

Case 1: The Nordic Outcomes Alliance

In 2026, a coalition of Scandinavian health authorities created a shared outcomes registry for oncology therapies. Data were anonymised and pooled across countries, enabling faster reassessment of reimbursement decisions.

Manufacturers participated voluntarily, sharing performance data in exchange for predictable pricing.

Within two years, decision timelines shortened by 30 percent, and patient access improved.

Lesson: Collective transparency creates efficiency.

Case 2: Singapore's Dynamic Pricing Pilot

Singapore's Ministry of Health introduced a pilot programme linking reimbursement to real-time utilisation and outcomes data. Prices automatically adjusted based on observed benefit.

The system rewarded manufacturers for sustained outcomes while reducing payer exposure.

Lesson: In a digital economy, price becomes a live variable, not a fixed number.

Case 3: The Latin American Access Pact

In 2027, several Latin American countries launched a joint negotiation platform to pool purchasing power and harmonise health technology assessments.

This collaboration reduced duplication, accelerated access, and increased negotiation leverage.

Lesson: Regional integration is the new frontier of access equity.

Case 4: Germany's Early Access Redesign

Germany's AMNOG system, long considered the benchmark for evidence-based pricing, evolved to include long-term real-world follow-up. Manufacturers must now submit periodic outcome data to maintain reimbursement status.

Lesson: Access no longer ends at launch; it continues through life-cycle evidence.

Data as Infrastructure

In the post-2026 landscape, data are no longer support tools; they are the infrastructure of access.

Health systems increasingly require real-world performance tracking as a condition of market entry.

Pharmaceutical companies must therefore evolve into evidence enterprises — integrating clinical, commercial, and policy data in a single feedback loop.

This integration enables adaptive pricing, risk-sharing, and faster re-evaluation. But it also demands governance maturity: secure sharing, data ethics, and patient consent management.

Companies that treat data as a public good, not a proprietary asset, will gain long-term legitimacy.

The Ethical Economy of Access

Post-2026, access decisions are being reframed around ethics as much as economics. Three ethical imperatives now define the legitimacy of pharmaceutical innovation.

1. **Transparency of Value**

   Stakeholders expect clarity on how prices relate to public investment, R&D costs, and patient outcomes.

2. **Equity of Reach**

   Access metrics must demonstrate inclusion across demographics, geography, and income levels.

3. **Accountability of Impact**

   Companies must report not only units sold but health gains achieved — a shift from marketing metrics to moral metrics.

Access-first innovation is not only about faster launches but fairer systems.

Framework – The System Resilience Index

To measure readiness for this new era, organisations can assess themselves using the **System Resilience Index (SRI)**.

Dimension	Definition	Indicators	Target State
Evidence Resilience	Ability to generate and integrate data continuously.	RWE integration, adaptive trials.	Real-time evidence loop.
Financial Resilience	Flexibility to adapt payment models.	OBA participation, multi-year budgeting.	Predictable affordability.
Operational Resilience	Capacity to maintain supply and delivery in crises.	Local manufacturing, digital logistics.	Redundant, decentralised supply chains.
Ethical Resilience	Trust and legitimacy among stakeholders.	Transparency, ESG metrics, access reporting.	Institutional credibility.

Table 21.2 The System Resilience Index

Post-2026 success depends not only on scientific excellence but systemic resilience.

The Role of AI and Automation

Artificial intelligence is reshaping access faster than any policy reform.

AI enables predictive pricing, automated contracting, and real-time patient segmentation. It helps payers identify which therapies deliver the most measurable benefit and helps manufacturers predict reimbursement success before submission.

However, AI also introduces new risks — algorithmic bias, opaque decision-making, and data inequality.

The access-first response is governance: transparent algorithms, ethical audits, and inclusion in training datasets.

AI can be the industry's greatest ally or its most powerful critic, depending on how it is managed.

Scenario – The 2030 Access Simulation

Imagine a near future where a therapy launches not with a price tag, but with a performance profile. Payers subscribe to it as a service.

Outcomes are tracked in real time through digital registries. The price updates quarterly based on verified benefit. If results decline, the cost automatically adjusts.

Patients see outcomes data published online. Governments use the same dashboards to plan budgets.

In this system, transparency becomes the invisible regulator.

Access is no longer negotiated in closed rooms but co-created in open systems.

This is not fantasy. Pilot projects in Scandinavia, Singapore, and Canada already point in this direction.

The post-2026 decade will likely see these ideas become infrastructure.

Cultural Transformation – From Power to Partnership

The next era of access demands a profound cultural change inside pharmaceutical organisations.

From Advocacy to Empathy – Access teams must listen as much as they lobby.

From Defence to Design – Policy engagement should be proactive, not reactive.

From Isolation to Integration – Market access, medical, and RWE teams must operate as one.

The companies that thrive will be those that treat access not as a department but as a design principle.

As one senior policymaker put it, "We don't need faster innovators. We need better listeners."

Strategic Implications for Leadership

Executives will need to manage a new type of portfolio — one measured not only by revenue potential but by access resilience.

This means integrating access metrics into investment decisions, corporate reporting, and leadership evaluation.

The CEO of the future will not ask, "What is our market share?" but "What is our access share?"

Boards that understand this shift will build companies capable of thriving under scrutiny and scarcity.

The Global Policy Horizon

By 2030, several global policy trends are likely to define access strategy:

1. **Outcome-Based International Pricing Reference** – Countries may begin comparing not only list prices but outcome-adjusted value.
2. **Global Data Trusts** – Shared registries governed by multilateral agencies will track therapy performance across borders.
3. **Sustainability-Linked Approvals** – Regulatory fast-tracks may be tied to commitments on affordability and carbon neutrality.

4. **Access Equity Indexes** – Investors and analysts may rate companies based on access equity performance.

The boundaries between health policy, trade, and climate will blur. Access will sit at the intersection of all three.

Key insight

The future of access will be shaped less by breakthrough science than by mounting systemic pressure. Fiscal constraint, political scrutiny, demographic change, and rising expectations are converging to narrow room for manoeuvre. Organisations that fail to adapt how they design, justify, and sustain access will find their options shrinking over time.

Reflection

Think about the pressures currently shaping access decisions in your environment. Which are temporary, and which are structural?

Notice whether your organisation is responding defensively to pressure, or deliberately redesigning how decisions are made under constraint.

Try this

- Identify three pressures most likely to affect access over the next five years.
- Examine which current practices are least resilient under those pressures.
- Ask where flexibility could be built into evidence, pricing, or partnerships.
- Reflect on how early decisions constrain or expand future options.
- Consider what access resilience would look like as an explicit objective.

Summary

- Access pressures are increasing, not easing.
- Constraint is becoming the normal operating condition.
- Early decisions shape long-term resilience.
- Flexibility must be designed deliberately.
- Defensive strategies narrow future options.
- Sustainable access requires system-level thinking.

As pressures intensify, technical competence alone will not be enough. The final measure of access-first thinking is whether it remains anchored to the people it exists to serve. The next chapter returns to the patient as the moral centre of access decisions.

CHAPTER 22

EPILOGUE: THE PATIENT AT THE CENTRE OF EVERYTHING

"When access works well, it feels unremarkable.
That ordinariness is its greatest success."
– Egbert Floppercough

Throughout the book, access has been treated as a system problem. This chapter returns to the patient as the moral centre of those systems. It reflects on how access decisions are experienced in real lives and why patient outcomes remain the ultimate measure of success.

The Quiet Room

The consultation room was small, barely large enough for the doctor, a patient, and the nurse who sat quietly taking notes. A plastic model of a heart sat on the desk beside a stack of leaflets about clinical trials.

The patient, a retired teacher, listened as the doctor explained the treatment options for his rare cardiac condition. The latest therapy had just been approved, a first-in-class medicine hailed in medical journals as transformative.

The patient nodded politely but asked only one question: "Will it let me walk my dog again?"

The doctor paused. "We hope so. That's what the data suggest."

For the patient, that was all that mattered. For the industry that developed the therapy, that simple question contained the essence of everything this book has argued: access is not about approval, price, or policy. It is about life continuing in ordinary ways.

Every dataset, every health technology assessment, every negotiation ultimately converges on moments like this — a conversation in a quiet room between a person and a possibility.

That is where the meaning of innovation is tested.

The Shift from Patient as Beneficiary to Patient as Partner

For decades, "patient-centricity" appeared on corporate slides and annual reports. It was well-intentioned but often rhetorical — an ethical flourish rather than a design principle.

The access-first era has changed that. Patients are now integrated into every part of the innovation lifecycle — not as symbols, but as collaborators.

They help define endpoints, co-design trials, shape reimbursement models, and monitor real-world outcomes. Their lived experience is now evidence, not anecdote.

Yet the transition from sentiment to structure remains incomplete. Many organisations still treat patient involvement as a compliance step rather than a source of strategy.

To truly place patients at the centre, three fundamental shifts are required.

1. **From Representation to Participation**

   Involve patients in protocol design, governance, and advisory boards from day one.

2. **From Feedback to Co-Creation**

   Engage them not to validate ideas but to generate them.

3. **From Empathy to Accountability**

   Measure success not by stated intent but by demonstrated impact — faster access, improved outcomes, reduced inequity.

When patients help shape the definition of value, the system naturally becomes more human — and more efficient.

The Paradox of Progress

Pharmaceutical science has never been more advanced. Gene editing, cell therapies, AI-designed molecules, and digital biomarkers promise precision unimaginable a decade ago.

And yet, the lived experience of patients often lags behind that promise. Treatments exist but remain unreachable. Approval comes, but adoption stalls.

The paradox of progress is that the faster science moves, the more the system reveals its friction.

Every leap in discovery creates new gaps in delivery — gaps that only patient-centred design can close.

The patient at the centre is not a metaphor. It is a corrective mechanism for systemic myopia.

Framework – The Patient-Centred Access Loop

The **Patient-Centred Access Loop (PCAL)** describes how patient insight sustains access through continuous feedback.

Phase	Traditional Focus	Access-First Focus	Patient Contribution
Discovery	Biological targets	Real-world need	Identify meaningful outcomes
Development	Trial endpoints	Quality-of-life metrics	Define relevance
Market Access	Pricing and reimbursement	Value communication	Shape benefit narrative
Post-Launch	Sales metrics	Real-world performance	Report lived experience

Table 22.1 The Patient-Centred Access Loop

This loop replaces the linear "bench-to-bedside" model with a cycle of learning that begins and ends with the patient.

The Voice in the Data

Modern healthcare systems generate enormous amounts of data — genomic sequences, registry entries, wearable device outputs. But the voice behind that data can easily disappear.

Patient-reported outcomes and real-world experience must be treated with the same rigour as laboratory metrics.

A recent European study found that therapies designed with patient input in endpoint selection were 40 percent more likely to achieve market access within the first year of approval.

The reason is simple: when evidence aligns with human experience, payers listen faster, regulators decide faster, and adoption happens naturally.

Data are persuasive only when they tell human stories accurately.

Case Studies – When Patients Redefined Access

Case 1: The Cystic Fibrosis Advocacy Model

In the United States, patient advocacy groups for cystic fibrosis did what no corporate strategy could: they built an ecosystem.

They funded early-stage research, engaged regulators, co-designed trials, and created real-world evidence registries.

When breakthrough modulators arrived, the pathway to approval and reimbursement was already built.

Lesson: Patient movements can be infrastructure.

Case 2: The United Kingdom's NICE and Patient Relevance Framework

In 2026, the UK's NICE introduced a formal mechanism for incorporating patient-defined "impact domains" into its appraisals. Patients helped define what outcomes mattered most: symptom relief, independence, and dignity.

Manufacturers that aligned trial designs with these domains achieved faster evaluations.

Lesson: Patient relevance accelerates value recognition.

Case 3: India's Digital Patient Platforms

India's digital health networks now include patient communities that report medicine access issues in real time. These data influence procurement decisions at the state level.

Lesson: Patient data are not just feedback; they are a governance instrument.

Ethical Rebalancing – Patients as Citizens, Not Consumers

The access-first philosophy redefines patients not as customers but as citizens with rights and responsibilities in shaping health systems.

This view has deep ethical implications. It challenges the industry to move beyond customer satisfaction metrics toward public accountability.

Transparency in pricing, inclusion in trials, and fairness in access are not public relations strategies; they are obligations under a social contract that grants the pharmaceutical industry its legitimacy.

As one policymaker in Canada put it, "Patients don't owe the system gratitude. The system owes them clarity."

Practical Tools – Embedding Patient Centricity in Access Strategy

1. **The Patient Advisory Framework**

   Establish multi-disciplinary advisory boards with patients as equal decision-makers in study and policy design.

2. **The Value Narrative Map**

   Translate clinical endpoints into patient stories — showing how each metric changes daily life.

3. **Access Equity Dashboard**

   Monitor inclusion metrics across age, gender, geography, and income in real time.

4. **Transparency Charter**

   Publish patient-relevant pricing rationales and access commitments publicly.

5. **Lived Experience Audit**

   Use periodic patient panels to review not satisfaction, but lived barriers to access — transport, literacy, affordability.

   Each tool transforms empathy into evidence.

The Role of Trust

Trust is now the most valuable currency in healthcare. Without it, even the most effective therapy will struggle to achieve adoption.

Trust is built through honesty about uncertainty, responsiveness to feedback, and humility in communication.

Patients no longer expect perfection; they expect participation. The companies that share data, admit limits, and engage openly will earn enduring legitimacy.

As one patient advocate said during a roundtable on pricing transparency, "We don't mind if innovation takes time. We mind if we're left out of the conversation."

Case Reflection – The Oncology Forum in Paris

In 2027, a coalition of oncology patients and clinicians in France co-created a public "Access Charter" outlining what timely, equitable access should look like.

It defined clear expectations: maximum 90-day reimbursement decisions, mandatory early payer-patient dialogue, and open access to trial results.

Within two years, most major manufacturers voluntarily signed on.

Lesson: When patients write the charter, trust follows.

The New Definition of Success

The success metrics for pharmaceutical innovation are evolving.

- **Past:** Approval, revenue, and market share.
- **Present:** Real-world outcomes and payer acceptance.
- **Future:** Patient equity, trust, and continuity of care.

True success will be measured by how far the system closes the gap between discovery and delivery, between clinical potential and lived reality.

An access-first company understands that every therapy is a promise — and every delay a broken one.

Framework – The Access Human Impact Index

The **Access Human Impact Index (AHII)** helps organisations measure what truly matters: the human consequences of their performance.

Dimension	Metric	Example Indicator
Reach	Percentage of eligible patients treated.	Uptake by population segment.
Speed	Time from approval to first patient treated.	Median launch lag.
Equity	Distribution across socio-economic groups.	Regional access parity index.

Dimension	Metric	Example Indicator
Satisfaction	Patient-perceived improvement.	Quality-of-life score change.
Trust	Patient confidence in company transparency.	Public sentiment score.

Table 22.2 The Access Human Impact Index

Companies that track these indicators demonstrate not only accountability but humanity.

The Global Patient Perspective

Across the world, patient expectations are converging.

In Europe, advocacy groups demand transparency and sustainability.
In Africa, patients ask for infrastructure and dignity.
In Asia, they expect technology to close distance and cost gaps.
In Latin America, they call for inclusion in decision-making.

Despite differing contexts, the message is consistent: "Nothing about us without us" has moved from slogan to structure.

This global shift represents the most profound transformation in the history of the pharmaceutical industry — one where legitimacy flows from listening.

The Spiritual Core of Access

Every major transformation in medicine begins with a moral insight. In the 20th century, it was "do no harm." In the 21st, it is "leave no one behind."

Access-first innovation embodies that shift. It connects science with solidarity. It recognises that the worth of a therapy lies not only in how well it works in trials but in how widely it works in life.

This is not idealism. It is precision ethics — aligning incentives, systems, and empathy toward a common purpose.

When a therapy reaches every patient who can benefit, the entire system becomes not only efficient but just.

Key insight

Patient-centredness is not demonstrated through language or intent. It is revealed through outcomes. When access strategies succeed, patients experience care as timely, fair, and meaningful. When they fail, patients experience delay, exclusion, and frustration, regardless of how innovative the science may be.

Reflection

Think about how patients experience the systems you help design. Where do they encounter friction, delay, or opacity?

Notice whether those experiences are visible in decision making, or discussed only after problems emerge.

Try this

- Trace a patient journey from diagnosis to treatment for one therapy.
- Identify where access breaks down or slows.
- Ask which of those points are within organisational control.
- Reflect on how success would look from the patient's perspective.
- Consider how patient experience could be used as a design input.

Summary

- Patients experience outcomes, not intentions.
- Access defines whether innovation is meaningful.
- Delay and exclusion undermine trust.
- Patient-centredness must be operationalised.
- Systems reveal their values through access.
- The patient remains the ultimate measure of success.

Recognising the patient as the moral centre is necessary, but not sufficient. The final step is translating reflection into sustained action. The closing chapter focuses on how access-first thinking can be embedded, maintained, and renewed over time.

CHAPTER 23

FROM REFLECTION TO ACTION

"When access works well, it feels unremarkable.
That ordinariness is its greatest success."
Egbert Floppercough

Reflection alone does not sustain change. This final chapter focuses on how access-first thinking can be embedded, reinforced, and renewed over time. It frames access not as a programme or transformation initiative, but as an ongoing practice that requires stewardship, attention, and care.

Books can inspire, but systems only change when people act. The chapters before this one traced a familiar pattern of discovery, delay, and design, showing that access is not a technical function to be optimised at the end, but a shared moral and strategic responsibility shaped throughout development.

Now the task passes to you.

If you work in research, your challenge is to ask earlier how your discoveries will reach people, not just whether they can be proven. If you work in access, your challenge is to look beyond speed to approval and ask how far a therapy actually travels once it exists. If you lead teams, your challenge is to reward integration over control, curiosity over certainty, and evidence over assumption.

The appendices that follow are not an afterthought. They are a continuation of the argument, translating reflection into method. They contain practical frameworks, examples, and tools drawn from situations where good intentions met real-world constraint. Treat them not as checklists to complete, but as prompts to think differently about how decisions are made.

Access work is never finished. It evolves with every dataset, every policy shift, every clinical guideline, and every patient experience. That is what makes it difficult. It is also what gives it meaning.

Somewhere, right now, a patient is waiting for a medicine that exists but has not yet reached them. The next decision you make can shorten that distance. That is what access-first innovation truly means.

Key insight

Access-first thinking only endures when it becomes part of everyday practice. Without reinforcement through governance, incentives, and leadership behaviour, even strong commitments fade. Sustained access depends on stewardship, learning, and the willingness to revisit decisions as contexts change.

Reflection

Think about how change has unfolded in your organisation in the past. Which initiatives endured, and which quietly disappeared once attention moved elsewhere?

Notice whether access-related improvements are embedded in systems and routines, or whether they depend on individual effort and goodwill.

Try this

- Identify one access-first practice you want to sustain over time.
- Examine what currently reinforces it and what undermines it.

- Ask how governance, metrics, or incentives could support it more reliably.
- Reflect on who acts as steward when priorities shift.
- Consider what would make access-first thinking self-renewing rather than fragile.

Summary

- Access-first thinking requires active stewardship.
- Change fades without reinforcement.
- Governance and incentives shape behaviour more than intent.
- Learning must continue after implementation.
- Responsibility does not end with delivery.
- Access is a practice, not a destination.

Closing

There is no final chapter in access. Each decision reshapes what is possible next. The question is not whether uncertainty will persist, but whether we choose to navigate it deliberately, responsibly, and with patients firmly in view.

FRAMEWORKS INTRODUCED IN THIS BOOK

Framework / Model	Purpose	Core Components	Location
The Access Equation	Defines impact as innovation multiplied by adoption	Impact = Innovation × Adoption	Chapter 1
Access Maturity Matrix	Diagnoses organisational stage of access integration	Approval-first → Access-aware → Access-integrated → Access-first	Chapter 3
Continuous Learning Loop	Embeds lifecycle evidence adaptation	Insight → Evidence → Feedback → Adaptation	Chapter 5
Value–Affordability Matrix	Aligns pricing strategy with system capacity	Value potential vs affordability quadrants	Chapter 7
Early Payer Engagement Planner	Structures proactive payer dialogue	Advisory input → Scenario testing → Value rehearsal	Chapter 7
Equity Dashboard Framework	Measures real-world access readiness	Geographic, diagnostic, financial, knowledge, systemic equity	Chapter 8
Access-First Development Blueprint	Integrates innovation, evidence, and system design	Discovery-to-delivery integration model	Appendix B

GLOSSARY: ACCESS-FIRST INNOVATION

This glossary is designed for cross-functional readers.

- **Executives** can use it to align teams around a shared language.
- **Scientists and HEOR professionals** can use it to integrate economic reasoning early.
- **Policy experts and payers** can use it to understand how companies structure value demonstration.
- **Students and new entrants** can use it to navigate the complex vocabulary of modern access strategy.

Purpose: To clarify the essential terms, frameworks, and concepts introduced in the book for quick reference and cross-functional understanding.

Access-First Innovation

A development philosophy that designs evidence, pricing, and policy alignment from the start so that medicines reach patients faster and more fairly.

Access Metrics

Quantitative indicators used to measure how quickly and widely patients gain access to approved therapies, such as time-to-reimbursement, patient uptake, and equity of distribution.

Adaptive Pathways

Regulatory and evidence-generation approaches that allow staged approval based on early data, with additional evidence collected post-launch.

Affordability Threshold

The level of cost that a health system can sustain for a therapy without compromising other areas of care.

Amortised Payment Model

A financial structure where high one-off therapy costs are spread over several years to make budgets predictable.

Benchmark Pricing

A method that compares the price of a therapy to those of similar products or to international reference prices.

Clinical Endpoints

Measured outcomes used in clinical trials to determine whether a treatment works, such as survival rate or symptom reduction.

Comparator

The standard treatment or placebo against which a new therapy is tested in a clinical study.

Cost-Effectiveness Analysis (CEA)

An assessment comparing the cost of a therapy with its health outcomes, usually expressed as cost per QALY gained.

Coverage with Evidence Development (CED)

A reimbursement approach granting temporary access to a therapy while further data are collected.

Diagnostic Equity

Ensuring all patients can be tested or identified for treatment eligibility regardless of geography or resources.

Equity in Access

Fair distribution of healthcare resources so that all patients, regardless of income or location, can benefit from innovation.

Evidence Generation Plan (EGP)

A structured roadmap for collecting data across regulatory, payer, and real-world settings to demonstrate value.

Health Economics and Outcomes Research (HEOR)

The discipline that evaluates economic, clinical, and humanistic outcomes to inform pricing and access decisions.

Health Technology Assessment (HTA)

A formal evaluation by national or regional authorities that determines whether a therapy provides sufficient value for reimbursement.

Incremental Cost-Effectiveness Ratio (ICER)

A calculation comparing the difference in cost and outcomes between two therapies to determine value for money.

Managed Entry Agreement (MEA)

A contractual arrangement between a manufacturer and payer that allows access under specific conditions, often linked to performance or outcomes.

Market Access

The set of processes and negotiations that ensure a therapy is reimbursed, adopted, and used by patients after regulatory approval.

New Value Triangle

A framework introduced in this book describing how clinical, economic, and societal value must align for true healthcare impact.

Outcomes-Based Pricing

A payment approach where the price depends on the therapy's real-world results rather than its theoretical promise.

Payer

Any organisation that finances or reimburses the cost of healthcare, including national health systems, insurers, and social funds.

Patient-Reported Outcomes (PROs)

Data provided directly by patients about how a therapy affects their quality of life or daily function.

Precision Policy

The concept of tailoring reimbursement, pricing, and access rules as precisely as the therapies themselves, ensuring alignment between innovation and system readiness.

Pricing by Design

Integrating pricing strategy with evidence generation and payer input from early development stages.

Quality-Adjusted Life Year (QALY)

A measure combining length and quality of life used to assess the value of medical interventions.

Real-World Evidence (RWE)

Data on how a therapy performs outside controlled clinical trials, often drawn from electronic health records, registries, or insurance claims.

Regulatory Approval

The formal authorisation by a medicines agency (such as EMA or FDA) confirming that a therapy is safe and effective for use.

Reimbursement

The process by which a therapy's cost is covered by payers or health systems so patients can access it without direct payment.

Stakeholder Alignment

The process of creating shared understanding among regulators, payers, clinicians, and patients about a therapy's value and use.

Systemic Equity

The capacity of a health system to deliver consistent quality of care across different populations, regions, and income levels.

Tiered Pricing

A pricing strategy that adjusts cost according to a country's economic capacity to promote global affordability.

Value-Based Healthcare

An approach that links payment and performance to patient outcomes rather than volume of services delivered.

Value-by-Design Model

The three-part framework from Chapter 7 that integrates early definition of value, matching evidence, and joint pricing design.

Value-Affordability Matrix

A tool that plots therapy value against system affordability to guide realistic pricing and access strategies.

Value Dossier

A comprehensive document submitted to payers summarising clinical, economic, and quality-of-life evidence supporting reimbursement.

Willingness-to-Pay Threshold

The maximum amount a payer is prepared to spend per unit of health benefit, often expressed as a cost per QALY limit.

APPENDIX A – GLOBAL HTA AND PAYER LANDSCAPE SUMMARY

Purpose

This appendix provides a concise but practical overview of how major Health Technology Assessment (HTA) systems and payer frameworks operate across regions. It is designed to help teams anticipate access hurdles early in development and to align evidence generation with real-world decision criteria.

Introduction

HTA agencies now sit at the centre of access decisions worldwide. They evaluate not only whether a product works but whether it delivers value for money within constrained budgets.

Although regulatory approval confirms clinical efficacy and safety, HTA determines whether that innovation will translate into reimbursement and use.

Understanding the diversity of HTA systems is therefore essential to building an access-first strategy.

Key Themes

1. **Convergence and Divergence**
   While global principles of value-based assessment are converging,

methodologies remain divergent. The UK, Germany, and Australia have established frameworks; emerging markets are adapting hybrid models.

2. **Transparency and Participation**
Many HTA bodies now include public and patient representatives. Decision-making is gradually becoming more transparent, although processes and timelines still vary widely.

3. **Evidence Expectations**
Comparative effectiveness and real-world evidence are increasingly critical. Static clinical data alone no longer satisfy most HTA bodies.

4. **Economic and Societal Value**
The trend is shifting from narrow cost-effectiveness to broader measures of societal impact — productivity, equity, and quality of life.

Regional Overview

Region / Country	Key HTA Body	Core Focus	Distinctive Features
United Kingdom	NICE (National Institute for Health and Care Excellence)	Cost-effectiveness, quality-adjusted life years (QALYs), and affordability.	Patient input integrated via Citizens Council; highly transparent appraisal reports.
Germany	G-BA and IQWiG	Comparative benefit assessment and early benefit analysis (AMNOG).	Manufacturers must submit evidence within three months of launch; rapid timelines.
France	HAS (Haute Autorité de Santé)	Clinical benefit (SMR) and improvement (ASMR) ratings.	Determines price negotiations with CEPS; qualitative assessment of innovation.

Region / Country	Key HTA Body	Core Focus	Distinctive Features
Italy	AIFA	Clinical and economic value, budget impact, and regional alignment.	Dual central–regional structure; managed entry agreements widely used.
Spain	AEMPS and regional HTA agencies	Cost-effectiveness and budget impact.	Regional disparities remain; outcome-based contracts growing.
Sweden	TLV	Cost-effectiveness, ethical principles, and equity.	Incorporates ethical review explicitly; national reimbursement conditional on value.
Canada	CADTH and INESSS (Quebec)	Clinical effectiveness, economic modelling, and societal impact.	Increasing focus on patient-reported outcomes and disinvestment strategies.
United States	ICER (Institute for Clinical and Economic Review) and payers.	Cost-effectiveness benchmarking and value-based contracting.	Not binding but influential; outcomes-based pricing gaining traction.
Japan	Chuikyo and PMDA collaboration	Cost–benefit re-evaluation post-launch.	Pricing reassessed based on real-world performance.
Australia	PBAC	Cost-effectiveness and clinical need.	Structured, transparent deliberation; strong link between HTA and reimbursement.
China	NHSA and CMDE	National negotiation and cost–utility analysis.	Increasingly sophisticated HTA; price-volume agreements common.
Brazil	CONITEC	Cost-effectiveness and equity within SUS system.	Public consultation mandated; emphasis on equity and regional access.

Region / Country	Key HTA Body	Core Focus	Distinctive Features
South Africa	NEMLC and SAPHRA	Essential medicine inclusion and affordability.	Access policies aligned with universal health coverage goals.

Emerging Global Trends

1. **Integration of Real-World Evidence**
   More agencies now require post-launch data submission. RWE is evolving from optional to mandatory.
2. **Outcome-Based Reimbursement**
   Dynamic contracts linking payment to performance are expanding, particularly in oncology and rare diseases.
3. **Equity and Sustainability Criteria**
   HTA bodies are experimenting with multi-criteria frameworks that factor in equity, environmental impact, and innovation sustainability.
4. **International Collaboration**
   Joint assessments such as the EU's *EUnetHTA 21* and regional initiatives in Latin America aim to reduce duplication and harmonise methodology.

Implications for Access-First Strategy

- **Early HTA Dialogue:** Engage at least 18–24 months before submission to align endpoints and comparators.
- **Adaptive Dossier Design:** Build modular evidence packages that can evolve post-launch.
- **Real-World Readiness:** Plan data collection systems before approval.
- **Global Value Consistency:** Maintain a coherent narrative across markets while adapting for local context.

Access-first success depends on anticipation. Companies that map HTA requirements early will not only accelerate reimbursement but build trust as transparent partners.

Editorial Note

Appendix A translates the philosophy of access-first innovation into a practical understanding of how payers and HTA bodies shape real-world access. It shows that success depends as much on procedural fluency as on scientific proof. Knowing how the system decides is the first step to designing innovation that fits within it.

APPENDIX B – THE ACCESS-FIRST DEVELOPMENT BLUEPRINT

Purpose

This appendix provides a step-by-step framework for embedding access thinking into every stage of pharmaceutical development. It offers a structured model for aligning scientific, economic, and societal value from discovery through post-launch.

The blueprint can be used by R&D teams, Medical Affairs, HEOR, and Market Access functions as a shared reference point. Its purpose is to ensure that access is designed, not retrofitted.

1. **Introduction – From Pipeline to Pathway**

Traditional development follows a linear pipeline: discovery, clinical development, regulatory approval, launch.

The access-first approach replaces that with a **continuous pathway**—a cycle of learning where regulatory, payer, and patient insights inform design from the start.

This blueprint is built around five design pillars:

1. Early access integration
2. Evidence alignment
3. Economic validation

4. System readiness
5. Post-launch learning

Each pillar contains key actions, decision points, and deliverables that can be tracked across development milestones.

2. **Pillar One – Early Access Integration**

Objective: Make access a founding principle of every development programme, not an afterthought.

Key Actions:

- Appoint a cross-functional *Access Steering Group* before Phase I. Include representatives from Market Access, HEOR, Regulatory, Medical, and Clinical.
- Define target population and value hypotheses early, using payer and patient insights to prioritise outcomes.
- Conduct an *Access Feasibility Assessment* alongside the scientific feasibility study.

Deliverables:

- Early Access Map (outlining major payer expectations by region).
- Value Hypothesis Document linking anticipated outcomes to payer-relevant endpoints.
- Stakeholder Engagement Plan including payers, patients, and policymakers.

Decision Gate: Proceed to Phase I only when scientific and access feasibility are both confirmed.

Implementation Insight: Companies that formalise access governance early report up to 40 percent shorter reimbursement timelines post-approval.

3. **Pillar Two – Evidence Alignment**

Objective: Design clinical programmes that generate both regulatory and payer-relevant evidence.

Key Actions:

- Align endpoints with HTA and payer priorities.
- Incorporate health resource utilisation, quality-of-life, and real-world data capture mechanisms in pivotal studies.
- Use simulation models to test how trial results will perform in HTA assessments.

Deliverables:

- Integrated Evidence Plan (regulatory, clinical, economic).
- Payer-aligned Endpoint Catalogue.
- Real-World Data Readiness Checklist.

Decision Gate: Phase II progression contingent on evidence plan endorsement by Market Access and HEOR leads.

Best Practice Example: An immunology company redesigned its Phase IIb trial after simulated HTA reviews revealed gaps in cost-effectiveness data. This led to a stronger value proposition and reduced post-launch negotiation time by nine months.

4. **Pillar Three – Economic Validation**

Objective: Embed health economics, pricing, and affordability analysis into the design of clinical and commercial strategy.

Key Actions:

- Build early economic models using available efficacy and epidemiology data.
- Test different price–value scenarios through payer advisory boards.
- Conduct budget impact simulations across priority markets.

Deliverables:

- Preliminary Cost-Effectiveness Model.
- Pricing Scenarios Report with elasticity analysis.
- Payer Feedback Summary.

Decision Gate: Phase III initiation conditional on confirmed economic feasibility across target markets.

Common Pitfall: Waiting until Phase III to begin pricing discussions leads to misaligned expectations and reimbursement delays.

Humour note: "If your first conversation with payers happens after approval, you're not late — you're irrelevant."

5. **Pillar Four – System Readiness**

Objective: Ensure that the healthcare system can deliver the therapy effectively at launch.

Key Actions:

- Map system capacity: diagnostics, infrastructure, workforce, logistics.
- Identify potential bottlenecks (cold chain, testing, referral pathways).
- Co-develop solutions with local partners (training, equipment, digital tools).
- Build patient support programmes that address non-clinical barriers (travel, literacy, financial).

Deliverables:

- System Readiness Report.
- Infrastructure Partnership Plan.
- Patient Access Programme Design.

Decision Gate: Market preparation complete only when delivery capability matches expected demand.

Example: A cell therapy manufacturer created pre-launch hospital certification programmes in 12 countries. By launch day, 80 percent of sites were already authorised to administer treatment, avoiding the typical one-year lag.

6. **Pillar Five – Post-Launch Learning**

Objective: Treat launch as the start of continuous learning, not the end of development.

Key Actions:

- Establish post-launch evidence systems linking patient outcomes, utilisation, and cost data.
- Use adaptive contracting models (e.g. managed entry or outcomes-based agreements).
- Integrate real-world evidence into future label updates and pricing renegotiations.
- Deliverables:
- Post-Launch Learning Framework.
- Data-Sharing Agreements with payers and health systems.
- Real-World Outcomes Dashboard.

Decision Gate: Annual review of access KPIs — coverage, equity, affordability, satisfaction — as part of corporate performance reporting.

Insight: The most successful access-first companies treat post-launch data not as compliance but as strategy. Continuous evidence sustains continuous access.

7. **The Access-First Development Blueprint in Practice**

Stage	**Traditional Focus**	**Access-First Focus**	**Key Outputs**
Discovery	Biological novelty	Value and population need	Value hypothesis and early access map
Preclinical	Proof of concept	Proof of relevance	Early cost-effectiveness model
Phase I	Safety	Feasibility of delivery	Access Steering Group activation
Phase II	Efficacy	Payer-aligned endpoints	Integrated evidence plan

Stage	Traditional Focus	Access-First Focus	Key Outputs
Phase III	Confirmation	Validation of value and affordability	HTA-ready data package
Submission	Regulatory approval	Access feasibility confirmation	Modular submission dossier
Launch	Commercialisation	System readiness and equity	Access toolkit and affordability programmes
Post-Launch	Sales tracking	Real-world outcomes and trust	Continuous evidence dashboard

Takeaway:

Each development phase contributes not only data for regulators but evidence for society. Access-first design turns development into a social contract — transparent, evidence-based, and equitable.

8. **Governance Framework for Access-First Organisations**

An access-first organisation requires formal governance to sustain cross-functional collaboration.

Governance Model:

- **Access Board:** Executive-level body overseeing integration of clinical, economic, and access strategies.
- **Evidence Integration Committee:** Ensures data generation aligns with payer and patient needs.
- **Equity and Ethics Subgroup:** Reviews global launch plans for fairness and sustainability.

Performance Metrics:

- Time from approval to reimbursement (median and range).
- Patient reach rate (% of eligible population treated within first year).
- Equity index (variation across socioeconomic or regional groups).
- RWE integration score (frequency and quality of post-launch updates).

Governance sustains culture. Without it, access-first intent dissolves into rhetoric.

9. **Practical Toolkit**

To apply the blueprint, teams can use the following practical tools:

1. **Access Readiness Checklist**
   - Have we defined payer-relevant outcomes?
   - Have patient representatives reviewed the design?
   - Do pricing and affordability models exist for all major markets?
   - Have infrastructure constraints been assessed?
   - Is a post-launch learning system in place?
2. **Access Integration Timeline**
   A visual roadmap aligning clinical, economic, and system milestones.
3. **Cross-Functional Review Template**
   Used to review alignment at each phase gate.
4. **Access KPI Dashboard**
   Monitors key metrics: coverage, speed, equity, trust.

Each tool ensures that access is embedded into everyday operations, not just strategy documents.

10. **Summary**

The Access-First Development Blueprint is not a theoretical model. It is a management system for connecting innovation to impact.

By aligning R&D, evidence generation, and market access from the start, companies can shorten time to patient access, improve payer confidence, and reduce post-launch uncertainty.

An access-first product is not just approved — it is used, trusted, and sustained.

Editorial Note

Appendix B converts the Access-First philosophy into an operational guide. It shows that designing for access requires not more process, but smarter process — where scientific curiosity and societal responsibility move in parallel. In the end, access-first development is not about slowing science down; it is about ensuring it lands where it matters.

APPENDIX C – CASE COMPENDIUM OF ACCESS-FIRST SUCCESSES

Purpose

This compendium highlights real cases where companies achieved faster, fairer access through early alignment of evidence, economics, and ethics. The aim is not to celebrate perfect examples, but to show that success in access is possible when design replaces defence.

Each example has been anonymised for confidentiality, but the insights are drawn from published case studies, HTA assessments, and direct project experience across Europe, Asia, and the Americas.

Case 1 – The Adaptive Oncology Launch

Challenge:

A cancer therapy showed exceptional early clinical promise but carried high uncertainty about long-term outcomes. The traditional route would have been to delay market entry until all data matured, but that would have postponed patient access by years.

Action:

The company pursued early dialogue with regulators and HTA agencies in Germany, France, and the UK. They co-created an adaptive access plan that included conditional reimbursement linked to a five-year registry and annual data reviews.

Outcome:

The therapy reached patients 18 months earlier than forecast. Real-world evidence confirmed durable survival benefits, allowing the therapy to transition smoothly to permanent reimbursement.

Lesson:

Early engagement replaces speculation with structure. Regulators and payers are more willing to accept uncertainty when there is a credible plan to reduce it.

Case 2 – The Real-World Vaccine Revolution

Challenge:

A global vaccine manufacturer wanted to expand coverage in low- and middle-income countries but faced infrastructure and affordability barriers.

Action:

The company partnered with international donors and local ministries to introduce solar-powered cold-chain storage, pooled procurement models, and outcome-based payment contracts linked to coverage rates.

Outcome:

Vaccination rates in target regions rose by 45 percent within two years. Cold-chain wastage fell by 70 percent. The approach became a blueprint for future roll-outs by other manufacturers.

Lesson:

Access-first innovation is not just about new molecules; it is about solving the conditions that block delivery.

Case 3 – Early HEOR in Immunology

Challenge:

A new immunology therapy targeted a chronic condition with high prevalence but variable payer perceptions of value. Past launches in the category had struggled due to narrow clinical endpoints and unclear economic impact.

Action:

HEOR specialists were embedded in the Phase II design process. The team modelled cost savings from reduced hospitalisations and work productivity gains. They also aligned endpoints with HTA expectations in five European markets.

Outcome:

Reimbursement was granted in record time. Payers cited "clarity and relevance of data" as decisive factors. The therapy's adoption curve outperformed internal projections by 40 percent.

Lesson:

Economic insight belongs in the protocol, not in the PowerPoint.

Case 4 – Patient Pathway Co-Design in Rare Diseases

Challenge:

A gene therapy for a rare metabolic disorder required complex diagnostic and referral processes. Even after approval, uptake was minimal because most clinicians did not know how to identify or refer eligible patients.

Action:

The company co-designed the access pathway with patient groups and referral centres. They funded diagnostic awareness campaigns, streamlined genetic testing logistics, and created "access navigators" who supported clinicians and families through the process.

Outcome:

Patient identification rates quadrupled. The therapy moved from theoretical availability to tangible treatment within months.

Lesson:

Access begins when systems are designed for the people who use them, not for the people who present them at conferences.

Case 5 – Managed Entry Agreement in Cardiology

Challenge:

A novel cardiovascular treatment delivered unprecedented efficacy but raised payer concern over long-term affordability.

Action:

The manufacturer negotiated a managed entry agreement with payers across three European countries. Reimbursement was conditional on real-world outcome reporting through national registries.

Outcome:

The therapy gained coverage in record time. Real-world data confirmed cost savings through reduced hospital admissions, leading to permanent reimbursement and an expanded indication.

Lesson:

Shared risk builds shared confidence. Evidence gathered jointly is trusted collectively.

Case 6 – Tiered Pricing and Health Equity

Challenge:

A curative antiviral therapy was unaffordable for lower-income regions despite major public-health need.

Action:

The company implemented a tiered pricing framework based on GDP and health-system capacity. They also established voluntary licensing agreements for local generic production in selected countries.

Outcome:

Over five million patients gained access within three years. Global disease burden declined dramatically, and the programme became a case study in equitable pricing.

Lesson:

Equity is good economics. Long-term trust and reputation are worth more than short-term margins.

Case 7 – Diagnostic Partnerships in Precision Oncology

Challenge:

A targeted therapy required advanced genomic testing, available only in limited laboratories.

Action:

The manufacturer built a global diagnostic consortium to subsidise testing, train local staff, and standardise reporting. The programme included technology transfer to developing markets.

Outcome:

Testing availability expanded from 20 to 120 centres in two years. Eligible patient identification increased by 300 percent.

Lesson:

A therapy is only as strong as the diagnostic system that supports it.

Case 8 – The Telehealth Turnaround

Challenge:

A diabetes monitoring programme used a digital app for data collection, but rural patients lacked reliable internet or digital literacy.

Action:

The company redesigned its monitoring system to include paper-based options, SMS reporting, and nurse-led home visits.

Outcome:

Patient participation doubled. Clinical outcomes improved, and satisfaction among clinicians rose.

Lesson:

Inclusion is a design choice. Simplicity often beats sophistication.

Case 9 – The Local Manufacturing Pivot

Challenge:

A biologic therapy relied on fragile international supply chains that caused repeated stock-outs in several regions.

Action:

The company invested in regional manufacturing hubs and public-private partnerships for quality control and logistics management.

Outcome:

Lead times shortened by 60 percent, and product wastage fell dramatically. Governments publicly praised the model as a sustainable innovation policy.

Lesson:

Supply resilience is the most underrated form of access planning.

Case 10 – The Payer Collaboration Platform

Challenge:

Multiple companies were submitting similar therapies for the same indication, leading to payer fatigue and inconsistent evaluations.

Action:

A consortium of manufacturers created a joint pre-submission platform with national HTA bodies to harmonise evidence standards and align comparator choices before trials were finalised.

Outcome:

All participating companies benefited from reduced redundancy, faster reviews, and more consistent decisions.

Lesson:

Collaboration among competitors can accelerate access for all when the shared goal is patient benefit.

Case 11 – The Equity Metrics Pilot

Challenge:

A multinational company wanted to make equity measurable rather than rhetorical.

Action:

They developed an "Equity Scorecard" that tracked regional uptake, diagnostic coverage, and socioeconomic disparity across launches. The data were shared publicly in annual sustainability reports.

Outcome:

Policymakers recognised the transparency as leadership. Internally, the scorecard guided resource allocation toward underserved areas.

Lesson:

What gets measured gets improved — and trusted.

Case 12 – The Early Advice Alliance

Challenge:

An early-stage biotech lacked experience engaging with payers and regulators simultaneously.

Action:

They joined a joint scientific advice pilot involving EMA, FDA, and multiple HTA bodies. The resulting guidance reshaped their development plan, integrating health-economic endpoints and real-world data collection from the outset.

Outcome:

When the product reached submission, both regulators and payers were already familiar with the evidence plan. Reimbursement followed within six months of approval.

Lesson:

Joint advice compresses timelines and builds alignment. The best way to avoid rejection is to invite feedback early.

Case 13 – The Real-World Registry that Redefined Value

Challenge:

An orphan therapy faced scepticism from payers due to small trial size and limited long-term data.

Action:

The company co-created an independent patient registry, jointly governed by clinicians, payers, and patient advocates. The registry collected quality-of-life and utilisation data in real time.

Outcome:

Within two years, the therapy's perceived value increased significantly. Reimbursement expanded to additional markets, and the registry became a model for future launches.

Lesson:

Transparency transforms uncertainty into evidence.

Thematic Analysis – Patterns of Success

Across these examples, three success patterns appear consistently:

1. **Early Alignment** – Access success correlates strongly with payer and patient engagement before Phase III.
2. **System Readiness** – Infrastructure, diagnostics, and logistics determine how quickly a therapy moves from approval to use.
3. **Evidence Transparency** – Open sharing of real-world outcomes builds credibility and resilience.

The companies that achieve sustainable access are those that treat it as an organisational discipline, not a department.

Framework Synthesis – The Five Rules of Access-First Success

1. **Start Early:** Involve payers, patients, and HTA experts from concept to launch.
2. **Design Evidence Around Value:** Align endpoints and data collection with what matters to health systems.
3. **Build the Bridge, Not Just the Drug:** Prepare diagnostics, delivery, and digital pathways before approval.
4. **Share Risk and Credit:** Use adaptive pricing, outcome-based contracts, and shared data platforms.
5. **Measure Equity:** Track who benefits, not only how many.

Access is not a promise; it is proof of design.

Editorial Note

Appendix C grounds the book's philosophy in practice. These cases prove that access-first innovation is achievable when companies think systemically, plan collaboratively, and lead ethically. Every successful example began with the same question: *Who will actually receive this treatment, and how?*

When that question drives decision-making, innovation stops being theoretical and starts being human.

APPENDIX D – TOOLS & TEMPLATES

Purpose

Key Question: What can you use tomorrow? The appendices contain practical tools, templates, dashboards, and real-world case compendia to translate the Access-First approach into daily use.

Tool 1 – The Access Readiness Checklist

Purpose:

A rapid diagnostic tool for assessing whether a programme or asset is access-ready across evidence, economics, and system preparedness.

When to Use:

Before governance reviews, Phase II or Phase III design decisions, or major launch planning meetings.

Checklist:

Domain	Key Questions	Yes / No / Action Required
Evidence Fit	Do endpoints reflect what payers and clinicians value?	
Comparator Alignment	Is the trial comparator relevant to real-world clinical practice?	
Economic Validity	Have early cost-effectiveness models been built and tested?	
Payer Dialogue	Have HTA or payer bodies been consulted pre-Phase III?	

Domain	Key Questions	Yes / No / Action Required
System Readiness	Have we mapped infrastructure, workforce, and diagnostic capacity?	
Equity Consideration	Have geographic, socioeconomic, and literacy barriers been assessed?	
Post-Launch Learning	Is a real-world evidence system in place to monitor outcomes?	

How to Apply:

Run the checklist quarterly. Highlight red zones (No) and assign owners and timelines for resolution.

Tip:

When teams score themselves honestly, this checklist becomes a strategic advantage rather than an audit tool.

Tool 2 – The Access Integration Map

Purpose:

A planning template showing where each function contributes to access outcomes along the product lifecycle.

Stage	Primary Function	Access Role	Key Deliverables
Discovery	R&D	Identify unmet need and define population value hypothesis.	Early access concept note.
Preclinical	Market Access / HEOR	Test early pricing assumptions and economic feasibility.	Draft cost-effectiveness model.
Phase I	Regulatory / Clinical	Ensure protocol includes data relevant to payers and clinicians.	Early evidence plan.
Phase II	HEOR / Medical Affairs	Align endpoints with HTA standards and real-world relevance.	Integrated data collection plan.

Stage	Primary Function	Access Role	Key Deliverables
Phase III	Market Access / Payer Relations	Prepare submissions, value dossiers, and early engagement sessions.	HTA briefing materials.
Launch	Access and Commercial	Implement affordability programmes, system support, and training.	Market access toolkit.
Post-Launch	Medical / HEOR	Monitor adoption, outcomes, and equity metrics.	Annual access performance report.

Application:

Use during programme governance meetings to visualise integration gaps and reassign resources proactively.

Tool 3 – The Value–Affordability Matrix

Purpose:

To evaluate whether pricing and value perception are aligned with system affordability and budget impact.

How It Works:

Plot therapies along two axes — **Perceived Value** (clinical, societal) and **Affordability** (payer capacity, budget sustainability).

	Low Barriers	High Barriers
High Value	Optimise education and logistics to speed adoption.	Prioritise affordability models and managed entry.
Low Value	Maintain efficiency, monitor fit.	Reassess viability before scaling.

Example Application:

A cardiovascular therapy with strong long-term data but high short-term costs would fall into the top-right quadrant — "High Value, High Barriers." It would require creative payment models, phased launches, or annuity contracts.

Practical Tip:

Plot products quarterly and colour-code by region to visualise where affordability mismatches are emerging.

Tool 4 – The Early Payer Engagement Planner

Purpose:

To structure payer engagement before and during clinical development.

Stage	Objective	Engagement Type	Outputs
Pre–Phase II	Define payer expectations for endpoints and comparators.	Informal consultation or advisory board.	Early Payer Landscape Report.
Phase II	Validate clinical assumptions and identify evidence gaps.	Scientific advice meeting with HTA bodies.	Integrated evidence roadmap.
Phase III	Test preliminary cost-effectiveness models.	Joint HTA–industry workshop.	Payer-informed pricing scenarios.
Pre-Launch	Align reimbursement dossier structure and negotiation plan.	Policy and payer alignment meetings.	Final value proposition and response matrix.
Post-Launch	Maintain trust through data sharing.	Outcomes-based partnership review.	Updated evidence package.

Rule of Thumb:

If the first formal payer interaction happens after Phase III results, you are at least 18 months late.

Tool 5 – The Evidence Alignment Grid

Purpose:

To ensure data generation covers all decision-makers — regulators, payers, clinicians, and patients.

Stakeholder	Decision Criteria	Required Evidence	Timing
Regulators	Safety and efficacy.	Phase III RCTs.	Pre-approval.
Payers / HTA	Comparative effectiveness, cost-effectiveness, equity.	RCT + real-world data, budget models.	Pre- and post-approval.
Clinicians	Clinical relevance, usability.	Practical endpoints, peer education.	Continuous.
Patients	Quality of life, convenience, equity.	PROs, real-world feedback.	Continuous.

How to Use:

Plot each stakeholder's evidence expectations at programme start and verify at each phase gate. Update regularly as priorities evolve.

Tool 6 – The System Readiness Audit

Purpose:

To test whether the health system is capable of delivering a new therapy equitably and safely.

Key Components:

1. Diagnostic capacity (availability, turnaround time, affordability).
2. Infrastructure (equipment, storage, distribution).
3. Workforce (trained staff, regional availability).
4. Patient logistics (travel distance, support services).
5. Digital readiness (registries, interoperability).

Scoring Template (1–5 scale):

Dimension	Score	Action Plan
Diagnostics		
Infrastructure		
Workforce		
Patient Logistics		
Digital Readiness		

Interpretation:

Scores below 3 indicate a red flag requiring investment or partnership before launch.

Tool 7 – The Equity Dashboard

Purpose:

To monitor whether access is equitable across geography, demographics, and socioeconomic groups.

Example Metrics:

- Percentage of eligible patients treated by region.
- Diagnostic coverage rate (urban vs rural).
- Time-to-treatment disparity index.
- Adherence variance by income quartile.
- Patient satisfaction by literacy group.

Template Output:

Equity Dimension	Indicator	Baseline	Target	Current	Status
Geographic	% of patients treated (urban vs rural)	45%	80%	65%	⚠ Moderate

Equity Dimension	Indicator	Baseline	Target	Current	Status
Diagnostic	Test turnaround time	21 days	10 days	12 days	✅ On track
Financial	Cost to patient (non-drug)	£220	£100	£160	⚠ Delayed
Literacy	Understanding of treatment plan	70%	90%	80%	✅ On track

Insight:

When displayed quarterly, this dashboard transforms equity from aspiration to performance.

Tool 8 – The Continuous Learning Loop

Purpose:

To integrate post-launch data back into development and policy strategy.

Cycle Step	Key Activities	Output
Data Capture	Gather RWE from registries, claims, and patient reports.	Updated datasets.
Insight Generation	Analyse clinical, economic, and societal outcomes.	Real-world value dashboards.
Review	Conduct cross-functional access review.	Prioritised improvement plan.
Adaptation	Adjust pricing, guidelines, or study design.	Updated payer and policy engagement.
Recycle	Feed insights into future asset planning.	Institutional learning.

Outcome:

This loop turns every launch into a learning platform — the hallmark of an access-first organisation.

Tool 9 – The Access KPI Catalogue

Purpose:

To standardise performance measurement for access-first organisations.

Example KPIs:

- Time from approval to first reimbursement.
- Percentage of target population treated within 12 months.
- Number of HTA submissions aligned with payer feedback.
- Payer satisfaction (qualitative scoring).
- Proportion of launches using outcome-based models.
- Post-launch data update frequency.
- Equity gap index (variation in reach).

Application:

Embed these KPIs into annual business scorecards and tie leadership bonuses to patient reach, not just revenue.

Tool 10 – The Access Leadership Conversation Guide

Purpose:

To help senior leaders and teams frame strategic discussions around access alignment.

Five Core Questions for Every Decision:

1. Who decides whether this therapy is used?
2. What evidence will they trust most?
3. What uncertainty will they fear most?
4. How can we reduce that uncertainty before launch?
5. How will we measure adoption after approval?

Tip:

Ask these questions early and often. They take less than ten minutes to discuss but prevent years of delay.

Summary

Access-first thinking succeeds when teams have tools that translate principle into practice.

Each of these templates is simple by design — because complexity is not the measure of rigour. Consistency, curiosity, and coordination are.

When organisations apply these tools systematically, they replace chance with structure and build the muscle memory that turns innovation into impact.

Editorial Note

Appendix D provides the operational backbone of *Access-First Innovation*. It is not a library of forms but a library of habits.

Used well, these tools make access-first thinking visible — in plans, dashboards, and decisions.

Used poorly, they become paperwork.

The difference lies not in the templates but in the intent: whether the goal is to complete a checklist or to reach a patient.

REFERENCES AND FURTHER READING (2026 EDITION)

Purpose: To provide the verified research base behind every framework and idea in this book, including key regulatory, policy, and academic sources for continued learning.

Section 1: Foundational Frameworks and Policy Sources

1. **European Medicines Agency (EMA)** – *Parallel Consultation Guidance for Health Technology Assessment (HTA) and Regulatory Advice* (2024 Update).
   A key document formalising the joint advice process between regulators and HTA agencies. Explains the mechanism for aligning clinical evidence generation with payer requirements.
2. **U.S. Food and Drug Administration (FDA)** – *Framework for the Real-World Evidence Program* (2023).
   Defines standards for using real-world data in regulatory submissions and post-market surveillance. Provides guidance for evidence credibility and transparency.
3. **World Health Organization (WHO)** – *Fair Pricing Forum: Global Policy Framework for Equitable Access* (2024).
   Outlines international principles on fair pricing, transparency, and affordability in global health innovation.
4. **National Institute for Health and Care Excellence (NICE)** – *Methods Guide for Technology Appraisal* (2022, ongoing updates).
   Details methodological requirements for cost-effectiveness

modelling, comparator selection, and evidence assessment in the UK context.

5. **OECD Health Division** – *Value-Based Health Systems: Policy Pathways for Sustainable Innovation* (2023).
   Examines how OECD countries are integrating value-based payment models and performance-linked reimbursement.
6. **European Commission** – *Pharmaceutical Strategy for Europe* (2023).
   Focuses on regulatory harmonisation, equitable access, and the future role of digital health in market access.
7. **World Bank** – *Health Systems Under Pressure: Infrastructure and Access in the Post-COVID Era* (2024).
   Offers comparative data on diagnostic and treatment infrastructure across income levels and its relationship with equity outcomes.

Section 2: Key Academic and Industry Studies

1. Towse A, Garrison L. *Can We Make It Work? Managed Entry Agreements in Europe and Beyond* (Health Economics Review, 2022).
   A comprehensive analysis of outcomes-based and risk-sharing agreements in practice, highlighting both successes and pitfalls.
2. Wenzl M, Chapman S. *Performance-Based Managed Entry Agreements for New Medicines in OECD and EU Countries* (OECD, 2019; referenced widely through 2025).
   Maps the evolution of managed entry models and the growing demand for outcome-linked payments.
3. Drummond M, Augustovski F. *Economic Evaluation in Healthcare: Integrating Value, Affordability, and Equity* (Value in Health, 2023).
   A modernised view of cost-effectiveness analysis incorporating distributional impacts and societal preferences.

4. Sussex J, Mestre-Ferrandiz J. *Bridging Innovation and Access: The Role of Early Health Technology Assessment* (Office of Health Economics, 2022).
Presents frameworks for integrating payer perspectives into R&D before Phase III.

5. Claxton K, Briggs A. *Decision Modelling for Health Economic Evaluation* (Oxford University Press, 2023).
Core text for HEOR professionals on model building, uncertainty analysis, and real-world data integration.

6. Lehoux P, Silva HP. *Responsible Innovation in Health: Conceptual Foundations and Global Applications* (Cambridge University Press, 2023).
Discusses the societal dimension of innovation and how access, equity, and legitimacy underpin sustainable R&D.

7. Sorenson C, Chalkidou K. *Global Health Technology Assessment: Evidence, Ethics, and Policy in Practice* (World Health Organization and London School of Economics, 2023).
Global review of HTA frameworks and how they are evolving to include ethical and equity considerations.

Section 3: Case Studies and Industry Reports

1. **EFPIA (European Federation of Pharmaceutical Industries and Associations)** – *Patients Waiting: Benchmarking Access to Medicines in Europe* (2024).
Annual comparative analysis of access timelines, identifying bottlenecks between approval and reimbursement.

2. **IQVIA Institute for Human Data Science** – *The Global Use of Medicines Report 2025*.
Data-driven overview of access trends, launch sequencing, and affordability across markets.

3. **Pharma Innovation Index** (IDEA Pharma, 2024).
Ranks companies not only by pipeline strength but by real-world adoption and access outcomes.

4. **National Health Council (US)** – *Patient-Centred Value Framework 2.0* (2023).
Expands traditional HTA methodologies to integrate patient experience and equity impact.

5. **Access to Medicine Foundation** – *Access to Medicine Index 2024.*
Evaluates global pharmaceutical companies' performance on equitable access strategies, pricing transparency, and capacity building.

6. **McKinsey & Company** – *Bridging the Access Gap: How Pharma Can Redefine Success* (2024).
Analysis of access-first organisational models and the shift from compliance to capability in global market access.

7. **Deloitte Centre for Health Solutions** – *The Future of Value in Life Sciences* (2025).
Discusses how digital evidence, predictive analytics, and AI are redefining payer–manufacturer relationships.

Section 4: Digital Health, AI, and Real-World Data

1. European Medicines Agency – *Guideline on Artificial Intelligence in Medicinal Product Development* (2025).
Sets expectations for AI-assisted trial design, decision support, and ethical governance.

2. U.S. FDA – *Good Machine Learning Practice (GMLP) for Medical and Pharmaceutical Applications* (2023).
Framework for trustworthy AI across clinical and regulatory workflows.

3. Digital Medicine Society (DiMe) – *The Playbook for Digital Endpoint Development* (2023).
Practical guide for integrating digital biomarkers and remote monitoring into trials.

4. Real-World Evidence Alliance – *Operationalising Real-World Data for Regulatory and Payer Decision-Making* (2024).
Step-by-step playbook for credible RWE generation and sharing.

5. World Economic Forum – *AI and Health Equity: Building Inclusive Innovation Ecosystems* (2024).
   Explores how AI-driven tools can reduce or exacerbate access inequities globally.

Section 5: Equity, Ethics, and Patient Engagement

1. Marmot M. *The Health Gap: The Challenge of an Unequal World* (2023 Edition).
   Seminal text linking socioeconomic inequality to health outcomes, widely cited in global policy.
2. Global Health Council – *Equity by Design: Practical Frameworks for Inclusive Access Programmes* (2024).
   A pragmatic guide for embedding equity metrics in product development and delivery strategies.
3. Patient Focused Medicines Development (PFMD) – *Patient Engagement Quality Guidance* (2022).
   Benchmark for meaningful and measurable patient involvement throughout the product lifecycle.
4. European Patients' Academy (EUPATI) – *Toolkit for Patient Involvement in Medicines Research and Development* (2023).
   Offers concrete tools for involving patients in clinical and policy decision-making.
5. Global Bioethics Forum – *Innovation and Equity in the Genomic Era* (2024).
   Discusses fairness, data sovereignty, and representation in global research.

Section 6: Recommended Reading for Practitioners

These resources are recommended for professionals applying access-first principles in daily practice. They blend strategic, operational, and cultural perspectives.

- TT. Akiwumi, *How to Lead when You're Not the Boss: Influence Without Authority* (2026).
- J. Porter, *Building Market Access Excellence* (2024).
- A. Talmor, *From Efficacy to Impact: The New Language of Value in Pharma* (2023).
- TT. Akiwumi, *Tales of Innovation, Illusion, and Patient Access to Medicines* (2025).
- P. Hawkes, *Rethinking Reimbursement: The New Economics of Adoption* (2024).
- G. Lewis, *The Health Systems Innovator's Handbook* (2023).
- M. Greer, *How to Design Access Metrics That Matter* (2025).
- C. Garrison, *The Payer Perspective: Balancing Evidence, Economics, and Ethics* (2024).
- J. Pita, *The Science of Access: Lessons from Global Implementation* (2025).

Section 7: Online Resources and Networks

For readers seeking practical tools, dialogue, or collaboration opportunities:

- **Access Observatory (www.accessobservatory.org):** Public platform tracking global access initiatives and outcomes.
- **HTAi (Health Technology Assessment International):** Global network advancing HTA and access science.
- **Ispor.org:** International Society for Pharmacoeconomics and Outcomes Research – key hub for HEOR and access innovation.
- **WHO Fair Pricing Forum:** Repository of policy papers and stakeholder updates on pricing equity.
- **Access Leaders Network (Substack and LinkedIn Group):** Community of professionals implementing access-first strategies across regions.

- **The Digital Health & RWE Alliance:** International initiative promoting credible digital endpoints and data transparency.

Closing Note

Access-first innovation depends on constant learning. The references above represent only a snapshot of an evolving field where science, policy, and ethics meet.

Readers are encouraged to use this list not as an academic appendix but as a **navigation guide**, a set of signposts pointing toward the frontier of evidence-based, equitable healthcare.

The most important reference of all, however, remains the patient, who is the ultimate validator of whether innovation truly delivers impact.

- HTAi. *Global Policy Forum Report 2024: Evidence, Trust, and Transparency.* https://htai.org
- WHO. *Global Health Data Governance Framework.* 2023.
- OECD. *Pharmaceutical Pricing and Reimbursement Policies in a Changing Environment.* 2023. DOI 10.1787/9789264939238-en

Narrative and Cultural Perspectives on Pharma Innovation

- **Akiwumi TT.** *Egbert Floppercough and The Chronicles of Pharma: Tales of Innovation, Illusion and Patient Access to Medicines.* Independent Press, London, 2025.
- **Akiwumi TT.** *The Same Molecule: Two Different Fates – How Mindset, Strategy and Culture Decide the Destiny of a Drug.* Access-First Publishing, London, 2025.
- Bloor D. *Knowledge and Social Imagery.* 2nd ed., University of Chicago Press, 1991.

- Marks HM. *The Progress of Experiment: Science and Therapeutic Reform in the United States, 1900-1990.* Cambridge University Press, 1997.
- Petty J, Kitson A. *Narrative and Sensemaking in Health Innovation. Soc Sci Med* 2024; 333: 116123. DOI 10.1016/j.socscimed.2023.116123

Chapters 13–22

(As already listed: Kolb 2015; Schön 1983; EUPATI 2023; Domecq 2014; Staniszewska 2017; Gerber 2024; WHO Europe 2024, etc.)

ABOUT THE AUTHOR

I work at the intersection of pharmaceutical development, market access, and health policy, and throughout my career I have helped organisations close the gap between scientific innovation and real-world patient access by working across R & D, health economics, medical affairs, and payer engagement where strategy, evidence, and decision making meet.

My work centres on designing evidence plans, organisational models, and decision processes that enable faster, fairer, and more sustainable access to medicines, with a particular focus on how early development choices shape downstream outcomes and how leadership behaviour influences access decisions under uncertainty.

This book draws on practical experience across multiple therapy areas and health systems rather than reflecting a single organisation or geography, and I wrote it for people responsible for turning scientific promise into real-world use because I believe innovation only matters when it reaches the people it was made for.

Thankfully, more people across the industry are coming to the same view, but this book is intended to move that shared understanding from passive agreement to deliberate, proactive action.

ACKNOWLEDGEMENTS

This book would not exist without the patience, generosity, and support of many remarkable people.

I am deeply grateful to Anthony J. Yanni, MD, MBA, Founder and Chief Executive Officer of Lucid Health Solutions, for his generosity in contributing the foreword to this book. His leadership in advancing patient-centred healthcare and his longstanding commitment to strategic innovation have been both instructive and inspiring.

To my friends, colleagues, mentors, and collaborators across the pharmaceutical industry, thank you for your honesty, insight, and time. The conversations we shared and the experiences you described have shaped this book in ways that extend far beyond the page. Your willingness to speak openly about both triumphs and frustrations has reminded me that progress in our field is built as much on resilience as on brilliance.

I also wish to acknowledge the patient advocates, healthcare professionals, payers, and regulators whose perspectives have grounded this project in its true purpose. You reminded me, time and again, that the measure of innovation is not in the molecule itself but in the people whose lives it changes. Your voices have given this book its balance and its conscience.

To my embattled editorial team, peer reviewers, and trusted friends, thank you for your thoughtful questions, sharp observations, and commitment to clarity. Your efforts refined every chapter. To the friends who read drafts, offered encouragement, and reminded me to rest when I forgot to, thank you for your kindness and humour.

Above all, my love and deepest gratitude go to my family and loved ones. Writing this book has been one of the most rewarding experiences of my life, and also one of the most demanding for those who shared it with me. Living with someone whose mind rarely switches off and who finds inspiration at inconvenient hours is not easy. Thank you for your patience through the late nights, the notes scattered across every surface, and the constant hum of ideas that filled the house. You brought calm, perspective, and strength when they were most needed.

Innovation has never been the work of one person. It is the product of shared vision, honest dialogue, and the courage to keep improving. This book is dedicated to everyone who pushes boundaries with integrity, compassion, and belief in what is possible.

www.ingramcontent.com/pod-product-compliance
Lightning Source LLC
LaVergne TN
LVHW052032200926
848481LV00005B/1652
* 9 7 8 1 8 3 5 5 6 9 8 7 0 *